EUROPEAN POLITICAL COOPERATION

Butterworths European Studies is a series of monographs providing authoritative treatments of major issues in modern European political economy.

General Editor

François Duchêne   Director, Sussex European Research Centre, University of Sussex, England

Consultant Editors

David Allen   Department of European Studies, University of Loughborough, England

Hedley Bull   Montague Burton Professor of International Relations, University of Oxford, England

Wolfgang Hager   Visiting Professor, European University Institute, Florence, Italy

Stanley Hoffmann   Professor of Government and Director, Centre for European Studies, Harvard University, USA

Hanns Maull   Journalist, Bavarian Radio, Munich. Formerly European Secretary, Trilateral Commission, Paris

Roger Morgan   Head of European Centre for Political Studies, Policy Studies Institute, London, England

Donald Puchala   Professor of Government and Dean, School of International Affairs, Columbia University, USA

Susan Strange   Professor of International Relations, London School of Economics, England

William Wallace   Director of Studies, Royal Institute of International Affairs, London, England

Already Published

An Electoral Atlas of Europe 1968–81 by John Sallnow and Anna John
Europe and World Energy by Hanns Maull
Europe Under Stress by Yao-su Hu
European Environmental Policy: East and West by Josef Füllenbach
The Mediterranean Basin: A Study in Political Economy by Glenda Rosenthal
Monetary Integration in Western Europe: EMU, EMS and Beyond by D. C. Kruse
Pay Inequalities in the European Community by Christopher Saunders and David Marsden

Forthcoming Titles

The Defence of Western Europe
The EEC and the Developing Countries
European Integration and the Common Fisheries Policy
Political Forces in Spain, Greece and Portugal
Britain in the European Community

European Political Cooperation:

Towards a foreign policy for Western Europe

David Allen, Reinhardt Rummel and
Wolfgang Wessels

Butterworth Scientific

London   Boston   Sydney   Wellington   Durban   Toronto

First published 1982

© Institut für Europaische Politik, Bonn, FRG 1982

British Library Cataloguing in Publication Data

Allen, David
    European political cooperation: towards a foreign
    policy for Western Europe.—
    (Butterworths. European studies)
    1. International cooperation 2. European Community
    countries—Politics and government
    I. Title II. Rummel, Reinhardt III. Wessels, Wolfgang
    327.1'7'094   JC362

    ISBN 0-408-10663-8

Photoset by Butterworths Litho Preparation Department
Printed by Mackays of Chatham, Chatham, Kent

Contributors

David Allen,	University of Loughborough, UK
Gianni Bonvicini,	Istituto Affari Internazionali, Rome, Italy
Götz von Groll	Wirtschaftskommission für Europa Genf, früher: Auswärtiges Amt, Bonn, West Germany
Prof. Beate Kohler,	Technische Hochschule, Darmstadt, West Germany
Dr Beate Lindemann	Forschungsinstitut der Deutschen Gesellschaft für Auswärtige Politik, Bonn, West Germany
Nicholas van Praag,	Istituto Affari Internazionali, Rome, Italy
Reinhardt Rummel,	Stiftung Wissenschaft und Politik, Ebenhausen, West Germany
Dr William Wallace,	Royal Institute of International Affairs, London, UK
Wolfgang Wessels,	Institut für Europäische Politik, Bonn, West Germany

Introduction to the English edition

This book was originally published in German in 1978. It represents the conclusions of a study group on European Political Cooperation convened in Bonn by Wolfgang Wessels at the Institut für Europäishe Politik. The study group consisted of researchers from several Community countries and was greatly assisted by contributions from officials in the German Foreign Office and from the Commission of the European Communities. Although the case studies and the conclusions refer to the period from 1970 to 1977 it was felt that together they represent a complete history of the first critical years of this new experiment in European cooperation and that as such they would be of interest despite the passage of time and the developments of new concerns within the framework of European Political Cooperation. It is hoped that the study group will be reconvened in the future to reassess the findings of this volume in the light of recent developments in Europe and the wider international system.

The editor of the English edition would like to thank Jeremy Leaman and Martha Wörsching for their assistance in translating those chapters originally written in German. Particular thanks go to Angela Midworth for typing and correcting the manuscript.

Loughborough   David Allen

Contents

European Political Cooperation: a new approach to European foreign policy

WOLFGANG WESSELS

1.1   Introduction

One can say today that the goals implicit in these texts [the Luxembourg and Copenhagen Reports] have to a large extent been achieved and that the procedures recommended by them have become accepted practice[1].

The contemporary politics of West European integration is usually described in terms of crises and disappointments. The current achievements of the EEC – the *aquis communitaire* – are seen to be under threat; ambitious programmes which sought to establish an economic and monetary union as well as a European union by the end of the decade have already foundered. Nevertheless, politicians and observers both counter this negative assessment with the successes of West European 'foreign policy'. They point out as particular advances the Lomé Convention, the common position maintained by the Nine*at the Conference on Security and Cooperation in Europe (CSCE), the Euro–Arab Dialogue, the system of EEC agreements with the Magreb and Mashrek states of the Mediterranean area, the Community representation at the Paris Conference on International Economic Cooperation (CIEC), the increasing unanimity of the Nine's voting behaviour at the UN, as well as a number of declarations by the Nine with reference to the conflict in the Middle East and in Southern Africa. Some observers conclude from such lists that the Community has already in the field of foreign affairs made a qualitative leap into a new phase of integration – a leap that has never been adequately described[2].

If we look at this assessment more closely two separate strands of European foreign policy can be identified. Apart from the 'external relations' of the EEC which are based on the Treaties and shaped by Community institutions, the governments of the Nine member-states of the Community have developed the organization for European Political Cooperation (EPC), within which the foreign ministries work together 'intergovernmentally' on the basis of non-binding agreements that do not provide for formal or permanent institutions. The goals of this cooperation are threefold;

---

* Until 1981 there were nine countries in the EEC. Greece has now joined the Community and negotiations are taking place for the entry of Spain and Portugal.

(1) 'To ensure a better mutual understanding of the major problems of international politics through regular information and consultation';
(2) 'To promote the harmonization of views and the coordination of positions'[3]; and
(3) 'To attempt to achieve a common approach to specific cases'[4].

If the goals and structure of EPC appear at first modest, the extent and intensity of EPC activities appear to justify a closer analysis both conceptually and politically. Thus:

(1) Every week an average of a hundred communications are transmitted over the telex system (COREU);
(2) The political directors of the Nine foreign ministries meet at least once a month to exchange information and views and to attempt to develop common standpoints in informal and confidential sessions;
(3) Working groups of national diplomats analyse the most important problems of international politics at more than a hundred sessions per year;
(4) Declarations concerning areas of international tension are regularly made in the name of the Nine;
(5) The Nine arrange to be represented as one at international conferences and in international organizations;
(6) The heads of state and government of the EEC meet three times a year in the European Council to discuss EPC questions where necessary;
(7) Foreign states are turning increasingly to the Nine as an accepted and important actor in the international political system[5].

Despite these concrete developments, EPC is often excluded from descriptions and analyses of the international role of Western Europe, of European integration or or the foreign policies of the member-states[6]. On the other hand, political assessment of EPC has up to now, ten years after its creation, been remarkably favourable. Thus for the Federal Republic of Germany EPC is an 'essential instrument of the politics of European unification'[7] whilst Mr Callaghan, then the UK's Foreign Secretary, saw EPC as 'the best model for future European cooperation'[8]. The foreign ministers of the Nine themselves stress that 'the European "esprit de corps" is increasingly becoming a determinant element of international politics'[9].

Academics and observers either describe EPC as a pillar of the present European system of equal importance to the Community itself[10] or see it as representative of what has been described as the 'Second Europe', distinguished from the Community by dint of its flexibility, confidentiality and informality[11].

Critical voices, however, judge EPC to be a diversion from the real economic and social problems of Europe[12]. They see it as an exclusively intergovernmental procedure, the integrational quality of which goes no further than that of the Vienna Congress or Metternich's diplomacy[13]. Strict federalists assess EPC only in terms of attempts to prop up what they regard to be an obsolete system of nation-states in Europe[14]. In this debate about EPC two aspects in particular have to be distinguished: (1) the achievements of EPC as a political and administrative structure for managing foreign policy issues, and (2) the relationship between EPC and the politics and theory of integration. Both aspects shall be pursued in greater depth below in order to develop an introductory framework for the later case studies.

1.2   EPC and the management of foreign policy

EPC was created to deal with problems of foreign policy, with which the member-states of the EEC are increasingly confronted. The aims of EPC is to put the Nine into a position whereby they can speak with one voice on international questions. To achieve this aim, reciprocal consultation is intended to encourage and establish the basis for the harmonization of views, the coordination of positions and, in concrete instances, a common line and common action. Have the Nine used EPC to realize these aims? Beyond this, has EPC fulfilled further functions within or for the West European system? By pursuing these questions one can distinguish the different functions which EPC has fulfilled, on the one hand with regard to the internal relations of the Nine, and on the other hand in terms of the Nine's position within the international system.

If one attempts to find provisional answers to these groups of problems one comes up against a series of methodological difficulties. A central precondition for analysis and assessment is an adequate level of information. Compared with the EEC decision-making process, EPC is surrounded by an unusually high degree of confidentiality[15]. A second and far greater difficulty is in registering and explaining reciprocal relationships between changes in national positions on the one hand, and developments in the framework of EPC on the other. To what extent can common views held by the Nine be traced back to their cooperation within EPC, or are changes in national affairs or in the international arena equally responsible for closer positions among the Nine? The question of effectiveness within the international system can be answered methodologically even less satisfactorily. In order to assess whether and how outside states are influenced by the policies of the Nine one requires the sort of information which is generally not accessible to the ordinary observer.

In ultimately assessing EPC the selection of criteria is decisive. Frequently EPC is judged exclusively in terms of an ideal-type model in which common institutions are in a position to make and carry through all necessary foreign policy decisions for the Community and thereby replace the national foreign policy of the member-states. This criterion cannot be applied in an absolute way to EPC where the participants are, at least in the initial state, legally sovereign states, since the criterion negates the initial conditions and cannot register possible processes of development. By dividing up the EPC functions into those which relate to the internal affairs of the Nine and those which evaluate the role of the Nine in the international system, an attempt is made to do greater justice to the particular conditions and qualities of EPC than would be possible using an ideal type. Any concluding assessment will have to return to more subjective criteria relating to desired levels of achievement. As the differences between the individual contributions in this volume will also show, these should at least include real case histories. The undifferentiated usage of simple indicators can also be misleading. Thus an analysis-in-depth of the role of the Nine in the General Assembly of the UN shows that a united front is not necesarily the most important objective to be pursued[16]. More importantly, outward signs of a common approach, indicated by, for instance, the statistics of voting behaviour of the Nine, have to be checked against their respective political usefulness and the real degree of substantive agreement. Thus the argument that 'strengths and weaknesses in political cooperation on an international level are rarely more obvious than in the behaviour shown in votes on motions presented to the plenary assembly of the UN'[17] has to be modified with respect to the political circumstances.

These problems should not mean withholding assertions on the internal and external efficiency of EPC. The results of the contributions presented in this volume concerning the structure of EPC and the case studies on the most important areas of activity represent an advance on the present state of information and more profound consideration of the assessments of EPC.

1.2.1   Internal factors

From the endeavours of the Nine to improve mutual understanding through regular contact there arose a steady flow of information and constant exchange of opinions on essential questions of international politics. A routine has developed which is now frequently described as a 'coordination reflex'[18]. Thus, 'In my view, the main success of political cooperation consists in its having injected this reflex into diplomatic behaviour, so that one considers it useful when confronted with a political problem to get to know what the partners are undertaking before one establishes one's own position'[19]. As a result of this reflex, the foreign policies of the other member-states have become more transparent and predictable and the number of surprising changes of position has decreased. Furthermore, in cases of open disunity there is now an expectation by the Nine that divergent positions will be revised[20].

A particular area in which this practice of reciprocal information and consultation can be observed occurs after the Nine practise political cooperation towards outside states, in international organizations and during international conferences. Diplomats of the Nine thus emphasize the special value of cooperation in the General Assembly of the UN[21]. Information transmitted in good time combined with a rapid clarification of positions on the spot are of great tactical value. These measures of coordination are of central significance for the conference management of the Nine. At the Helsinki Conference in 1975 and the subsequent Belgrade Conference (1978) as well as for the Euro–Arab Dialogue, a finely graduated but also intensive procedure of consultation and coordination of views was developed[22] which integrated national and EEC officials into a negotiating machinery which acted coherently. At the same time, the Community together with EPC developed its negotiating machinery to a high level of organizational 'perfection'. The most finely tuned procedure was followed by the EEC at the Paris Conference on International Economic Cooperation[23].

The exchange of information and opinions by the embassies in outside states functions with variable intensity and effectiveness. In a number of outside countries the ambassadors of the Nine meet regularly, with the result that their positions develop into common views which are identified as such by the governments of the outside states. In the major capitals this process is less obvious because of particular national points of emphasis, the desire to retain an independent profile and because of 'direct' diplomacy by ministers and heads of government. Thus in Washington, whilst exchanges of information do take place they lead to united positions and coordinated action to a far lesser degree than in less significant outside countries, countries which are also given less attention by national politicians. Despite the positive nature of these developments the preconditions for the establishment of common embassies of the Nine[24] or of representative agencies in which the member-states with particular ties to outside states also take care of the interests of the other partners do not exist. Differences of political priorities and the increasing role of embassies as sales agencies for national products place narrow limits on such plans.

Although the exchange of views and information is part of the daily bread of diplomats the 'coordination reflex' within and through EPC has achieved a special quality far beyond levels previously achieved[25].

Information and consultations which lead to an effective coordination reflex are necessary but not wholly sufficient procedures for 'achieving an harmonizing of views and a coordination of positions'.

Although some have argued that the emphasis on procedure in EPC entails an avoidance of substance[26], it is possible to identify a moving together of views from originally differing positions of the member-states in important areas of international politics. With regard to the Atlantic Alliance and the politics of détente, above all during the CSCE and the subsequent Belgrade Conference, in relation to the Arab countries and in declarations concerning the conflict in the Middle East, during the Cyprus crisis and in the approach towards Southern Africa as well as in the General Assembly of the UN, harmonized points of view have developed. The degree of approximation in views differs according to the particular problem area and according to the particular questions posed. The *aquis politique* is not defined as unambiguously and as bindingly as the Treaties and subsequent legislation of the EEC[27]. Despite common declarations, differences of interpretation and realization can be identified time and again in real day-to-day politics. Harmonization on a few basic questions does not necessarily lead still to agreement on specific matters and on all diplomatic fronts. Thus whilst it is possible to share the views of many of the ministers and officials in EPC that EPC can demonstrate considerable progress in the harmonization of points of view, such positive results can be traced back essentially to the influence of national or international factors rather than to the dynamic effects of the EPC itself[28]. The Nine have produced in EPC a structure which favours and facilitates such approximation of points of view but does not necessarily produce them.

This trend towards harmonization can be seen as a progressive development whereby the process of approximation leads to the creation and filling out of a package of unified basic foreign policy standpoints – a *communauté de vue*. If one follows this thesis through, governments 'learn' to approximate and give depth to their positions within EPC in more and more areas of international politics so that they develop a broad and sound basic consensus concerning the international role of the Nine. This basic view does not necessarily lead to a common European foreign policy. However, national foreign policies and the foreign relations of the Community can then be developed along the lines of such a broad basic consensus.

This view of possible future developments of EPC presupposes that the harmonization process both encompasses the fundamental concepts of national foreign policy and also achieves a stability which can weather serious crises within the Nine. Both conditions are at present still not met by EPC. Despite a number of declarations concerning the foundations of European politics, one cannot observe any essential harmonization of views concerning the basic conceptions of the role of Europe in world politics[29]. With regard to stability in fundamental views, it is a clear disadvantage that cooperation within EPC is limited to foreign ministers and diplomats. Domestic, social and political forces are not involved, either actively or passively. The discussions with the political committee of the European Parliament and the even more sporadic discussions in national parliaments or their committees do not add up to any real involvement in the opinion-making and decision-making processes[30]. Thus EPC produces few major inputs into the political debates on basic issues relating to the future of European foreign policy[31]. The discussion on the relevant chapters of the Tindemans Report has again shown that fundamental differences of opinion continue to exist between political forces in the Community concerning the international role of Europe[32]. EPC is a structure within which foreign ministers can bring their positions closer together, an important task which, however, is limited in terms of its effect in depth. The confidentiality of EPC work is, seen in the short term, one of the most important factors behind the unproblematic mode of operation in EPC. In the long term, however, it could handicap EPC. The EPC structure is thus not suitable for the establishment of an all-embracing and stable community of fundamental foreign policy views. For this future task, hopes are laid on a directly elected Parliament which, together with the European party federations, could initiate a comprehensive debate on foreign policy questions and thus perhaps contribute to a greater level of basic agreement which would then broaden the political base of EPC. However, it is quite possible that such debates could accentuate differences of opinion and have a disturbing effect on EPC.

The close network of numerous and different reciprocal relations between the Nine, inside and outside the framework of the EEC, is constantly subject to heavy pressures which are particularly reinforced in the case of international crises and outside provocation. Differing national reactions which appear logical and natural to governments in accordance with their understanding of national interest can endanger the Community, the policies of the Community or the general relations between the member-states. Thus the effects of the graduated Arab oil boycott (in 1973) led to considerable tension between the member-states and threatened the existence of the Community in central areas. In cases of this nature EPC offers an extensive and familiar system for the internal management of crises in which special crisis consultations (*consultations d'urgence*) are envisaged. In less serious cases EPC can, as a result of its coordination reflex, help towards neutralizing at an early stage the negative effects of any policy of 'divide and rule' from outside states or groups of states.

The coordination measures of EPC also accompany, support and reinforce Community policies in the field of external relations. Political questions, which are dealt with in close connection with Community policies or are dealt with inadequately by the EEC bodies, can be discussed within the framework of EPC. A political consensus was produced in the EPC towards the Arab States adjoining the Mediterranean, towards the USA, towards Cyprus, Portugal and South Africa which made it easier to develop specific EEC policies[33]. This supplementary and reinforcing role became particularly necessary when outside states, such as the US government with its notion of the 'Year of Europe', the Soviet Union with the CSCE, and the Arab States with the oil boycott, combined economic, monetary and in some instances military demands, so that neither the Community nor the member-states alone could react adequately. The Community countries were able to use the EPC structure as a focus in order to reduce the deficiency of their internal coordination and to improve the coherence of their policies[34].

1.2.2   External factors: the role of the Nine in the international system

On the diplomatic stage the Nine are confronted by the problem of developing unified action under the cloak of EPC while they continue at the same time to act as independent states and as members of the EEC. They have to present the independent but at the same time limited role of the EPC, and introduce it in a clearly identifiable way into international politics. With this form of action the Nine have themselves produced a relationship of tension between expectations and possibilities. On the one hand, the Nine are reluctant to place those tools of foreign policy at the disposal of the EPC, with which normal nation-states operate in international politics: on the other hand, they are identified as a 'power' by many outside states who, as a consequence, expect them to act as such.

The daily routine work of international diplomacy consists in the main of the exchange of information, of the exposition of points of view and of the painstaking process of bringing positions closer together through negotiation. Official declarations, often the first sign of diplomatic activities for the outside observer, are as a rule only employed when these normal channels have been exhausted. In EPC the Nine have developed a machinery through which they can participate collectively in the daily work of diplomacy. EPC lives within and through the traditional diplomatic apparatus of the member-states. On the other hand, the EEC does not possess an adequate diplomatic infrastructure, so that it cannot participate in *all* the essential aspects of the important business of 'diplomatic trade'.

The function of EPC – to make the Nine a recognized partner in daily diplomatic business – is particularly apparent in international conferences (CSCE and the Euro–Arab Dialogue) and in the General Assembly of the UN. The Nine has become an important participant in the process of diplomatic clarification at these conferences and as such has to be recognized in the negotiating and coordinating process by Western, Eastern and neutral bloc states. But outside these institutionalized negotiating processes the Nine involve themselves increasingly in daily diplomatic business[35]. Particular forms of this display of unity can be seen in collective intervention measures or in official visits by the presidency[36]. The Nine have, however, not yet merged as a unit in this process. Access to the Nine proceeds in part via the particular government with which the respective outside state fosters particularly intensive contacts. The presidency is also being increasingly regarded as an essential channel, for example by the USA and Japan, who strengthen their embassies in the countries of the presidency. To preserve continuity, which is made difficult by the biannual change of the presidency, the Nine have developed rather bizarre forms of foreign representation involving representatives of the previous, present and future presidencies.

This continuing function of EPC as an international partner for the daily business of diplomacy is of considerable value, even if it has not had spectacular results. The Nine are increasingly regarded as an independent unit which cannot be (or cannot easily be) divided. This development is initially only effective in the atmosphere of diplomatic contacts[37] but it is already becoming a fact of international political life, entailing as it does the building up of networks which can be of particular value at times of crisis[38].

The most visible signs of EPC activities are official declarations of the Nine. Declarations represent an essential instrument of international diplomacy, frequently used by international groupings, such as the group of non-aligned countries, NATO, OECD and the Warsaw Pact in order to raise demands, express warnings and give indications as to the direction of their policies. Frequently these declarations have emerged primarily as aspects of consensus-formation within the above groupings. EPC is no exception. A number of declarations of the Nine served initially to harmonize viewpoints within EPC. These declarations do, however, represent points of reference for the foreign policy of the Nine to which national diplomacy can relate in its day-to-day work and behind which it can 'hide' if the need arises. In some cases declarations like those concerning the situation in the Middle East in the summer of 1977 and those concerning South Africa clearly signal that the positions of the Nine have changed or have become more resolute. It is difficult to estimate what effect these declarations have on the states or groups of states to which they refer; this depends to a large degree on the significance which these states accord to the position of the Nine and on the potential influence which the Nine possess. It is obvious, however, that attention is being increasingly given to the positions of the Nine. Thus one can observe that in questions concerning the Middle East the states involved comment particularly intensely on declarations of the Nine and even urge the publication or the non-publication of these declarations.

The role of the Nine in the daily process of diplomacy and the respect which their declarations receive internationally is determined to a high degree by the availability of the means of implementation. EPC only has direct control of diplomatic instruments such as *démarches*, declarations and support or rejection of proposals in international conferences and in the General Assembly of the UN. The deployment of these tools of diplomacy has proved particularly useful in multinational negotiations, especially in comparison with the limited capabilities of individual member-states. Beyond these direct diplomatic means the question of the employment of positive or negative sanctions on the part of the Nine, particularly with regard to the economic potential of the EEC, becomes open-ended and unpredictable. For outside states, this insecurity can be an important factor in the negotiating process since, under certain circumstances, a declaration in the name of the Nine can have positive or negative consequences for the shaping of economic relations with the EEC.

The instruments of the Community are, however, not simply a tool in the hands of EPC they are part of a process related to the independent aims of the Community even if, in important instances, close relations exist between the aims of the EEC and EPC. The basis of EEC external relations are to be found in the Treaties, which cannot, in the short term, be placed at the disposal of political and diplomatic interventions. Central areas of the EEC, such as customs, trade and association policies, can only be used diplomatically in the negotiating phases with outside states. Financial aid granted under particular political conditions proved a flexible instrument at least in the case of Portugal[39]. Presenting the prospect of EEC membership as an incentive for outside states to behave in a particular way cannot generally be used as an instrument of influence. The prospect of EEC membership was indeed a significant factor in the domestic political development in Greece, Portugal and Spain, and was exploited by the Nine. However, at the same time, the EEC was not thereby obliged to honour the promises given. Beyond the southern European circle of states the use of the prospect of EEC membership is at present irrelevant. In other aspects of the Community's policies in which possible membership for outside states is useful (the Lomé Convention, association agreements, etc.) the regulations on entry are generally fixed, so that it is not possible to demand any particular type of behaviour from outside states in the sense of foreign policy goals. The employment of the EEC instruments in support of EPC can as a rule only be considered within a limited framework. The Nine can also place those instruments and channels of influence which lie exclusively or primarily under national control at the disposal of EPC. The breaking off or opening up of diplomatic relations, the development of special bilateral relations, arms exports or embargoes, military aid and development aid are all potential instruments for coordinated deployment by the Nine. As a number of case studies show[40], it can be assumed that some of the Nine consciously cultivate such instruments alongside EPC.

EPC is not an independent and isolated form of European foreign policy. Rather it represents an additional and supplementary structure within a complex configuration of national, EEC, West European and Atlantic policy-making. One important success of EPC lies in its having reduced deficiencies of coordination between various levels and agents of European foreign policy, a success which is of benefit both to the external relations of the EEC as well as to national diplomacy.

With EPC the Nine have extended, differentiated and strengthened the potentiality of a European foreign policy – both internally and externally. In internal relations the Nine have developed EPC into a structure within which the 'coordination reflex' and the 'harmonization of positions' have created the preconditions for a coordinated diplomacy. In the international system the Nine have established themselves as an accepted partner in daily diplomatic affairs with the help of this coordinated diplomacy – a partner whose common declarations and other means of diplomacy are generally well regarded.

The Nine have developed and upheld positions in areas and zones of tension in international politics in which they were, until recently, not represented by one voice. In many cases some member-states had not even formulated positions before or would not have developed them so explicitly without encouragement through EPC. Compared with the extraordinarily carefully formulated Luxembourg and Copenhagen Reports. EPC has developed a broad and differentiated capacity as a foreign policy structure. 'The practice of political cooperation has become more enduring and more scrupulous than the actual texts intend'[41]. The Nine have thereby used EPC, as this book's case studies show, with variable success in constellations and situations which differ widely from one another. In crises (Cyprus) as in long drawn-out negotiations (CSCE, Euro–Arab Dialogue), in the immediate geographical environment (Cyprus, Portugal), as in more distant centres of tension (Southern Africa), the Nine have developed in EPC a degree of unanimity in analysis, opinion-making and action hitherto unknown.

However, the studies also show clear limits regarding the capacity of EPC. With EPC the Nine are less flexible than other agents of international politics. Diplomacy can as a rule only consist of reactions to developments in outside states which cannot themselves be predetermined[42]. Thus EPC can primarily be directed only towards damage-limitation and the neutralization of conflict. Preventive reduction of conflict in all areas of tension which could affect Western Europe goes far beyond the capabilities of the Nine. It is also becoming clear that as a result of the internal processes of coordination delays occur which notably limit the effectiveness of EPC. The expense in terms of organization and time involved in opinion-making and decision-making within EPC compares unfavourably with the expected effects of a common approach in a number of cases.

The balance-sheet of EPC also shows tendencies towards selectivity and discontinuity in the treatment of international problems. If sensitive and crucial interests of individual member-states are touched on, above all during election campaigns, then problem areas can either be pursued with particular emphasis or can be completely excluded. The capabilities of EPC in terms of anticipating impending problems of international politics are thus further limited by chance political occurrences and national frailties.

The actual substance of EPC politics frequently gets stuck in unbinding declarations, since clear discrepancies exist between declarations of position on the one hand and complementary Community policies on the other. This weak point of European foreign policy will continue to exist as long as the coordination between individual fields of action and between EPC and EEC decision processes is not improved more systematically at a European and national level[43]. If the Nine wanted to use the Euro–Arab Dialogue seriously and comprehensively to achieve a settlement with the group of

Arab states, they would at least have to develop certain forms of common energy, industrial and monetary policies in order to facilitate the realization of obligations towards this group of states. There is a growing tendency in multilateral diplomacy to bunch together various problem areas into negotiating packages. However, despite initial successes, the Nine and the Community do not yet possess even in EPC a suitably reliable political and administrative structure in order to become a negotiating partner that acts cohesively in all instances[44]. EPC cannot, thus, be regarded as a foreign policy structure of a third superpower either from its disposition or its performance[45]. Rather, EPC can be judged as an incomplete and painstaking endeavour to extend the role of Europe as a civilian power in the field of international diplomacy[46]. Alongside the exclusive civilian means of EPC diplomacy the internal decision-making process is also characterized by a principle of consensus whereby each of the Nine, whether large or small, can operate on an equal basis. Thus with EPC the Nine have up to now developed a structure more suited to the exchange of information for analysis and opinion-formation than to decision-making and united action.

From the point of view of the governments of the member-states EPC offers the possibility of strengthening and refining national foreign policy. With the help of this additional European level their own interests can be articulated not only more emphatically in international politics but also more ambivalently and thus less vulnerably. The satisfaction of many national figures with current achievements and the *status quo* can also be understood in terms of this perspective of self-interest. The weakness and strengths of EPC as a foreign-policy structure are characterized by various factors, as other contributions to this book will demonstrate, among which particular significance has to be attached to the interests and role of the USA, the political, economic and military dimensions of the respective problem areas, the context of diplomatic procedure (multi- or bilateral), the time factor (short-term crises management or conferences arranged over the longer term), the political interest of the member-states and the international position of the negotiating partner.

1.3   EPC and European integration

The usefulness of EPC lies in its direct task and function as a machinery of European foreign policy. The aspect of EPC relating to integration theory and integration policy is considered just as significant. In the context of this volume the integrative quality of EPC decision processes, its value as an institutional model and as integration strategy, as well as inferences for integration theory, are of particular interest.

EPC is frequently characterized as an intergovernmental process which is clearly distinguishable from federal models, or from the supranational or neo-functionalist interpretations of the EEC decision processes[47]. In order to identify the integrative quality of EPC more closely one can turn to a comparison of the structure of EPC decision-making and that of the EEC. Both structures display essential similarities in their central elements. Decisions are made after painstaking and frequently long drawn-out processes of consultation, negotiation and coordination which are characterized by a complex interbureaucratic network between the member-states. Both rely upon a pronounced vertical hierarchical structure at national level with the foreign ministers or heads of government as the main agents of decision-making. The functioning of the machinery is made possible by close horizontal contacts which connect the various corresponding levels of officials and politicians of the national administrations with one another. The close horizontal ties at European level have a retroactive effect on the national decision-making process. The search for common formulations at the European level often influence, imperceptibly, the views and positions which are then held in the process of national opinion-formation. The special 'club character' of EPC contributes beyond this towards developing loyalties towards the European group-loyalties which are also still discernible in national decision-making processes. This 'process of socialization of the main actors towards a common framework and common views must not, however, be overestimated. Integration via group constraint comes up against the specific interests of the member-states and is limited by the dominating processes of socialization in the national framework. A pronounced shift of loyalties to a new centre of decision-making with jurisdiction over the national level cannot be identified[48]. Despite unarguable European commitment, activities are primarily directed towards the furthering of national foreign-policy goals and interests[49]. Transnational coalitions which break through the decision-making monopolies of the member-states are not to be found in EPC. In the EEC, transnational interest groups and parties have developed but their influences on decisions is limited to only a few sectors (for example, agriculture) and do not challenge the national monopoly on decision-making in all the essential problem areas. EPC decision processes are thus completely subordinate to the political control of national governments, just as EEC processes are when it comes to important matters.

Informality and confidentiality, the characteristic elements of EPC, are increasingly becoming significant in the framework of the EEC. Informal meetings of the heads of government and of foreign and finance ministers which are arranged without a strict agenda, without documents ready for ratification, without a large number of national and European officials and without making formal decisions have supplemented the formalized decision processes of the EEC in the last few years.

Apart from the identical or similar elements of both structures one can identify noticeable differences, even when one takes into account that the actual decision-making processes in the EEC vary from sector to sector and according to the actors involved[50]. The stipulations of the Community Treaties often fix the procedure and content of the EEC decision-making processes to a considerable extent. On the other hand, the stipulations of the Luxembourg and Copenhagen Reports in relation to EPC were more flexible and less binding; legalistic discussions which aim to avoid or produce precedents occur rarely in EPC. These differences are, however, determined by the nature of the decisions. While EPC concentrates essentially on the exchange of information, coordinated diplomacy and declarations, the work of the EEC bodies is, to a large part, directed towards the passing of legally binding acts. The consequences of EEC decisions are thus more incisive and more binding; after their passage in law they are placed beyond the unlimited control of the member-states. Beyond this, the differences are felt in the political controversiality of the sectors. EEC agricultural policy, which directly affects politically active groups of the population or fundamental decisions of external policy which have consequences for whole branches of industry and the trade unions, excite more attention and come up against stronger domestic political obstacles than the sensitive items of EPC policy. The political constellations which affect the EEC are accordingly different as a rule to those which influence EPC. As the establishment of a code of conduct for European firms in South Africa indicates, EPC can also become involved in sensitive areas of domestic politics. With an extension of EPC activities it will not be possible to maintain any insulation of EPC processes[51].

In the EEC decision-making processes there are some institutions which have no equivalent in EPC. No parallel has been created within EPC to the role of the Commission as 'motor', 'agent', 'guardian of the treaty' and 'executive body' which can rely upon a bureaucracy with continuity, experience and specialized knowledge. This is also the case for important functions which the European Parliament and the European Court of Justice fulfil for the Community. Two conclusions can be drawn from this comparison. First, EPC is not a regression to an obsolete anachronism but a method of common policy-formation which is characterized by a number of essential elements similar to those of EEC processes. Nevertheless, clear differences from EEC processes can also be identified. EPC is thus a part of European integration and not the relic of an historical epoch.

A second conclusion aims to modify the current classification of EPC as 'intergovernmental'. Within EPC, governments do work together without a legally binding framework while applying strictly the rule of unanimity and producing legally unbinding decisions. Even if EPC shares these conceptual elements with historically familiar forms of diplomatic cooperation, the intensity and quality of EPC activities, however, go beyond these accepted concepts in the way that makes this characterization appear no longer applicable in any satisfactory way. An essential feature of EPC lies in its *interdiplomatic* structure which does not simply limit EPC to cooperation at the highest level but anchors it firmly in the diplomatic machinery of the Nine. These direct institutionalized intercommunications are essentially different from other forms of multilateral diplomacy, the cooperative nature of which has more of an *ad hoc* character and proceeds indirectly via permanent representatives and embassies. This 'anchorage' is also an essential precondition for the reliability and continuity of cooperation, which is becoming more approximate to something legally binding. 'A kind of law of custom has emerged between the countries of the Community which naturally does not envisage any sanctions but which has nevertheless taken on the character of a recognized rule which can be occasionally broken but whose existence one still recognizes[52].' The habitual practice and the self-obligation (coordination reflex) which is predominantly seen as a matter of fact leads to a *de facto* binding quality whereby the mechanism of sanctions does not rest upon any legal basis but on group expectations of mutuality. In the interdiplomatic srructure there is a clear mobilization effect which allows diplomats to cultivate a system of European cooperation on several levels. Thus an important group of actors, as well as maintaining national loyalties, orients itself towards the development of common European positions. Diplomats have indeed already worked on the process of integration; however, with EPC, increasingly more departments are being integrated into a common network. The term 'intergovernmental' in common parlance stresses the national lines of separation and negates aspects relating to the development of a new potential such as has been created with EPC. Even the regularly practised reference to unanimity stresses only one aspect of the reality; the principle of consensus does not mean an automatic inflexibility of national positions but leads to dynamic processes of adaptation as a result of consistent interest in EPC activities. The limits of national control are, however, clearly preserved. The latent danger of fragility and non-obligation which existed in previous cases of intergovernmental cooperation is far less pronounced with EPC. In particular parallel membership in the EEC and the linking of EPC and Community politics have had a stabilizing effect. The characterization of EPC as intergovernmental is not 'wrong' but it is inadequate and thus less useful. In important elements it is possible to identify features of integration; in EPC, among other things, by dint of the close actual connection with the EEC. These features make classification into this customary conceptual scheme appear incorrect; the multidiplomatic structure with its socialization process and mobilization effect, reliability and continuity, the *de facto* binding character, the practice of the principle of consensus and the capacity of the process make EPC a phenomenon whose essential integrational quality can be described as less than supranational but more than intergovernmental.

If the characterization of the features of EPC has to be developed beyond traditional concepts it is also the case that the explanatory value of customary integration theories are limited[53]. The approaches of neo-functionalism, communications theory, intergovernmental or politico–economic theories, the theory of multinational politics and system theory does not offer an adequately coherent basis for explanation which can trace the evolution, method and mode of operation of EPC. Although these theories offer an extensive list of categories to describe and measure the progress of integration and of explanatory factors and their causal connections, no adequate points of reference for the central characteristics of EPC can be identified. The theories either concentrate on the European level divorced from national decision-making processes, and thus exclude the complex relations between the member-states and between national and European levels, or they take economic or social structures as their point of departure; the differing interests, goals and methods of various actors are taken into consideration as derivative factors.

Some categories and theories, like elite socialization, spill over, and interdependence can be employed in a limited way. Factors which can particularly help to explain EPC, like external pressure and the interests and motivations of governments, are not as a rule employed or, if they are, only unspecifically. The intergovernmental approaches which place the role of national governments at the centre of their considerations employ categories which, as was demonstrated above, do not do justice to EPC. The theory of multinational politics diverts attention onto actors who compete with governments in the shaping of international relations through their own transnational relations. This approach also describes transgovernmental bureaucratic alliances. Despite these categories, the involvement of national political motives and interests[54] as well as an adequate perception of the EPC method for an adequate explanation of EPC are missing. Since EPC is an independent but not isolated European phenomenon, the reality of EPC could be an additional incentive to revise theories of integration and to look for new approaches.

1.4   Conclusions

A number of actors and observors assess the value of EPC as a model for the institutional development of the Community towards European unity. Informality, confidentiality, the absence of a new bureaucratic apparatus, the first positive results and the experience that national control of European decision-making processes is not reduced or disturbed by 'unpredictable' bodies like the Commission, the European Parliament and the Court of Justice, all make EPC an attractive model for the pragmaticians and defenders of national sovereignty. The results of the case studies show, however, that the capabilities of institutional procedure are closely linked to the area of operation. The work and effects of EPC are essentially determined by the specific qualities of diplomatic work. A mechanical transposition of this model onto other sectors of European politics ignores the fact that the structure of EPC has developed from the specific reality of foreign policy action and international diplomacy. Applying this procedure to questions of European economic and social policy could not achieve comparable results and would probably have negative effects on common policies in these sectors. However, for the medium term it is not so much the question of competition between the two models which is the main constructive task but how the existing coexistence and the developing complementarity of both models can be shaped and extended[55]. In the long term a new-style institutional model could develop out of the experience gathered within these differing frameworks in specific sectors and out of lessons drawn from the complementarity of their approaches. At present the contours of such a model of synthesis cannot be made out with sufficient clarity.

The dynamic perspective of EPC as a paradigmatic strategy of integration can be distinguished from the static consideration of EPC as an institutional model. These considerations are not directed at the institutional capacity of EPC but at its method of furthering or obstructing processes of integration[56]. If at first it was predominantly feared that EPC could cause disintegrative effects as a process aimed against the Community[57] EPC can now, despite its initial difficulties, be seen as a refined strategy through which common positions can be developed in an area that was previously the exclusive domain of the individual states. The recipe for success à la EPC could be based on the following rules: the common enterprise has to begin with a loose, non-binding and modest formula, through which a process of developing trust can be initiated. Ambitious and binding plans only lead to early arguments on the ideology of integration which block and overtax any future cooperation. Without these disturbances a 'natural' procedure will develop which, in a particular situation (as for EPC in the Copenhagen Report) can perhaps be recorded in writing. Gradual development does justice to the individual interests of the participants and is flexible enough to avoid deviation and special requests without any irreparable breaks. If the process is thus flexibly organized the actors can accumulate an increasing body of common positions if they are confronted with the 'right' challenges which ultimately create the preconditions for qualitative changes of cooperation. Within this perspective EPC could be assessed as a strategy for the achievement of the conditions necessary for more far-reaching shifts towards integration .

Compared with the debates surrounding the Fouchet plans at the beginning of the 1960s or economic and currency union in the 1970s, the EPC method has proved itself to be a superior strategy for initiating and developing common endeavours in the sensitive area of foreign policy.

The area in which such a strategy can be applied is, however, limited. In the economic and social sectors of European politics this procedure is only reliable in the initial phase. Although it creates certain political and administrative preconditions for further steps EPC will not be in a position to spur on the integration process by itself.

In conclusion, EPC opens up perspectives which make a stubborn reliance on traditional concepts of integration policy appear unreasonable. EPC has proved itself to be a useful structure for foreign policy opinion-formation, decision-making and action, and a helpful stimulus towards a reassessment of traditional conceptions of European integration.

Notes

1 Henri Simonet: President in office of the Council of Ministers. European Parliament, 15 November 1977
2 Eberhard Rhein, 'Die Europäische Gemeinschaft auf der Suche nach einer gemeinsamen Aussenpolitik'. *Europa-Archiv*, 6/1975, p. 172.
3 The First Report of the foreign ministers to the heads of state and government of the member-states of the EEC, 27 October 1970 (Luxembourg Report)
4 The Second Report of the foreign ministers to the heads of state and government of the member-states of the EEC, 23 July 1973 (Copenhagen Report). See also David Allen and William Wallace, Chapter 2
5 Thus the Russian anbassador at the UN approached the Nine with the request for a common meeting and greeted them with the only slightly ironic appellation 'Mighty Nine'
6 See, for example, Werner Feld, *The European Community in World Affairs*, New York, 1974 (he devotes four pages to EPC out of a total of 353); Alfred Grosser (Ed.), *Les Politiques Extérieures Européennes dans la crise*, Paris 1976; (the contributions on the foreign policy of the larger Western European states mention EPC either in passing or not at all). Kenneth J. Twitchett, 'External Relations or Foreign Policy', Twitchett (Ed.), *Europe and the World*, London, 1976 (he devotes only four of a total of 34 pages to EPC; the other contributions to this collection leave EPC largely out of their deliberations)
7 Report by the Federal Government of West Germany on Integration in the European Communities for the period April 1975 to September 1976, Bonn, 1976

8 See David Allen and William Wallace, *Die europäische politische Zusammenarbeit, Modell für eine europäische Aussenpolitik*, Bonn, 1975, p. 32
9 Copenhagen Report. See footnote 4
10 Hans von der Groeben, 'Die Europäische zwischen Föderation und Nationalstaat', Groeben, Boeckl and Thiesing (Eds.), *Handbuch für Europäische Wirtschaft*, October 1977, p. 1ff.
11 Ralf Dahrendorf, 'Wieland Europa'. *Die Zeit*, 9 July 1977, p. 3
12 See Lothar Broack, 'Integration nach aussen? Die EG im globalen Konfliktfeld', a paper presented at the annual colloquium of the 'Arbeitskreis Friedens und Konfliktforschung', Bonn 1976, p. 2ff.
13 Thus, among others, C. C. Schweitzer at a meeting of the 'Arbeitskreis Europäische Integration' in Bonn, Spring 1977
14 This was the tenor of some voices in the circle of the Union of European Federalists (UEF)
15 This also applies to those parts of the EEC Commission involved in EPC
16 See Beate Lindemann, Chapter 9
17 Case study on the voting behaviour of the member-states of the European Community and the countries Greece, Turkey, Cyprus, Spain and Portugal, produced by the General Directorate for Science and Documentation of the European Parliament for the Political Committee, 15 November 1976, PE 46, p.3
18 This concept was probably first coined by the Political Committee; Callaghan, at that time Foreign Secretary, first introduced it into the public debate
19 Vicomte Davignon, one of the founders of EPC, quoted by William Wallace, 'A Common European Foreign Policy: Mirage of Reality', in *New Europe*. Spring 1977, p. 26

20 Thus when France broke ranks and recognized Angola or when Denmark voted in the UN General Assembly to condemn West Germany, France and the UK for arms sales to South Africa, it was made clear in subsequent EPC meetings that such actions were perceived as 'deviant' by the rest of the Nine

21 See Beate Lindemann, Chapter 9

22 See Götz Von Groll, Chapter 5 and David Allen, Chapter 6

23 Wolfgang Wessels (Ed.), *Europa und der Nord–Süd-Dialog, Erste Bilanz der Konferenz über internatioanale wirtschaftliche Zusammenarbeit*, Bonn, 1977, in particular the articles by Jonathan Carr and Wolfgang Hager. See also Stephan Taylor, 'Die Europäischen Gemeinschaften als Verhandlungspartner im Nord–Süd-Dialog', *Europe-Archiv*, 20/1977, p. 721ff.

24 This proposal was made by H. Wischnewski, then Minister of State in the German Foreign Office

25 Some effects have, for example, become noticeable in relation to the role of the embassies of the Nine in member-states. They feel themselves occasionally excluded from the process of harmonization which operates directly between the Nine foreign ministries. See David Allen and William Wallace, Chapter 2

26 The relationship between procedure and substance in EPC is described critically in David Allen and William Wallace, 'Political Cooperation: Procedure as Substitute for Policy', in H. Wallace, W. Wallace and C. Webb, *Policy Making in the European Communities*, London/New York, 1977, p. 277ff.

27 This is also a particular problem for the enlargement of the EEC: How can the new members be tied down to the *acquis politique*?

28 See the case studies in this volume and Allen and Wallace, *Policy Making*

29 See, for example, the Copenhagen Document on European Identity, published in *Europäische Politische Zusammenarbeit, Eine Dokumentation der Bundesregierung*, 3rd edn, 1978, p. 78ff.

30 Report of the Political Committee on European Political Cooperation (Blumenfeld Report), Doc. 427/77 of the European Parliament

31 One example is the declaration to the Copenhagen Summit in 1973 on 'European Identity', which was the result of a process of diplomatic formulation but which was wholly ignored in the political debate in the member states

32 Wolfgang Wessels, 'Die Europäische Union im Tindemans-Bericht, Bilanz einer einjänrigen', *Aus politik und zeitgeschicht* (Supplement of the weekly paper *Das Parlament*), B 52/76, 24 December 1976, p. 21ff.

33 Otto von der Gablentz, 'Auf der Suche nach Europas Aussenpolitik', *Die Zeit*, 28 November 1975, p. 32

34 See Beate Kohler, Chapter 7

35 One example: When the Ethopian government wanted to check the diplomats' post, the Netherlands, in its capacity as the presidency, successfully intervened in the name of the Nine. See *The Economist*, 29 January 1977, p. 49

36 For instance, on the occasion of visits by the Dutch Council President, Van der Stoel to Yugoslavia and to Turkey in the second half of 1976

37 See Beate Lindemann, Chapter 9, and David Allen, Chapter 6

38 The Euro–Arab Dialogue is viewed from this perspective as a forum for possible Euro–Arab crisis management

39 See Nicholas van Praag, Chapter 8

40 See Nicholas van Praag, Chapters 8 and 10

41 Simonet, the acting President of the Council before the European Parliament, 15 November 1977; *Proceedings of the European Community*, Appendix No. 223, November 1977

42 One can thus attach some limited validity to the criticism contained in the Blumenfeld Report that 'it [EPC] has up to now hardly succeeded in foreseeing the possible development of events within the framework of the mechanisms of EPC'

43 See Gianni Bonvicini, Chapter 3, and William Wallace, Chapter 4

44 See Reinhardt Rummel, Chapter 11

45 The notion of the third superpower is introduced into many general debates as a demand. Referring to the power of its structures and its resources, Galtung regards the EEC as being already on the way to becoming a superpower; cf. Johan Galtung, *Kapitalistische Grossmacht Europa, oder die Gemeinschaft der Konzerne*, Reinbek, 1973

46 For details of the substance of the 'civil power' concept, see Francois Duchène, 'Die Rolle Europas in der Welt: Von der regionalen zur planetorischen Interdependenz', M. Kohnstamm and W. Hager (Eds.), *Zivilmacht Europa*,

Supermacht oder Partner, Frankfurt, 1973, p. 19ff.

47 These conceptual subdivisions are generally adopted in most of the discussions concerning EPC. For one of the latest resumés of these traditional interpretations, cf. Carol Webb, 'Introduction, Variations on a Theoretical Theme', Helen Wallace, William Wallace and Carol Webb (Eds.), *Policy Making in the European Community*, London, 1977, p. 17ff.

48 See Ernst B. Haas, 'International Integration – the European and the Universal Process', *International Organisation*, Vol. XV, 1961, p. 367. This shift of loyalties is often used as an indicator of 'integration'

49 Thus also the Blumenfeld Report

50 William Wallace, 'Walking Backwards towards Unity', Wallace, Wallace and Webb, *Policy Making*, p. 309

51 See William Wallace, Chapter 4

52 Simonet before the European Parliament, see Note 41

53 In this section the relevant theories of integration cannot be dealt with anew. For details see in particular: Charles Pentland,

International Theory and European Integration, London, 1973; Reginald Harrison, *Europe in Question*, London, 1974; Rudolf Hrbek, 'Eine neue politische Infrastruktur? Zum Problem transnationaler Kooperation und Koalition politischer Parteien in der EGm', *Zussamenarbeit nder Parteien in Westeuropa*, Bonn, 1976, p. 345ff.; Carol Webb, 'Introduction, Variations on a Political Theme', p. 6ff.; Heinrich Schneider, 'Integration – gestern, heute, morgen', 'Integration' supplement to *Europäische Zeitung*, No. 1/1978, p. 3ff.

54 See, in particular, David Allen and William Wallace, Chapter 2

55 See also Reinhardt Rummel, Chapter 11

56 For general remarks on integration strategy, cf. Wolfgang Wessels, 'Die Integrationsstrategie des Tindemans-Berichtes', Heinrich Schneider and Wolfgang Wessels (Eds.), *Auf dem Weg zur Europäischen Union, Diskussionbeiträge zum Tindemans-Bericht*, Bonn, 1977, p. 219ff.

57 See David Allen and William Wallace, Chapter 2

European Political Cooperation: the historical and contemporary background

DAVID ALLEN and WILLIAM WALLACE

2.1   Introduction

The establishment of a system of political cooperation represented a significant landmark in the continuing debate about the character of political integration and the formal or informal nature of European institutions. It was entirely outside the competence of the Treaties, without any legal framework beyond the text of the Communique of The Hague Summit at which it was conceived[1]; it had no definite institutional basis; it had no secretariat; it had, at best, tenuous links with the existing institutions of the European Communities; and it had no fixed meeting place, and was condemned instead to travel in succession round the capitals of the member states. The objectives it was to pursue were couched in the cloudiest rhetoric, thinly disguising the underlying disagreements about its purpose and its future development. There was no mention of 'common policy', even as a distant aim, and no hint of deadlines for the completion of intermediate or final stages of an outline plan, as in the Werner Plan for Economic and Monetary Union or in the original programme for the customs union set out in the Treaty of Rome – indeed, there was no plan at all, and only the flimsiest of guidelines for activity. As set out in The Hague Communique and in the Luxembourg Report of July 1970, political cooperation represented the *reductio ad absurdem* of the lowest common denominator principle in European integration. Unable to agree about policy objectives or about the institutional framework appropriate to cooperation in this new issue area, but accepting the need to give an added impetus to the 'relaunching of Europe', the heads of state or government at The Hague agreed to establish a new procedure instead.

2.2   Prehistory of EPC

Many of the problems and confusions that surrounded political cooperation at its inception in 1970 can only be understood by an examination of previous attempts at cooperation in the area that has become known as high politics. The attempt in the early 1950s to leap from the economic to the political sphere had failed when the French Assembly refused to ratify the plans for a European Army (the European Defence Community) and hence also the more grandiose concept of the European Political Community. After the establishment of the European Economic Community in 1958 the question of the development of political union in Europe was taken up again, primarily at the urging of Jean Monnet's Action Committee for the United States of Europe. By now, however, France was governed by de Gaulle who was, and remained, actively opposed to any further integration moves that implied an increased surrender of national sovereignty. De Gaulle's opposition to the further expansion of the 'Community method', whereby power was transferred to the supranational institutions of the EEC, was formally expressed by his Prime Minister, Michel Debré, in a speech to the National Assembly in January 1959 in which he warned that any future European construction 'cannot be based on repudiation of the idea of the nation'. In proposing the alternative concept to the EEC of a *Europe des patries*, Debré, at de Gaulle's bidding, was drawing the battle-lines for all future discussion of political cooperation. To prepare for the political union of Europe he suggested in 1959 a 'regular and continuing consultation of the heads of government'.

Despite the suspicions of the Belgians and the Dutch that this suggestion for ministerial consultation would undermine the newly established institutions of the EEC, agreement was reached, in November 1959, to hold quarterly meetings of the foreign ministers for consultation on foreign policy matters. Under this agreement meetings were held in 1960 at which subjects such as the Congo crisis and the forthcoming summit conference were discussed, but during that year de Gaulle indicated that he was keen to expand further the scope of these intergovermental meetings. There then followed, accompanied by the growing suspicion of the other four members of the EEC, a period of intense Franco–German negotiation in which de Gaulle managed to obtain the support of Adanauer for his idea of establishing a permanent political secretariat, based in Paris, to coordinate discussion not only of foreign policy but of other 'political' matters that fell outside the competence of the Treaties of Rome. The Franco–German discussions were followed both by attempts to reassure France's other EEC partners and by further contemptuous speeches by de Gaulle in which he attacked the workings of the supranational Community institutions.

At the very first conference of the 'Heads of State and Government and Foreign Ministers' of the six member-states in February 1961, de Gaulle's ambitions were frustrated by the Dutch Foreign Minister Joseph Luns, who refused to let a Study Commission set actual dates for regular meetings of heads of government. The Dutch, in expressing a concern shared by all the other EEC member-states, were worried both that de Gaulle sought to undermine the institutions of the Community and that his emphasis on 'national' policies would prove disruptive of harmonious relations with the USA within the NATO framework.

Both these concerns were to arise again in the 1970s when the present system of political cooperation was being developed. There then followed twelve months of argument, primarily between the French government and its partners about the shape of the proposed 'Political Committee', the status of its secretariat and its relationship with the existing institutions of the Communities. A Study Commission was set up under Christian Fouchet, and at a meeting in Bonn in July 1961, following a further round of Franco–German discussions, the six heads of government accepted its proposals for regular meetings to 'compare their views, to harmonize their policies and to arrive at common positions in order to further the political union of Europe, thus strengthening the Atlantic Alliance'. It was when the Fouchet Commission, having been charged with drawing up proposals to give the 'union' institutional status, produced a revised version of the plan (which France's partners had resigned themselves to accepting) that disagreement once again surfaced. In direct opposition to the stated desire of the other five states to merge the Community executives (EEC, ECSC and Euratom) and increase the powers of the European Assembly, Fouchet proposed giving a new 'council of heads of state or government' powers to 'harmonize, coordinate and unify the foreign,economic, cultural and defence policies of the Six' whilst at the same time *reducing* the role of the European Assembly.

The result of these new 'Fouchet' proposals was a deadlock which de Gaulle, despite further talks with the West Germans and Italians, was unable to break. In April 1962 the foreign ministers met in Paris, and Spaak, suspicious that the smaller EEC countries were being presented with a *fait accompli*, finally vetoed all further discussions of the proposals. The result of this meeting was to increase further French hostility to the Community institutions, which in turn ensured that future proposals for foreign policy coordination would be inextricably intertwined with arguments about the eventual nature of any full European Union.

The Community crisis of 1965–1966 which ended in the 'Luxembourg Compromise' raised similar issues about the future shape of European cooperation and left them similarly unresolved. Thus when at the end of the 1960s the heads of government met once again at The Hague to consider both the British application and the next stage of integration, political cooperaton was less a novel departure than an already familiar subject which carried with it a large number of sensitive and contentious issues, raising again the threat posed in earlier discusions to the 'Community method' and the Communities themselves. Pierre Werner, the only statesman at The Hague who had attended the Paris and Bonn Summits of 1961, voiced his own doubt as to whether the time had yet come 'to reopen the dossier on political cooperation as such'[2].

2.3   The Luxembourg and Copenhagen Reports

Nevertheless, the subject was reopened. The Hague Conference declared its intention to pave 'the way for a united Europe capable of assuming its responsibilities in the world of tomorrow and of making a contribution commensurate with its tradition and its mission . . .' and 'instructed the Ministers of Foreign Affairs to study the best way of achieving progress in the matter of political unification within the context of enlargement' and 'to make proposals before the end of July 1970'[3]. The Ministers, in their own report, 'felt that efforts ought first to concentrate specifically on co-ordination of foreign policies in order to show the whole world that Europe has a political mission . . . Desirous of making progress in the field of political unification, the governments decided to co-operate in the sphere of foreign policy'. 'The objectives of this co-operation are as follows:

– to ensure, through regular exchanges of information and consultations a better mutual understanding on the great international problems;
– to strengthen their solidarity by promoting the harmonization of their views, the co-ordination of their positions, and, where it appears possible or desirable, common actions.'

The modesty of these proposals is evident in comparison with the language of the draft treaty presented by the French during the earlier discussions of 1961, which had declared that: 'It shall be the aim of the Union . . . to bring about a common foreign policy in matters that are of common interest to member states.' The modesty of the stated objectives of consultation, coordination and 'where possible or desirable common action' also stood in sharp contrast to another of the decisions taken at The Hague, the ambitious commitment to economic and monetary union. The foreign ministers' procedural proposals (formulated by a committee of the political directors of the six foreign offices, under the chairmanship of the Belgian political director, Vicomte Davignon) were similarly less ambitious than those of the Werner Plan. Foreign ministers were to meet 'at least every six months . . . on the initiative of their chairman'. The main institution proposed was a Political Committee, composed of senior officials from national foreign ministries. They were given the loosest of mandates, to 'meet at least four times a year, to prepare the ministerial meetings and carry out any tasks delegated to them by the Ministers', and to have authority to set up 'working groups' and 'groups of experts', or to institute 'any other form of consultation' necessary. Secretarial and organizational arrangements for meetings were 'as a general rule' to be the responsibility of the country holding the presidency of the Council of Ministers. Meetings would take place in that country's capital, rather than in Brussels, with the host country providing the chairmanship. Disagreements about the Parliament were tempered by a commitment to invite the Commission 'to make known its views' when questions of overlapping competence with the Communities were discussed. It was also agreed to hold an informal 'biannual colloque' with the Political Committee of the European Parliament, which would not, however, report to the full Parliament in plenary session. As a procedure, it promised everything or nothing. There was no commitment to agree but simply to 'consult on all important questions of foreign policy' or on 'any question of their choice' which member-states might propose. National governments might thus, in the words of one sceptical observer, 'both have their cake and eat it' – both to pursue common policies and to preserve the freedom to opt out when it suited them. Scepticism, indeed, seemed to be a fairly widespread reaction. Maurice Schumann, summing up as chairman the second of these new 'Conferences of the Foreign Ministers of EEC Countries', concluded defensively that 'far from splitting (as had been expected) we have, on the contrary, considerably narrowed the gap between our points of view'[4].

The Luxembourg Report had argued that the applicant countries would 'have to accept the goals and procedures of political cooperation' as soon as they became Community members. In practice all the new members (including Norway, until its referendum) had been participating in political cooperation as 'observers' for some months before. Paradoxically, the UK and German governments suddenly became the most enthusiastic about further development, with the French government apparently urging caution because it found itself so often isolated[5]. The Paris Communique directed that consultation should be intensified at all levels, with the foreign ministers meeting quarterly in future[6]. The aim of their cooperation was now more ambitiously stated as 'to deal with problems of current interest, and, where possible, to formulate common medium and long-term positions'. They were able also to keep in mind, *inter alia*, 'the international political implications for and effects of Community policies under construction', and to maintain 'close contact' with Community institutions on matters 'which have a direct bearing on Community activities'. The foreign ministers were asked to prepare by June 1973 a second report on methods and procedures for improving political cooperation. Although, as before, it was possible to agree on procedural measures, the Paris Summit recorded continuing disagreement on most other policies. The preamble asserted that 'Europe must be able to make its voice heard in world affairs, and . . . must affirm its own views in international relations, as befits its mission to be open to the world and for progress, peace and cooperation'. This opaque language masked the continuing inability of the member governments to agree on what that voice should affirm in its dealings with the outside world.

The Copenhagen Report approved one month later by the foreign ministers in July 1973 set out as much to describe an already developed machinery as to lay down plans for its further development. This studied generality contrasted with the detailed proposals for future progress laid down in many Community plans in other fields. It noted that 'the characteristically pragmatic mechanisms set up by the Luxembourg Report have shown their flexibility and effectiveness'. The 'habit of working together,' it claimed, had become a 'reflex of coordination . . . which has profoundly affected the relations of the Member States between each other and with third countries. This collegiate sense in Europe is becoming a real force in international relations'[7]. Confusingly, many of its 'proposals' for improving cooperation had already been attained – as the report itself noted in an Annexe entitled 'Results obtained from Political Co-operation'. Thus, for instance, the group of 'Correspondents' which the Report announced was to be established had already begun to meet regularly. It was to follow through the implementation of decisions, to meet the absence of a secretariat by dealing with 'problems of organization and problems of a general nature' and to provide a link between the growing number of 'groups of experts' and working parties. Similarly, the proposal to increase the frequency of meetings of foreign ministers and of the Political Committee formalized existing practice. In addition, in each capital of the Nine, officials from the embassies of the other member-states were designated as 'correspondents' to the foreign ministry of the country to which they were accredited. In Third World countries, cooperation among the embassies and missions of the Nine was to be encouraged. A special network of communications among foreign ministries was established based on the COREU system of telegrams. Guidelines for relations with the Commission, the Council and the European Parliament were laid down, emphasizing still that 'Political Cooperation Machinery, which deals on the intergovernmental level with problems of international politics, is distinct from and additional to the activities of the institutions of the Community'. The presidency's responsibility for ensuring 'that the conclusions adopted at meetings of Ministers and of the Political Committee are implemented on a collegiate basis' and for calling and servicing meetings at all levels was recognized as an increasing administrative burden, but nothing concrete was proposed to alleviate it. With the rhetoric that so often camouflages continuing disagreement about content, the Report added that 'the ministers consider that cooperation on foreign policy must be placed in the perspective of European Union'.

Finally, to conclude this section on the 'formal' reports relating to European political cooperation it should be noted that the Belgian Prime Minister Tindemans, in the Report on European Union he presented to his colleagues in January 1976, called bluntly for 'an end to the distinction which still exists today between ministerial meetings which deal with political cooperation and those which deal with the subjects covered by the Treaties', though he also made it clear that 'the current procedures for preparing the diplomatic discussions of the Ministers' through the separate Political Committee structure should, in his opinion, remain unaffected[8].

His Report admitted the Commission's charge that in political cooperation 'we are equipped to react rather than to act'. His only remedy, however, was that 'the Ministers of Foreign Affairs will have to see that the existing machinery is improved'[9].

2.4   Interests and motives

The interests and objectives of the different member-governments (and indeed the existing Community institutions) were extremely mixed when it came to consideration both of the Davignon proposals and the political cooperation machinery that was eventually set up. For the French government, adjusting its European policy slowly after President de Gaulle's resignation, the acceptance, at The Hague, of enlargement needed to be balanced by a renewed emphasis on other articles of the Gaullist covenant: by resistance to any expansion of the roles of the Commission and the European Parliament; and by the creation instead of an intergovernmental structure for European cooperation and the pursuit of a common policy for Europe distinct from (and if necessary opposed to) that of the USA. The Dutch and German governments were prepared to yield to the French on this point in order to gain acceptance of the principle of admitting the four applicant-states, hoping that it would prove only a temporary arrangement which could in time be brought closer and closer to the established institutions. All the Six saw the advantages of moving towards a common policy towards Third World countries in terms of greater influence and status for the Community members in their relations with the USA, with the Soviet Union and Eastern Europe, and with the Arab countries of North Africa and the Middle East. All were painfully aware of the major obstacles which lay in the path of a common policy. The West German government also had other interests in promoting political cooperation, 'at a time when we are trying to bring East and West together', as Herr Brandt emphasized at The Hague. The Germans were concerned both with balancing their *Ostpolitik* with an active *Westpolitik* and with creating a vehicle for the more active foreign policy they now aimed to pursue[10].

Both national and Community attitudes to the new procedure were coloured by the suspicion that political cooperation was as much a threat to the established procedures of the Communities as a means of widening the area of collaboration among member-governments. Its link with the ill-defined concept of 'political union' reinforced the fears of those who saw this as a renewed Gaullist onslaught on the Community method and on the Community structure as the basis for a future European union. In the first three years those involved were therefore often just as concerned with questions of institutional status and procedural details as with the substantive problems under discussion. The distinction between 'political' and 'economic' issues, between those within the competence of the Communities and those that went beyond it, was fundamental to the establishment of political cooperation as a separate procedure. It was to deal with issues of high politics in the traditional Gaullist sense, rather than with technical problems falling within the legal framework of the treaties. The Commission's reaction was at first defensive, concerned to maintain the boundaries of its legal competences against any attempts at encroachment and to insist that it alone was entitled to represent the common interest in areas of established Community policy. For some within the Commission the term 'political' still had pejorative connotations, implying a threat to all that the Communities had so far achieved. The French government was just as concerned to keep the new procedure untainted by the insidious atmosphere of Brussels and to prevent the Communities from encroaching on an area of policy so central to national sovereignty. The dispute over the possible creation and location of a political secretariat and its relationship with the existing Community institutions distracted attention from the question of what such a secretariat might do. The differentiation between the 'Conference of Foreign Ministers of the EEC Countries' and Council of Ministers was seen at its most absurd in the midday trek from Copenhagen to Brussels between meetings in November 1973. Moreover, it prejudiced the chances of achieving coherence with related areas of Community activity. The rigidity of this distinction was consistently opposed by both the Dutch and German governments[11]. The European Parliament, too, soon began to express its irritation at the formalistic refusal of successive foreign ministers, while holding the presidency, to discuss with the full Parliament matters which 'do not fall within the competence of the Council'. The Parliament's anger reflected a determination to extend its competence and its representative role to this new area of collaboration, and a continuing feeling that political cooperation represented a threat to the Communities. Some Danish representatives, in contrast, insisted at the same time on the principle of democratic control and on limiting the Communities' competence to economic and welfare issues. They argued rather that political cooperation should be made subject to the control of national parliaments – an alternative which would have risked the disclosure of confidential multilateral discussions[12]. Although several member-governments did not fully accept the distinction between political and economic relations or between high and low policy on which the political cooperation procedure rested, their foreign ministries had little difficulty in adjusting to them. Throughout the Six, the division of foreign relations into 'political' and 'economic' categories was institutionalized in these ministries' division into political and economic directorates, with the latter responsible for Community matters – a division most marked in the French and German foreign ministries. Political directors were already accustomed to the principle of multilateral consulta-tion within the NATO framework. They were, however, not involved in the network of relations through which governments coordinated national policy towards the Communities. This also meant that they had little or no contact with the Permanent Representations in Brussels. Political cooperation for the first time gave political directors and their staff an opportunity to play a role in the Community arena. The readiness, even enthusiasm, with which officials in foreign ministries and embassies abroad took to the development of political cooperation may also have reflected a bureaucratic instinct to expand their functions. Within the Community framework the traditional foreign ministry role of overseeing the whole spread of external relations, of acting as gatekeeper between national policy-making and international cooperation, had been threatened and eroded by the direct involvement of domestic ministries in the Community process. The political cooperation procedure, in contrast, focused upon the central concerns of diplomacy; and foreign ministry control of that procedure was neither challenged by other powerful ministries or by domestic constituencies. It was thus hardly surprising that within the foreign offices of Europe there was considerable enthusiasm and support for the development of political cooperation. In addition there were, of course, some tangible gains for the participants in this purely intergovernmental process. The quality of the information about each others' attitude to forthcoming issues had been immeasurably improved. 'There are no longer any surprises among the Nine', 'we all know each other's minds', were the responses from foreign ministry to foreign office. One embassy official in London in 1973 complained that the desk officer on Vietnam in the Foreign and Commonwealth Office was better informed than he was about the thinking within his home foreign ministry on South-east Asia.

Finally, one might conclude that the development of the political cooperation machinery served, particularly during a rather sticky period for the European integrative enterprise, both the interests of those who wished the EEC to develop rapidly into some sort of European Union and those, like the UK, who were unenthusiastic about such progress. For the supporters of Europe, political cooperation proved to be an area where at least some progress could be reported, despite the stalemate and deadlock within the formal Community institutions – as such it was something of a morale-booster. For the British in particular, and perhaps also the French, political cooperation as it developed represented an area of European activity that caused no offense to their firmly held objections to further extensions of the principle of supranationality. Thus political cooperation proved to be an issue that all states could agree to, albeit for widely differing motives.

2.5   The general political context

Although the case studies in this volume examine in considerable detail the political background of specific issue areas we should conclude with a short analysis of the general political context in which political cooperation developed. The starting point must, of course, be the resignation of General de Gaulle in 1969 and the consequent easing of French opposition both to the enlargement of the EEC to incorporate the UK and to an extension of the scope of European integration. At The Hague Summit at the end of the 1960s the stalemate that had existed since the failure of the Fouchet proposals of 1962 and the Community crisis of 1965–1966 was broken and a second 'relaunching of Europe' embarked upon, with at least the tacit support of Pompidou, the new French President. Nevertheless, many of the basic tenets of Gaullism continued to be adhered to and this was reflected in the French insistence, during the early days of political cooperation, on the continued separation of Community and EPC affairs. Thus although an advance had been made in that political cooperation did get underway after 1970 it still remained until 1974 the prisoner of the continuing theological debate about the future shape of a United Europe.

This uneasy internal situation was not much assisted by the generally divisive attitude of the USA[13]. The difficulties that arose, both over Kissinger's 'Year of Europe' initiatives and the Middle East war and subsequent energy crisis, undoubtedly held up the general development of political cooperation (as indeed had doubts and fears about Europe's relationship with the USA in the past). Given the long-established nature of the two problems mentioned above, it was thus rather surprising to find that by the end of 1974 a marked change in the general context of political cooperation had come about. The transformation can be dated fairly precisely between February and June. In February Herr Scheel told the Political Affairs Committee of the European Parliament that cooperation was proving difficult and that he saw no hope of an early *rapprochement* between France and the Eight on relations with the USA. In June his successor, Herr Genscher, announced to a surprised press that the foreign ministers had found agreement on 'all' issues so easy that they had concluded the business of a two-day meeting in one day[14]. The Gymnich meeting had clearly played a role in untying the tangle of disagreements, and in persuading the new UK Foreign Secretary, Anthony Crosland, of the value of political cooperation – an interesting example of rapid socialization. His enthusiasm removed a potential source of friction after the change of UK government, particularly with the prospect of renegotiation. Similarly the arrival of Helmut Schmidt as Brandt's successor in West Germany seemed to ease a number of potential tensions in intra-European relations. But the decisive event, without doubt, was the death of President Pompidou on 2 April 1974. Two 'pro-European' candidates were the front-runners in the French presidential election campaign, from which Giscard d'Estaing emerged victorious on 9 May. The changed tone of French policy was rapid enough to throw its diplomatic representatives into some confusion. M. Sauvagnargues, the new Foreign Minister, made it clear from the start that he saw no harm in blending Community issues with political cooperation.

The fruits of French – and UK – pragmatism were evident in the handling of the Cyprus crisis during July, when for the first time foreign ministers conferred informally on political matters within the Council chamber.

However, whilst the above example suggests that the decisive factors influencing the progress of political cooperation were national policies and national attitudes rather than, for instance, the habits of consultation built up over three and a half years, it is important to stress that the most important influences have come from outside the Nine. Thus the improvement in relations with the USA was also much assisted by the declining confidence of the Nixon administration once the full extent of the Watergate affair became apparent. It should also be noted, and this point perhaps serves to place EPC in some sort of perspective, that the US attitude towards the foreign policy activities of the Nine seemed to become more tolerant once Washington was satisfied that political cooperation was a process more notable for its procedure than its substance.

Within Europe much the same analysis can be applied: national policies were important for establishing EPC and getting it over the two fundamental hurdles discussed above. This apart, though, it is difficult to find any significant relationship between the general political situation and the development of political cooperation. Such a relationship is far more likely to be found in Brussels within the Community institutions, for the very bureaucratic nature of EPC, particularly its secrecy, protects it to a certain extent from the disturbances caused by changing political attitudes to and enthusiasm for progress at the European level. Nevertheless it is certainly the case that when European enthusiasms are running high within the member-states this is felt in EPC, mainly because of its established role in the preparation of summit conferences and proposals for institutional change within the EEC.

Despite the considerable advance publicity, little was expected of the Tindemans Report on European Union for it was seen by most participants as a holding operation rather than a manifestation of any renewed political will on the part of the member-states of the European Community. As we have noted above, the Report adopted a firm *communitaire* line, calling for the absorption of the political cooperation machinery into the legal framework of the Treaties of Rome, but this evoked little positive response. To sum up, then: the general political context of EPC has been essentially favourable, particularly to the extent that cooperation in foreign policy has come to be regarded as useful in its own right rather than merely as a symbol of movement towards a European Union; there was a clear injection of enthusiasm around 1974 but one is still left with the conclusion that the fortunes of EPC still seem, as the following case studies make clear, to be more related to the nature of specific external stimuli than to any general integrative mood in Europe.

Notes

1 Communique of the Conference of Heads of State and Government of the European Community's Member States of 2nd December 1969 in The Hague; Article 15

2 *Bulletin of the European Communities*, 1–1970, p. 52

3 The Hague Communique, pp. 3 and 15

4 *Bulletin of the European Communities*, 6–1971, p. 21

5 *Guardian*, 18 January 1973

6 'Declaration of the Conference of the Heads of State and Government of the European Community's Member States of October 21st 1972', *Bulletin of the European Communities*, 10–1972

7 'Second Report on Political Cooperation', *Bulletin of the European Communities*, 9–1973, p. 14–21

8 *Bulletin of the European Communities* (Supplement), 1–1976, pp. 14 and 31

9 Ibid., p. 32

10 *Bulletin of the European Communities*, 2–1970, p. 35

11 Berndt von Staden, 'Political Cooperation in the European Community', *Aussenpolitik*, 23, No 2, 1972, pp. 123–133

12 Official Journal, *Debates of the European Parliament*, July 1974, p. 90

13 See Chapter 6 in this volume on the Euro–Arab dialogue (pp. 69–82)

14 *Bulletin of the European Communities*, 6–1974, p. 124

The dual structure of EPC and Community activities: problems of coordination

GIANNI BONVICINI

The history of political cooperation between the nine EEC member-states runs parallel to the work of the European Community and has at times been seen as a political alternative to this form of integration. The factors separating and differentiating the two approaches have thus continually prevailed over any factors tending towards their unification. Nonetheless, since 1971, the year in which the concept of political cooperation was first translated into concrete institutions alongside existing Community institutional structures, the finding of a solution to the problem of coordination between them has become a practical necessity. To be more precise, two factors tend to favour coordination between political cooperation and Community activities.

The first of these is that the declared aim of political cooperation is the same as that of Community cooperation: the political unification of Europe. It was the final communique of The Hague Summit Conference in 1969 which launched the idea. The Community foreign ministers were entrusted with the task of studying, in view of the prospective enlargement of the Community, how best to realise progress in the field of political unification[1]. In the first Davignon Report in 1970 they declared that the best way of making progress towards this goal was 'a concrete effort towards foreign policy coordination to show the world that Europe has a political mission'. At the same time, the first steps were taken towards economic and monetary union. The ministers proposed a stage-by-stage programme with a deadline set in 1980 for the achievement of European sovereignty in monetary policy and in the coordination of economic policies. Compared with the aims of political cooperation, those in the field of economic and monetary union were much more ambitious. But even though the means for attainment took on an entirely different form, its final objective, nevertheless, was the political unification of Europe

In the second place, from a negotiating point of view the close links between foreign and economic policy were there from the beginning. It is hard to consider energy policy, Mediterranean policy, the Euro–Arab Dialogue, relations with the USA and the European Security Conference (to give a few examples) as problems where the economic aspects of policy are rigidly separated from the foreign-policy questions. At the 1972 Paris

Summit the EEC heads of state officially recognized the interdependence of economic and foreign policy. In paragraph 14 of the final communique they recognized the 'implications and consequences in the international political field of Community policies presently under debate'[2]. There can be no doubt that in practice, with the creation of the EEC the member-states created a body with exclusively economic responsibilities. At the same time, however, Community economic policy has profound effects on the outside world. The very existence of the Community is seen by the outside world not as merely an economic datum but as a fact of international politics. The beginning of cooperation in the foreign policy field can only reinforce this characteristic of the Community as a distinct international entity[3].

The Community heads of state have recognized the need for coordination between the two sides of the Community's activity. At the Paris Summit in October 1972 they repeated that 'in questions affecting the activities of the Community, close contact will be maintained with Community institutions'. At the next Paris meeting in October 1974 they were far more explicit. 'In order to guarantee the coordination of Community activities the foreign ministries are charged with initiating and coordinating Community activities within the Council of Ministers. During the Council Sessions they may also meet as a political coordination body.' At the same meeting the heads of state reserved a privileged role for themselves in the management of foreign policy 'in all sectors affecting the interests of the European Community'. The transformation of the Summits into European Councils gave a more systematic character to this resolution and allowed the heads of state to plan more easily their role as overall coordinators of foreign and economic policy[4].

Naturally, the government heads have not always acted in unison. Frequently, trends which run contrary to the aims of coordination have been displayed. There is, of course, a long history to the recurring idea of a secretariat for political cooperation, detached from Community institutions, which would hold extensive powers of initiative and coordination[5]. Although the proposal for the creation of such a separate secretariat has remained on the drawing-boards, and despite official declarations of concern, the two institutional structures – that of the Community and that of political cooperation – continue to follow independent procedures. Thus, periodic conferences (at least four per year) of foreign ministers, prepared by a committee consisting of their foreign-policy directors (the Political Committee) have been instituted in order to consider matters in the field of political cooperation. A so-called 'Correspondents' group' (a type of sub-group of the Political Committee) is in charge of the application of political cooperation decisions and of studying organizational problems. Individual issues of cooperation (e.g. the European Security Conference, the Middle East, etc.) are prepared within *ad hoc* working groups. In addition, ambassadors of the Nine also have some coordinative functions: they meet regularly in the various capitals of the world to coordinate their positions towards the host-country.

The purpose of this extensive network is to search for common ground on concrete issues which are of concern to the Community as a whole in the world at large. On these issues, 'in keeping with the terms of political cooperation, every nation-state seeks, *in general*, to refrain from definitively fixing its position without having first consulted other members'[6].

Until the present time little progress has been made in establishing consistent contact between this decision-making structure and the Community apparatus. The publication of the first Davignon Report in July 1970 was followed by a period during which those charged with the management of political cooperation and those dealing with Community activities fought jealously to defend their prerogatives and to avoid any 'polluting' contact with each other. The main reason for this attitude, quite apart from actual competition between institutions, is to be found in the differing political premises on which they are founded. Political cooperation represents, in practice, an alternative concept to that represented by the Community. It restores a prime role to the nation-state in the building of Europe and allows the latter more extensive control over Community activities. Thus the tendencies which have been manifested for some time within Community institutions have been further reinforced by a growing consolidation of intergovernmental management methods, in stark contrast to the supranationality outlined in the Treaty of Rome.

3.1 Coordination in the European Council and the Council of Ministers

However, despite the rigidity of the distinctions mentioned above, many issues are such that decision-making must follow the same line both within political cooperation and within normal Community institutions. This is especially true within the European Council. The role of this new, non-institutionalized organ has never been well defined. In any event, the declared political goal of the European Council is the overall coordination of European cooperation and the definition (at least in theory) of the basic strategic line guiding Community activity[7].

The European Council may discuss both EEC and EPC items. The distinction between the two fields is rendered even more artificial by the fact that it is the same people (the heads of government) who work in both. Often the very logic of the problems up for negotiation leads to confusion between the external and internal aspects of cooperation.

At least to some extent the same is true of the Council of Foreign Ministers, which was granted specific responsibilities for the general coordination of Community activities following the 1974 Paris Summit. Here,

too, however, the same individual plays two roles; one in political cooperation and one in Community activities. But if it is true that the foreign
ministers act simultaneously as interpreters of the discussions and decisions
which are reached in both fields of Community activity, it must be kept in
mind that the staffs which prepare the dossiers change, depending upon
whether political cooperation of Community-related topics are being considered. Consequently, it can be said that while in practice progress towards
coordination has been made (on the level of foreign ministers and heads of
government), from an institutional point of view responsibilities in the two
fields remain strictly divided. Although ministers are no longer obliged to
hold meetings in the two fields at separate times in order to emphasize this
distinction, the latter is carefully maintained by the Council which meets as
the Ministerial Conference when discussing political cooperation, and as the
Council of General Affairs when dealing with Community issues.

It should be added that the degree of rigidity in the classification of
questions on the agenda and in the issuing of invitations for Community
institutions to participate in political cooperation depends on the President's
will and his ability to persuade his colleagues.

As late as the end of 1973 the two sets of structures (Community
institutions on the one hand, political cooperation on the other) were kept
rigidly apart. During the Danish presidency of the Council of Ministers in
the second half of 1973 the European foreign ministers were forced to move
from one city to another, all in the same day, in order to emphasize this
separation[8]. From the beginning of 1974 onwards, however, the situation
gradually began to improve during the German, French, Irish and Italian
presidencies (1974–1975). There were a number of reasons for this more
favourable attitude towards the coordination of political cooperation with
Community activities. As far as the French were concerned, the change was
due to their newly-elected President Giscard d'Estaing's desire to distinguish himself from his predecessors by encouraging European political
integration.

The Irish, on the other hand, as well as favouring the advancement of
integration, wished to use the Commission as an additional source of
information, given their limited national bureaucratic resources.

3.2 Participation of the Commission in political cooperation

The greatest progress towards coordination has been the acceptance of
regular participation by the Commission in the political cooperation process. This is especially true for the European Council and for the Conference
of Foreign Ministers, in which the President of the Commission
or the Commissioner, with responsibility for external affairs, participates
regularly.

This changed attitude towards the Commission (and the changed attitude of the Commission towards political cooperation) can be traced back to a number of factors. The first of these was the positive experience of work in the preparatory committee for the European Security Conference. Even though it related in the main to the economic 'basket', the task of coordinating the Community position was carried out most successfully. Under circumstances which required considerable effort, Commission officials proved to be extremely competent in mediating between diverse national interests. Because this task brought such satisfactory results, after the Helsinki Conference the group continued to function regularly (as a follow-up working group), having been assigned the job of studying the Conference results and coordinating future Community positions. A second important development was the coming to power in France of Giscard d'Estaing and his more flexible approach to Community affairs. A third factor was the Nine's decision not to create a strong permanent secretariat for political cooperation. In the search for further administrative support more emphasis was placed on the functioning of the Community machinery. Events showed the usefulness of the Commission and of Community institutions in general, in the achievement of concrete results in foreign policies. Thus many misunderstandings have today been removed. The Commission itself has changed its views of political cooperation. Whereas once it was suspicious, jealously guarding its prerogatives, today it is collaborating fairly intensively, whilst still watchful for any attempts to encroach upon its area of activity.

The Commission has set up the necessary machinery to deal with this new mass of work. With regard to the institutional implications, general responsibility for political cooperation has been attributed to the President and to the General Secretariat. The Directorate-Generals for External Relations and for Development are responsible for the preparation of documents and dossiers and administrative problems. This division of labour in itself is significant for it calls for a high degree of coordination within the Commission between international economic affairs and political cooperation and a rationalization of the work to be done. Usually the Commission manages to arrive at a coherent policy position (unlike some of the member-states). It should be added that it is always the same officials who work on political cooperation. This reinforces their ability to influence the Political Committee and those working groups charged with the formulation of a common policy on a specific issue.

Within the Political Committee itself, the Commission has gradually become more involved in the elaboration of proposals which are to be presented to the foreign ministers in preparation for their various meetings, as well as the implementation of the decisions which have been taken. Commission officials now meet regularly with the political affairs directors in order to discuss the topics on the meetings' agendas. There is one exception to the, by now, firmly established procedures, namely the more informal working dinners that the political directors hold. Commission officials are not invited to these affairs, perhaps because the national foreign service officials wish to preserve one forum in which they feel free to exchange confidences and matters that the Commission would be sensitive to.

Nevertheless these informal meetings have proved to be less important than their confidentiality led one to expect. It has, however, helped to accentuate a strange psychological trait within the Commission. According to a report to the European Parliament prepared by Erik Blumenfeld, 'the Commission believes that on account of its position as a guest at political cooperation meetings, information received there should be used with discretion'[9]. The *rapporteur* emphasizes that this discretion is due not simply to the Commission's absence from the dinners but to its more general guest-status in political cooperation work.

The Commission's role at lower levels of political cooperation is less clear. The setting-up of the correspondents' group was an innovation suggested by the second Davignon Report in 1973[10]. The correspondents were to have a dual role. On the one hand, they were made responsible for the organization within each individual foreign ministry of dossiers concerning political cooperation. They thus came to play an indispensable part in examining the national side of each individual European problem and coordinating the assignment of tasks to the various directorates (primarily the economic and the political directorates) within national foreign ministries. Their second task is to manage the EPC aspects of the presidency, which is rotated between the member-states, each of which assumes this role for six months at a time. During this period, the correspondent in question receives additional help in order to fulfil his two roles. Nevertheless, the second of these, as well as being only periodic (once every four and a half years), is, given the lack of a well-defined European structure for the correspondents' group, relatively unimportant. The group is neither a 'mobile secretariat' nor yet a genuine working group. Obviously, in these conditions it is impossible even to discuss coordination between the positions of the Commission and those of the group. This does not exist at any level. The situation is not difficult to explain if one considers the essentially 'national' origins of the correspondents' group as well as the 'national' framework within which it works, essentially closed to any possible 'approach' from the Commission.

The working groups are a rather different case. They were first discussed in the first Davignon Report in 1970. Their task is the preparation of work for the Political Committee[11]. Here too, however, there is no general rule on participation by the Commission. There is nevertheless, a trend towards a gradual increase in the involvement of Community officials. Obviously this trend is not a continuous one. The decision as to whether the

Commission is to participate is normally taken at the beginning of each meeting. The problems which arise here are usually due to opposition from an individual national delegation to the presence of Community officials during discussion of specific issues. When this occurs, and it is impossible to reach unanimous agreement, the Chairman may request the temporary withdrawal of the Commission representative until the next item on the agenda. In some groups, however, there have been instances where participation by a delegation from the Commission has become the norm. This is the case in the group on the European Security Conference, where the Commission is now represented permanently. The number of groups where this applies, as opposed to those without officials from the Commission, is on the increase. It should be emphasized, however, that in this field everything depends on the decision of the group Chairman and on the unanimous acceptance of the Community presence by national delegations.

Finally, we come to the question of Community representatives' relations with the ambassadors of Community member-states located in Third World countries or in the headquarters of major international institutions. Above all, it must be made clear that in confronting the enormous network of national diplomacy the Commission has very few delegations to major countries of the world or to international organizations at its disposal. The Community officials who are able to follow political cooperation issues at this level are small in number. However, they usually participate in the meetings of the Nine's ambassadors, especially in routine meetings which deal with Community affairs and those concerning political cooperation. In any case, the participation of the Community representative in the meetings is decided upon by the ambassador who is acting as president. His decision is consequently subject to the wishes of his government and its will either to emphasize or to de-emphasize the Community's importance in collaboration of the Nine.

These last examples call for a number of comments. First, there is no precise rule establishing the Commission's right to participate in political cooperation. The Commission is invited to give its opinion on the grounds that this is 'current practice'. This does not mean, however, that it has a *right* to take part in work concerning political cooperation. Everything depends on the value attributed to 'current practice'. Certainly it is unlikely that we will return to the times when the Commission was totally excluded from political cooperation. Although the main trend is in the opposite direction it is not as yet firmly established.

Our second point is that the opinion of the Council presidency and of the Political Committee is of decisive importance in determining the Commission's role. Whereas the smaller Community members use the Commission to make up for their own weakness, this is not true for the large countries, who tend to rely on their own sources of information and their own diplomatic representatives.

In practice, the Commission's contact with political cooperation is still sporadic and superficial even if it is growing. Its role depends on custom and on a tacit invitation from the presidency, except, of course, in cases such as that of the CSCE, when the Conference of Ministers made an official request for the Commission's participation, subsequently confirmed and thus legalized by the Community Council.

3.3   COREPER and the European Parliament in political cooperation

Before concluding it would be useful to examine two other aspects in the coordination between Community institutions and the organs of political cooperation: the roles played by the Committee of Permanent Representatives (COREPER) and the European Parliament respectively.

Regarding COREPER, it could be said that this arm of the Community has suffered more than any other as a result of the establishment of political cooperation. COREPER had always been the filter between the initiatives of the Commission and the activities of the Council of Ministers. In the field of political cooperation the initiatives no longer come from the Commission (since this role has been delegated to the Political Committee) and COREPER's importance has thus become secondary. This fact becomes clear when the Council of Ministers has to decide upon to whom it wishes to delegate certain problems. It occurs fairly often that there are difficulties in establishing whether a given problem is political or economic in nature. Often the COREPER is put on the defensive. In the dispute which follows between the COREPER and the Political Committee the Commission has on occasion managed to play a role on account of its coherent position and the rapidity with which its administration gains access to necessary information. There can be no doubt that the Commission tends to defend the COREPER, if only because it is a Community institution. This is somewhat ironical if one remembers the bitterness with which the Commission fought to prevent the emergence of a strong role for the COREPER as a filter between itself and the Council. The Commission's intervention in favour of the COREPER represents an historical nemesis.

On the other hand, in order to explain certain difficulties which COREPER faces in trying to insert itself in the realm of political cooperation, one must retrace its origins, as well as those of the Political Committee. In other words, one needs to analyse the relations between national foreign offices and the Council, or, to be more precise, between specific branches of national foreign offices and the Council. In fact, the representatives of both COREPER and the Political Committee come from the ministries of foreign affairs, but their importance within the ministries and their relation with the

Council of Ministers differ. Furthermore, they are often formally separated. Therefore it could be that in many instances there exists a degree of jealousy and conflict over one or the other's competence in dealing with a given issue. Meetings between COREPER and the Political Committee have been called to try to resolve these disagreements, but so far there are no positive results to speak of.

A few words on the role of the European Parliament concerning the control of political cooperation are in order. Here, too, involvement is increasing. Originally, following the first Davignon Report the Parliament had a very restricted role in political cooperation activities. Everything was limited to twice-yearly meetings between the Parliament's Political Committee and the ministers of foreign affairs (though often the meetings were only attended by one minister at a time) and to a verbal report to the Parliament on progress in political cooperation work by the current President of the Council of Ministers. The number of meetings each year between the Political Commissioner and the foreign ministers has now increased to four. It is also possible for parliamentarians to address written or oral questions to the current President of the Council. The President is not, however, prepared to respond to questions orally; more often replies are in writing.

Despite some improvements, the European Parliament's role may be considered as irrelevant. Not only is parliamentary control exerted after decisions have been taken but this control is purely consultative. This means that while the Parliament has succeeded, after many years of struggle, in winning some limited but significant powers from the Council (for example, in the budgetary field), it has at the same time failed to control an extremely broad sector of activity.

The parliamentarians are themselves well aware of this gap. In a recent report on political cooperation they propose a number of measures to improve existing procedures[12]. The most insistent complaints concern the lack of information provided and the lack of sensitivity shown by the Commission and the Council of Ministers towards the requirements of parliamentary control, the lack of time and the fact that debates are always held after the relevant decisions have been taken. In some ways these are problems which affect all Western parliaments whose degree of control over foreign policy has always been somewhat limited. In the case of the European Parliament, however, even the basic tools are lacking. There is often, furthermore, great difficulty in determining to whom parliamentary questions should be addressed. In certain issues where economic and foreign policy issues seem to be mixed it is not clear whether responsibility lies with the Community Council or with the Conference of Foreign Ministers. Here we return to the problem of the formal dichotomy between those questions dealt with within the framework of political cooperation and those where responsibility belongs to the Community. This time the victim is the

European Parliament, which is forced to exert its limited and highly partial task of political control in an atmosphere of general uncertainty[13].

3.4   Limits of coordination

The fact that the need for coordination between political cooperation and Community activities has been clear from the beginning has obviously helped to bring the two sides of European activity together. Many problems concerning coordination or the assignment of responsibilities which a few years ago seemed to be insoluble are no longer of importance today. On several occasions we have seen the EEC's economic policy act as an active support for initiatives in the field of political cooperation (as in the case of aid to Portugal). The Commission has also taken independent foreign policy initiatives (such as the Ortoli Declaration on Spain), later supported by the Council (although these have been followed by protests). We have witnessed a continuous cooperation at a certain level of decision-making between the Commission on the one hand, and the Political Committee on the other. This shows the degree of flexibility and adaptability which has developed in political cooperation.

At the same time, however, as well as these positive aspects of the situation there are a number of unresolved issues. The first and most important of these is that decision-making in the field of political cooperation and in Community activities are two separate processes, both in terms of the way in which decisions are made and the way in which they are controlled. The Tindemans Report on European Union accepted the maintenance of this distinction[14]. This is highly significant if one considers that the Belgian Prime Minister was acting as a spokesman for the Nine when he prepared the Report. The future of political cooperation at least in the eyes of the governments would be to remain an instrument for collaboration which is different from that of the Community. It would thus continue to follow a path of integration which is strictly diplomatic and intergovernmental, making very few concessions to the notion of supranationalism.

The second weakness is the uncertainty which arises from the absence of precise rules. Given that fields of responsibility and roles have never been legally defined, everything is left to the member-states and to the presidency. Even the participation of the Commission in political cooperation work rests on a very precarious basis. Coordination depends on little more than goodwill. Levels of participation by Community institutions fluctuate considerably. At a low level there is practically no coordination. Correspondents, ambassadors and expert groups work independently with practically no support from Community officials[15]. This complicates problems of information between the two structures. The diplomatic network tends to escape all efforts of coordination. Problems of confidentiality tend to create new barriers such as the COREU network linking the nine Community capitals and reserved for use by the diplomatic services. The Commission is obviously excluded from this network. It is informed of the content of messages which have been transmitted many hours after – and only in cases in which the current president decides to release the information.

Finally, whilst in most cases the Commission provides information or takes part in the decision-making process it has never *initiated* action, which is actually the only role which distinguishes the Community context of the Commission's activity. Without this level of participation there can never be any substantial interpretation between the two decision-making structures, so that as far as the harmonization between Community and political cooperation activities and positions is concerned, it will be extremely difficult for their convergence to go beyond a certain limit.

Certainly, experience to date shows that improvements are still possible. It is not inconceivable, in other words, that technical measures might lead to a higher degree of cooperation between the two fields. It might be possible to consider a more authoritative role for the European Council, and thus the elimination of distinctions between different kinds of policy question, or the setting up of a political cooperation office at the Council Secretariat, or, more generally, a closer involvement of the Commission in the work of the Political Committee. Nevertheless, the real problem of how political cooperation can co-exist with Community activity remains. This was very honestly recognized by the Belgian Minister for Foreign Affairs, Henry Simonet, in a speech to the European Parliament in November 1977. He declared that in so far as absorption of political cooperation by Community institutions is concerned, it was necessary to realize that, while this remains a long-term goal, certain states remain unwilling to move beyond the present situation and wish to avoid involving themselves in a decision-making process leading to the formulation of a genuine European foreign policy[16]. A form of political cooperation based exclusively on national political wills is 'precarious, reversible and leaves many loop-holes'. This state of affairs could end up by having a negative effect on what has already been achieved, with great difficulty, in recent years. The definitive solution to the problem thus remains tied to a broad institutional reform both of political cooperation and of the Community; in a word, a qualitative leap towards European Political Union.

Notes

1 In paragraph 3 of the final communique issued by The Hague Conference (1–2 December 1969) the heads of government declared that 'Entering the final stage of the Common Market signifies not only consecration of the irreversible nature of the Community's achievements, but also the preparation of the way towards a united Europe, capable of assuming its responsibilities in tomorrow's world and making a contribution, corresponding to its tradition and mission'

2 *Bulletin of the European Communities*, No. 10, 1972

3 This latter concept was reconfirmed by the second report on European Political Cooperation in Foreign Policy, presented by the foreign ministers to the heads of government on 23 July 1973 (the so-called Copenhagen Report). This argued that for Europe to make her voice felt in world politics it was necessary for her to take her 'post in world affairs as an independent entity'. *Bulletin of the European Communities*, No. 9, 1973, pp. 14–21

4 On 9 and 10 December 1974 it was decided at the seventh and last summit meeting in the Community's history to transform the traditional summits into regular meetings of EEC heads of government (known as the European Council). This change was proposed by the new French President, Giscard d'Estaing, who worked to give fresh drive to the European integration process through the recognition of an official role for heads of government

5 The idea of a political secretariat dates back to discussions held in the period from 1960 to 1962 between heads of government, foreign ministers and officials. It was formulated for the first time in the so-called Fouchet Plan for Political Union in 1962. On this occasion, no agreement was reached. This did not, however, prevent similar proposals being advanced from time to time, i.e. Pompidou's idea, advanced in 1973, for a 'thinking secretariat' (with a high degree of political autonomy) to be based in Paris and the European Parliament's proposal for a Political Cooperation Office, based in Brussels (the Blumenfeld Report, 12 October 1977)

6 This somewhat vague commitment is contained in the second Davignon Report on political cooperation, published on 23 July 1973 (see Note 3). Since then, however, there have been numerous and often spectacular violations of the principle

7 As far as coordination within the European Council is concerned, it should be pointed out that in its brief history it has discussed and taken decisions of principle both on purely Community affairs (such as the Regional Fund and Employment Policy) and on questions of foreign policy (such as political relations with Portugal and Rhodesia)

8 A particularly famous occasion on which this occurred was 23 July 1973, when the foreign ministers of the Nine met in the morning in Copenhagen to examine points to be discussed with Nixon during his visit to Europe (later postponed) and in the afternoon in Brussels to discuss unresolved questions connected with the opening of international trade negotiations (the Nixon Round). The rigid Danish attitude was not, however, due simply to questions of principle, but rather to the poor relations between the Minister for Foreign Affaris (Anderson) and the Minister for European Affairs (Noorgard). That Denmark opposes any even minimal change in the present European institutional system is well known (for further information see Gianni Bonvicini, 'La Politica di Integrazione Europea', *L'Italia nella Politica Internazionale (1973–74)*, Instituto Affari Internazionali, Edizione Communita, Milano, 1974, pp. 335, 367ff.

9 The Political Committee of the European Parliament: draft paper on European political cooperation. Rapporteur Erik Blumenfeld – PE 49335/riv. 11–12/10/77

10 Point 3 in the second Davignon Report (23 July 1973) reads: 'A group is to be set up consisting of European liaison officials from foreign ministries and will be known as the "correspondent's group". The group will have the task of putting political cooperation into practice and of examining organisational and general problems. The group will also be responsible for preparing the work of the Political Committee on specific questions on the basis of the latters' directives'

11 Point 3 of Paragraph III of the Davignon Report of 27 October 1970 explains that 'the Political Committee can create working groups to handle particular tasks. It may set up groups of experts to collect material on a specific problem and to suggest possible solutions'

12 Ample space is given to relations between the parliament and tools of political cooperation in the central sections of the report by Erik Blumenfeld (pp. 19–23), PE 49335/riv II

13 The dichotomy between political cooperation and Community activity and its effect on the role of the European Parliament is mentioned in an informative note issued by the Christian Democrat Group within the European Parliament: PE – Christian Democrat Group – Secretariat. Informative note on the

Blumenfeld Report, Doc/6/1040/77/GP

14 In connection with the problem of a single decision-making centre, the Belgian Prime Minister, Tindemans, stated in his report on European Union that 'the existence of a single decision-making centre does not mean that Community activities and political cooperation must necessarily merge. The differing nature of these problems does not oblige us to deal with them through identical procedures'. *Bulletin of the European Communities*, Supplement 1/76

15 This opinion was also expressed in the informative note issued by the Christian Democrat group within the European Parliament (see Note 13). On pages 3–4, it is recalled that 'the greatest resistance to active Community participation in political cooperation is to be found not so much at a high level – that is at foreign ministry level – but rather among those high national officials who constitute the infrastructure of European political cooperation'

16 A summary of the debate held on 15 November 1977 is to be found in the official summaries of the proceedings of the European Parliament in *Agence Europe*, No. 2328, 16/11/77, p. 4, Brussels

CHAPTER FOUR

National inputs into European Political Cooperation

WILLIAM WALLACE

4.1 EPC and EEC: the question of separate procedures

There has been from the outset a two-way relationship between national structures and Community-level mechanisms in the parallelism of European Community policy-making and European Political Cooperation (EPC). The separation of EPC from the well-established procedures of the European Community, set out for fundamentally political reasons in the Davignon Report, reflected an existing and equally well-established division of competences within the foreign ministries of the member-governments – above all in Paris and in Bonn. This organizational division between political and economic directorates within each foreign ministry, the former outside the interdepartmental machinery for coordinating 'European' policy, the latter tied into a network which it shared with finance and economic ministries, had reinforced the distinctiveness between the two sets of procedures: the one in Brussels, the other travelling successively around the capitals of the member-states. Equally, as experience has shown the foreign ministers, the Political Committee, COREPER and the Commission that the international issues they face are too complicated to be parcelled neatly into separate 'political' and 'economic' compartments, so to one degree or another national foreign ministries have begun to adapt their structures to cope with the unavoidable overlap of policy-formulation and decision.

Part of the initial attraction of the political cooperation procedure, for foreign ministries, was that it was a process which called for the traditional diplomatic skills which was also entirely beyond the time-consuming and irritating requirement for interdepartmental consultation and bargaining which European Community questions forced upon them: that is, that it was entirely under foreign ministry control. Without the proposed political secretariat, without any 'supranational' agency to put forward initiatives or to present an alternative perspective, political cooperation rested *entirely* upon national officials – and, at that, entirely upon officials drawn from the traditional geographically-organized core of their foreign ministries, the political directorates.

At the outset, then, the Davignon procedure fitted relatively easily into the existing structures of national policy-making. Political directors took on a role which they had already played, if less intensively, within the framework of NATO's political consultations and – more infrequently – during General Assemblies at the UN. More junior officials within their directorates were designated to represent their governments on working groups, as these were established. In most cases the counsellor responsible for West European bilateral relations automatically became correspondent. As political cooperation spread to embassies in Third World countries and to missions to intergovenmental organizations, it was added to the range of responsibilities laid upon their political sections – while their economic sections remained responsible for Community matters. The convenient division of subjects within the framework of the Conference on Security and Cooperation in Europe (CSCE) into political and economic 'baskets', each serviced by separate working groups, fitted this organizational division fairly well; although there were occasions, during the Community's first discussions about contacts with Comecon and a concerted policy towards the East European countries, when Council committees consisting of representatives from national foreign ministries' economic directorates came close to conceding points which were being held firm as bargaining counters in Helsinki or Geneva.

Even at the start, though, there was a darker side to this picture. As one participant put it, 'all the interdepartmental jealousies were allowed to rage' over the establishment of a separate and exclusive network alongside the highly developed procedures of the EEC. In the absence of any institutional structure or secretariat, personalities and personal relations were necessarily of central importance to the workings of political cooperation in establishing the *rapport* between political directors which has formed the basis for the successful operation of the Political Committee and in building up the wider network of informal relationships between heads of division and desk officers in different foreign ministries which the working groups have promoted. These personalities brought with them their own preconceptions about the proper role of foreign ministries, their own pride and prestige, their own resentments at the encroachment of economic directorates upon the proper field of competence of the political directorate and, more widely, at the encroachment of domestic ministries upon the proper competences of foreign offices to which the Communities had led. Some, of course, felt and resented this encroachment more strongly than others. In one or two member-countries the reaction of permanent representations and of those concerned with the coordination of national policy towards the Communities to this new and independent body provoked bureaucratic rivalries which could not have been prevented, even if the officials concerned with political cooperation had wished to do so.

There was thus a significant degree of tacit support within other foreign ministries – even in the Netherlands, outwardly a stronghold of integrationist sentiment – for the position adopted by the French government that the procedures of political cooperation should be kept separate from those which concerned matters within the competences of the Treaties of Paris and Rome. Even in 1975, after five years of experience, the British government with its distinctive pattern of foreign-ministry organization was the only member-state regularly to send an official from its Permanent Representation to Political Committee meetings, and on occasion to include its Political Director in its delegation for a meeting of the Council of Ministers. Contacts between the French Permanent Representation and the Political Directorate of the Quai d'Orsay were only slowly improving, helped both by changes of personnel and by the more relaxed attitude of the Giscardien regime towards the European Community. Exchanges of information on problems of Europe's external relations appeared most difficult in West Germany, where administrative competences were strongly defended and where the Economics Ministry's leadership in questions of Community policy had yielded only gradually to the interventions of the Foreign Ministry. But in none of the foreign ministries of the Nine was the contact between parallel hierarchies responsible for political cooperation and for the internal and external aspects of Community policy yet perfect. Commission officials noted sadly that at the Political Committee meeting in June 1975 national representatives had discussed, among other items, the development of North–South relations without any prior knowledge of a Commission Proposal on this subject, or of working papers circulated to economic directorates and discussed within the Community framework some time before.

The initial modesty of the political cooperation procedure had been such that most national officials anticipated few problems of management or of coordination with other aspects of foreign policy. The leisurely pace of consultation envisaged in the Luxembourg Report, with foreign ministers meeting only twice a year, political directors quarterly and other groups 'envisaged where necessary . . . to deal with specific matters' did not suggest an enormous additional burden on foreign ministries. The more communitarian governments expected that this small-scale procedure, once under way, could without too much difficulty be slotted bit by bit into the existing machinery for formulating European policy. The less communitarian did not anticipate that it would pose major problems for their traditional foreign-ministry apparatus.

As the subject-matter and activity of political cooperation has expanded, most particularly since the crisis period of 1973–1974, two opposing pressures have affected foreign ministries: their recognition of the impossibility of separating the political from the economic dimension in the issues now coming to the fore, particularly in the Euro–Arab Dialogue, in monitoring and attempting to influence developments within Portugal and in relations with Greece and Turkey over the Cyprus question; and their appreciation that the increasing burden of work and travel upon those directly involved in political cooperation has made it impractical to integrate their responsibilities with those carried by the already heavily-burdened officials responsible for Community matters. Responses to these pressures so far have varied. Some have attempted to divide the management of bilateral relations from multilateral consultations, to spread the load; several have established special units, outside the regular foreign ministry hierarchy, to manage such complex exercises as the Euro–Arab Dialogue. Minor, or even major, reorganizations of internal structure have been carried out in several national foreign offices, in which the demands of political cooperation have been one of the factors working for change. One may anticipate that further adjustments in structure and in the distribution of responsibilities will be necessary as political cooperation continues to develop.

4.2   The burden of the presidency

The rotating presidency imposes the most severe burden on national governments. The procedures of political cooperation at the start placed the initiative for convening meetings and the administrative support for those meetings in the hands of the 'chairman' (as the presidency was still called in 1970). The Luxembourg Report's recommendation that 'the meetings will as a general rule be held in the country whose representative is in the chair', agreed to meet French insistence that EPC should be kept as far as possible separate from the contaminating influence of the Brussels institutions, increased the burden. During the first two or three years of operation, the president's role did not extend far beyond chairing the meetings, attempting to promote compromise among divergent viewpoints and meeting the press on behalf of his colleagues at the conclusion of each ministerial 'conference'. The failure to agree in 1972 upon President Pompidou's proposal for a political secretariat made it clear that as political cooperation expanded, so the presidency would play a larger role.

The Copenhagen Report of 1973 registered the by-now central role of the presidency 'as regards the internal work of Political Cooperation'. 'Experience has also shown,' it added, 'that the Presidency's task presents a particularly heavy administrative burden'. The weight of this burden was increased during the following eighteen months. The creation of the COREU network gave the foreign ministry of the presidency another coordinating and administrative task. The emergence under the German presidency of the 'Gymnich' meeting, that most informal of the European institutions in which the foreign ministers of the Nine are closeted in an attractive and secure chateau for a weekend, provides another responsibility (and an opportunity for competitive display of national treasures). The Ottawa Agreement with the US government on consultations between EPC and the US government naturally placed the responsibility of representing European views in the hands of the presidency. At the same time a representational role outside the European Community was emerging, with

M. Sauvagnargues' visits to Greece and Turkey and Mr Fitzgerald's visits to Washington, Lisbon and the Middle East. In international organizations and conferences, the CSCE has shown the way, with representatives of the presidency convening meetings and discreetly adding the Commission representative to their delegation for their six-months' stint; cooperation extended to the UN, so the demands upon the representatives of the presidency outside the Community grew further.

The French tenure of the presidency in the second half of 1974 found itself faced with the administrative consequences of this expanding burden. But few changes were made in the organization and staffing of the Quai d'Orsay and of the major missions; rather, it was expected that the regular staff could cope with this additional but temporary burden. For the Irish, who succeeded them in January 1975, the presidency as a whole, and in particular its political cooperation dimension, presented them with a major challenge. This challenge was made yet more weighty by the agreement at the Paris Summit of December 1974 that the European Parliament should be allowed to put questions to the presidency (in the person of the foreign minister of the country concerned) on matters of political cooperation, which required the group of correspondents to spend a good deal of time under the chairmanship of their 'president' consulting on agreed replies. Considerable scepticism had also been expressed within the US administration about the capacity of the Irish government effectively to represent its colleagues' views on complex matters of multilateral diplomacy in the consultative procedures between the US government and the Nine. The Irish Government had, however, made extensive preparations for its first tenure of the presidency. The three sections of the political division were increased to four, with a substantial increase in staffing (drawn partly from Irish missions abroad and partly from the cadre of additional personnel created by the expansion of the Irish foreign service then under way). The Irish Foreign Minister devoted by far the largest part of his working time during the first six months of 1975 to the duties of the presidency, both those which stemmed from his Community role and those which arose from political cooperation; and both the other members of the Community and the Americans adjudged the result as a considerable success.

Since then the administrative preparations for the assumption of the presidency in each national capital have laid particular stress upon the secretarial, administrative and representational responsibilities which political cooperation lays upon the country in the chair. Without any form of central secretariat, the Irish had recruited a small group of multilingual secretaries for their six-months' stint which they then passed on to the Italians, half-hoping that this might prove the nucleus of a small travelling secretariat which would improve the continuity of administrative practice and relieve the strain on successive national foreign ministries. But the Luxembourgers, who succeeded to the presidency in January 1976, declined to employ them, and the management of political cooperation thus returned purely to the officials of the foreign ministry of the country in the chair.

The preparations which the UK government made for its first period in the presidency in January–June 1977 therefore laid great emphasis on political cooperation. The larger of the three sections of the special Presidency Unit set up within the Foreign and Commonwealth Office in the autumn of 1976 was responsible for managing political cooperation, and the UK correspondent and her assistants were transferred to this unit for the duration of the presidency and given additional support. The Lancaster House conference centre, completely refurbished and remodelled during 1976, was extensively used for the long succession of working group and Political Committee meetings which for the first six months of 1977 gathered in London. Leeds Castle, a magnificent and securely moated medieval fortress only recently acquired by the government, was prepared for the 'Gymnich' weekend. Afterwards many of the UK officials involved felt that their conscientious preparations had been excessive, and the burden of management less than they had expected. As anxious as the Irish to prove themselved capable of effective management, they had even sent someone over to the The Hague in November 1976 to ask if they could now take over the files of the presidency; and were surprised to find that none existed. The pattern which the British displayed was, however, fairly typical of the requirements of the presidency. Consultations with their predecessors in the chair, and at later stages with their successors, were undertaken to ensure a certain continuity; extra staff were added to the foreign ministry section responsible for managing political cooperation. Conference centres were laid aside and press facilities improved; special consultations with the US embassy established the transatlantic link. The foreign minister and his ministers of state were briefed in advance on the presidential role, and its requirements in terms of preparation for meetings, attendance at Strasbourg and representation abroad. A great deal of extra activity was generated, both among ministers and officials; and after six months in the chair, all felt a mixture of exhaustion, achievement and frustration, uncertain quite what progress they had made but satisfied that they had made the machinery work smoothly.

The presidential role has thus become an important factor in national governments' involvement in political cooperation. The administrative responsibilities which it brings are a challenge to each Diplomatic Service, a test of its efficiency and stamina. The representational duties gives each foreign minister and his officials an opportunity to play for six months a larger and more visible role on the international stage. Each national capital becomes in turn the focus for more intensive diplomatic activity with its US embassy acting as the link between the US administration and European political cooperation, with embassies such as the Japanese reinforced to keep abreast of European diplomatic developments and with larger contingents of foreign journalists flocking around the visiting ministers and officials. In Third World countries and at international organizations diplomats throw themselves into the extra burden of administration and reporting, and relish the extra task of acting chairman and spokesman for the Nine. With the opportunities, however, come frustrations. Officials who have laboured hard for six months to establish the groundwork for a new agreement or statement of policy often find themselves, as the presidency passes on, watching their successors being given the credit for its achievement. The problem of ensuring continuity from one presidency to another, in the absence of a secretariat, has continued to exercise governmental attention. Very discreetly, at the close of the UK presidency, one official from the political cooperation section of the Presidency Unit was seconded to the Belgian Foreign Office, to be joined by a Danish official similarly seconded for six months before the Danish term of office[1].

4.3   The role of national parliaments

National parliaments are hardly engaged in the process of political cooperation; indeed, most members of parliament in all the member-states of the Community have only the vaguest awareness of what European Political Cooperation involves or the subjects which it covers. The Irish government includes references to political cooperation meetings in its six-monthly reports to Parliament; the subject is similarly touched on in written and oral reports to the foreign affairs committees of the Dutch, Danish and German parliaments. But the secrecy of these intergovernmental discussions is largely observed, so that even the minority of national parliamentarians who are actively interested in foreign policy questions are given only a general impression of the issues under consideration. Those who are members of the Political Committee of the European Parliament are better placed, in having the opportunity to question a foreign office minister from the government holding the presidency in closed session. Exceptionally, the president of the Foreign Affairs Commission of the French National Assembly was reportedly shown copies of COREU telegrams; and took the opportunity to protest regularly to the Quai d'Orsay, in deference to the memory of President de Gaulle, at references to the presence of Commission representatives in working group discussions.

4.4   EPC structures in the nine national capitals

The problems which have faced the larger foreign ministries have been different in quality from those in the smaller countries. For West Germany, France and Italy and the UK the size of their foreign ministry itself poses problems of internal coordination. In West Germany and France, in particular, hierarchical structures were firmly established and hard to alter; informal contacts between junior officials in different directorates had not traditionally been encouraged. Their wide range of perceived foreign-policy interests gave these larger countries a direct concern in all issues under discussion within political cooperation, involving a growing number of officials in different divisions of their foreign ministries in the formulation and presentation of national attitudes.

The structure of the Quai d'Orsay was in some ways most easily adapted to such a procedure. The political directorate, one of the three *grand* directorates which had dominated the Quai since the Second World War, was responsible for the management of political relations with all Third World countries. The political director could therefore speak with authority on all items on the agenda of the Political Committee, and all French representatives on working groups were responsible to him. The deputy political director shared the burden of multilateral work. Under them the West Europe *sous-direction*, whose head acted as correspondent and which was also responsible for bilateral relations with six of the eight member-states, played a watchdog role over the responsiveness of other *sous-directions* to the needs of political cooperation, and their observance of the *grandes lignes* of French policy towards its procedures – discouraging a continuing Commission presence, maintaining the distinctive areas of French interests, and so on. Here, as elsewhere, the formulation of national policy was entirely outside the procedures established for coordination on Community matters. On institutional questions the West European *sous-direction* would habitually liaise with officials in the legal directorate and the economic cooperation desk of the economic directorate; the larger questions of European Union necessarily involved interministerial discussions at a high level. But on matters of political cooperation *tout propre* the political directorate was its own master, under the overall guidance of the minister and his *cabinet* and with occasional interventions from the Elysée.

The reorganization of the Quai d'Orsay announced in October 1976 potentially alters this pattern of policy management fundamentally. The creation of several geographical directorates (as proposed by the committee of officials charged with the recommendations for reorganization) would separate the management of bilateral relations from multilateral cooperation – bringing together from the formerly dominant political, economic and cultural directorates the different dimensions of French relations with, for instance, Algeria or South Africa, and leaving only strictly multilateral matters with the functional directorates.

The dominance of the political director in the Quai d'Orsay, his undefined relationship with the Secretary-General and his enormous burden of work and travel was one of the several factors influencing the shape of the reorganization. But such newly-circumscribed responsibilities would create

for him a problem already familiar to his West German and UK counterparts: that he will be unable in Political Committee to speak with confidence
and authority on items which fall within the competence of his colleagues.

In the early summer of 1977 the reorganization was still under discussion,
with only the Asian sections of the functional directorates reorganized; the
future pattern of organization within the Quai d'Orsay therefore remained
in question. Meanwhile, the problems of managing the Euro–Arab Dialogue
had led to the creation of a small special unit, under a senior official
responsible to the Political Director but able to consult with the Economic
Directorate on an authoritative basis.

The division of responsibilities within the Auswärtiges Amt has followed
a rather different pattern. The German correspondent heads a small division
within the political directorate responsible only for multilateral questions of
European cooperation, uncomfortably separated from the main thrust of
policy-making towards the Communities, which is the responsibility of the
economic *abteilung*, reporting to a different *staatsminister* and in control of
the dialogue with the Economics Ministry and communications with the
Permanent Representation in Brussels. Relations with Third World countries are the responsibility of a third *abteilung*, with a different director, so
that on Third World items the German political director must speak in the
Political Committee with a certain diffidence. To circumvent the still
relatively rigid hierarchical structure of the Auswärtiges Amt, special units
had been created to handle both the CSCE and the Euro–Arab Dialogue,
with senior officials at their head to give them sufficient weight to intervene
authoritatively in discussions in the different *abteilungen*. So far this
structure has sufficed for the German input into political cooperation,
though not without some discontinuities between policy on Community
matters and political consultations. But it must be seen as a transitional
arrangement, unlikely to survive a greater intensity of operation.

The UK Foreign and Commonwealth Office is organized on a depart-
mental basis, without a superstructure of directorates to inhibit flexibility of
adjustment and obstruct communication among departments. Coming late
to political cooperation in 1972, the immediate responsibility was added to
the existing structure for formulating and managing Community policy. The
European Integration department was therefore split into two, responsible
respectively for internal and external questions; the head of the latter became
the UK correspondent, with subordinate sections responsible both for
Community external relations and for political cooperation – reporting to
the under-secretary for Community questions on matters with the competences of the Treaties and to the under-secretary for European, NATO and
East–West questions on political matters. The latter became the UK
'political director', a new concept for the Foreign and Commonwealth
Office, but one which had become an accepted title by 1975. Responsibility
for the CSCE was shared between this section and the East European and

Soviet department; for the Euro–Arab Dialogue this section again initially took the responsibility for coordination, though for a number of reasons a separate and special unit headed by an assistant under-secretary was created in the spring of 1976.

The advantages of these arrangements lay partly in the pulling together of Community and non-Community matters at desk level and partly in the lighter load which fell upon the designated political director. Its disadvantages, unavoidably, were that the political director could not always speak with knowledge and authority on all questions before the Political Committee, and that as the work of political cooperation spread through the Foreign and Commonwealth Office it became increasingly difficult for even this fairly large department to keep abreast of current business.

There was, however, no formal coordinating structure for political cooperation above this level. The Cabinet Office unit responsible for pulling together the threads of UK policy towards the European Communities did not concern itself with political consultations, and in 1975–1976 its members remained remarkably uninformed about the procedures of political cooperation as such.

In Italy, as in France, the existence of a strong Political Directorate within the Ministry of Foreign Affairs made for an easy adjustment to the initial demands of political cooperation. The Italian correspondent heads a small section within the Directorate of Political Affairs responsible for the Italian input to the COREU network, for assisting the political director in carrying out his EPC responsibilities and ensuring that other sections fulfil their obligations within the various working groups. The evolution of the European Council has given the Prime Minister's Office some standing in matters of political cooperation; but in preparations for meetings of the European Council the staff of the correspondent's section simply move across temporarily to the Prime Minister's office.

For the smaller countries, the problem of internal coherence and coordination is necessarily less worrying. For Luxembourg, indeed, it does not exist. One Luxembourg official during their presidency chaired four different working groups, providing in himself a thread of continuity and coherence between their separate discussions. Within the medium-sized hierarchies of the Dutch and Belgian ministries it was still possible to rely to a great extent on personal contact and informal discussion on the more limited range of issues which actively concerned their governments in political cooperation. In The Hague, the two directors responsible for 'European' and for 'political' questions met as a matter of habit every day to exchange views. In Brussels, until early 1976, the parallel divisions responsible for Community matters and for issues within political cooperation reported, as did the divisions responsible for bilateral political relations, to the then political director, M. Davignon; the division of the political directorate into bilateral and multilateral components, which then took place, was partly motivated by the imbalance within the foreign ministry to which this concentration of responsibilities on M. Davignon had led.

In such an uninstitutionalized structure as political cooperation the importance of personalities has from the outset been very considerable. At the national level, too, personalities and personal relations have markedly affectedthe style and effectiveness of policy-making in this field. In Italy, for example, the excellent personal relations between the political and economic directors greatly eased coordination and exchange of information between their subordinates in the early years of political cooperation; in France, reportedly, the opposite was at first the case. Ministerial interest, the extent to which officials are asked for briefs and expected to respond to active ministerial demands, is as important a variable. Fluency in French (and, increasingly, in English), a diplomatic manner combined with an appetite for detail and a hard-headed grasp of domestic constraints and interests will clearly be increasingly important requirements for politicians aspiring to the foreign minister's portfolio in the member-states.

4.5   The need for reform

Increasing convergence between the issues dealt with within the machinery of political cooperation and those which fall within the competences of the European Communities has forced national ministries to reconsider the relationship between the two. Those which grafted political cooperation onto sections of their foreign ministry scarcely at all involved in Community external relations have already begun to adapt, and are likely to have to adjust further. It should be noted that the pattern of foreign ministry adaptation is much more closely related to the bureaucratic traditions of each state and diplomatic service than to its government's attitude to European unity. In spite of the West German government's often repeated commitment to the ideals of European Union, with the Community structure as its core, its own Foreign Ministry presents internal problems of coordination at least as difficult to remove as those within the Quai d'Orsay.

If the workload of political cooperation continues to increase at the pace at which it has grown over the last seven years its implications for the balance of work within foreign ministries will become very considerable. The strain on political directors of the additional burden of travel is already noticeable. A further intensification of consultation would unavoidably restrict their ability to play a more general role within their own foreign ministries (from which they are already so frequently absent) and would support the suggestions that one or two political directors have already made informally for additional personal support. The UK pattern of a political director with only limited subject-responsibilities outside the demands of political cooperation itself, or the pattern proposed in the French reforms of a 'specialist' political director concerned primarily with multilateral relations and with EPC itself, seem models for the future, in spite of the attendant disadvantages which the loss of a general oversight of bilateral relations will bring. The role of the correspondent, which has in many ways become less clear as working groups have developed a life of their own, would then appropriately become one of assistant to the political director, forming in effect a private office attached to each political director to assist him in his European responsibilities. Such a direct attachment would also enable correspondents to regain influence over the more active working groups by bringing the weight of their political director to bear – and thus preventing working-group members from developing a commitment to their group which transforms what (in the views of most political directors) were intended to be consultative bodies into decision-making committees, and thus 'arrogating' to themselves decisions which should formally be reserved to the Political Committee or to the ministerial level.

As political cooperation develops further, the question of its relationship to the procedures for coordinating policy towards the European Communities is likely to be raised in each national capital. So far it has been acceptable to leave matters of political cooperation outside the extensive interdepartmental structures developed to reconcile divergent priorities towards the Communities as a whole. Most domestic officials concerned with specific Community policies have remained at best dimly aware of political cooperation; many are still almost completely unaware of its procedures or of the issues with which it is concerned. Those few home civil servants who actively follow the COREU telegrams and the national preparations for EPC are, with few exceptions, extremely sceptical about what they see as an entirely diplomatic exercise. But it is unlikely that this divorce of EPC from Community issues can long continue. When the political directors proposed in 1975 the use of loans from the European Investment Bank to assist the more moderate elements within the Portuguese military leadership finance officials and central bank staff were necessarily drawn in. When the future of Yugoslavia's relations with its Western and Eastern neighbours is under discussion, the importance of its agricultural trade with the Community requires reference to ministries of agriculture (as well as, of course, to the Commission itself), and the difficult issue of migrant labour brings in other domestic ministries. Political cooperation has so far been isolated, remarkably, from the bureaucratic politics of national administrations; but it is unlikely that it can remain isolated for much longer.

Further development of political cooperation will also raise questions about national representation in other Community capitals and in Third World countries. Already the role of embassies in other Community capitals has been affected by the growth of direct contacts among foreign ministries. The French have taken the line that embassy political sections have thus become less important as intermediaries among the Nine, and have in some cases reduced staffs; the West Germans and the British, by contrast, have maintained their staffs, while redefining their role as supplementary to the direct consultations among working groups. Even for those working groups which meet infrequently, however, the problem of keeping abreast of confidential discussions to which the accredited representatives of each national government have not themselves been a party is acute. The novelty of dealing with foreign ministry officials who often consider themselves better informed about the position of one's own government than a diplomat can hope to be himself is compounded by the novel experience for embassies of receiving copies of telegrams sent through the COREU network by their own government, not directly, but via the foreign ministries to which they are accredited, who will naturally have seen them first. In London the embassies of the other member-governments receive COREU telegrams by Foreign and Commonwealth Office messenger two or three times a day; in Bonn, by contrast, embassy officials must visit the Auswärtiges Amt to collect copies from pigeonholes provided. This disorienting process implies that the role of embassies within the Community itself as a vehicle for intergovernmental communication on political matters must come increasingly into question.

Outside the boundaries of the Communities increasing cooperation among national diplomatic services raises the question of duplication of effort in representation. Joint reporting, from Tokyo, from Moscow and from a limited number of other capitals, has already developed: this is regarded on the whole as a necessary but not very useful chore by the larger diplomatic services but of considerable value to the smaller members, whose resources for gathering information and assessment have thereby been expanded. As Portuguese Guinea approached independence the West German government floated the proposal that the Nine should appoint a single representative to the new state: but the idea rapidly foundered in the face of opposition from other members, in particular from the French and the British with their specific West African interests. Since then there have been more limited discussions on the sharing of facilities in smaller Third World countries, with West German officials the most enthusiastic and with British (and other) officials pushed towards the idea by the steady pressure of budgetary constraints. The obstacles in the path of shared facilities, or more ambitiously of jointly staffed missions, are very considerable. But if political cooperation continues to advance, national governments are likely to find themselves moving slowly towards this, at least as far as the smaller developing countries are concerned.

The development of political cooperation has thus modified the practices of national foreign ministries, and transformed the context within which they operate, in its first seven years. Its continued development can only modify their operating assumptions further, and force them progressively to adjust their structures to the collaborative European context within which they are already working.

Note

1 For further information on the role of the presidency see H. Wallace and G. Edwards, 'European Community: the Working Role of the Presidency of the Council', *International Affairs*, October 1976. See also their 'The Council of Ministers of the European Community and the President-in-Office', Federal Trust, 1977

CHAPTER FIVE

The Nine at the Conference on Security and Cooperation in Europe

GÖTZ VON GROLL

5.1 Problems of East–West relations

A novel feature of the CSCE negotiations, which started in November 1972, was the close cooperation of the nine states of the European Community: this cooperation was also prevalent in Belgrade and it resulted in the Nine making their mark on this conference from its very beginning. The problems that CSCE was to address were not, of course, new but prior to this conference they had been mainly managed by bilateral relations, multilateral military alliances or global international organizations.

When the foreign ministers of the then six states of the EEC approved the Luxembourg Report in Munich (1970) and thus created EPC, they decided to initiate the new organization in two problem areas of foreign policy, namely the conflict in the Middle East and the European Security Conference. The following is an attempt to describe the interests of the Community as a whole as well as the interests of individual member-states in terms of the substantive areas outlined in the Final Document of the CSCE.

With regard to the *principles of international law* governing relations between member-states, the interest of the East in emphasizing 'the inviolability of borders' caused the Nine to cooperate in seeking to write into the Final Document the possibility of peacefully agreed changes of borders. This was related to the fact that during the Paris Summit of October 1972 they had agreed to move towards the creation of a 'European Union'. In addition to this, there was the interest of the Federal Republic of Germany in giving expression to the option of a reunited Germany. The Nine insisted on a very thorough formulation of Principle VII (Human Rights), as a legal–philosophical basis for any improvements they tried to achieve in the humanitarian field of East–West relations. In order to be able to refer to the pre-eminence of the Rome Treaties they also laid particular emphasis on the question of adherence to existing treaties, i.e. on a clear formulation of Principle X. In addition, of course, other principles, like cooperation, prohibition of violence, non-intervention, self-determination and sovereign equality, were also related to EEC interests, and their preservation demanded careful formulation of the so-called 'Basket I' of the Final Document of CSCE.

Questions of military security have been and remain of vital interest to all EEC states. It was therefore in the common interest of the Nine to emphasize the 'complementary character of political and military aspects of security'. The special relationship of France within NATO meant, however, that the Nine gave NATO the lead in this area. Many of the participants, especially neutral and non-aligned states, wished to see a link between CSCE and the Vienna Talks on Troop Reduction (known in the West as MBFR): here the French position in particular meant that this had to be paraphrased in the Final Document in very vague terms.

Matters arising in the area of *economics, science, technology and the environment* (Basket II) applied not only to EEC member-states but also to the Commission of the Community in Brussels. The most important area, trade, was already the responsibility of the Community when in 1971 CSCE preparations started in the context of EPC. During the preparatory phase at Geneva the negotiating mandate for matters of trade during the conference was eventually transferred to the Commission. All other matters (science and technology, protection of the environment, transport, migrant labour) were at that time still in the 'grey area' of the gradual transition from national to Community jurisdiction. Thus from the start in terms of Basket II, the EEC Commission had to be involved in the deliberation in a decisive way.

It was, of course, the case that most of these questions were dealt with on a multilateral basis in the Economic Commission for Europe (ECE, a UN body) in Geneva, of which all CSCE states were members (Canada and Switzerland joined during the CSCE negotiations). It was thus necessary to strengthen the representation of the Community in this body and to institutionalize the right to speak for the representative of the EEC Commission. This was achieved during the Geneva phase of the CSCE. In response to criticisms from the East of an unwillingness to cooperate, the EEC Community countries came forward with numerous suggestions in Basket II, almost all of which were later taken into consideration in the Final Document of the CSCE.

Attention has already been drawn to the importance of *humanitarian questions* (Basket III) to individual EEC states and their citizens. It was regarded as essential in this area to maintain a demand for improvements concerning visits of relations, emigration with the aim of reuniting families and enabling marriages across borders, facilitation of travel and youth and sporting exchanges. With the help of other Western, neutral and non-aligned states it was possible to agree on very concrete measures, and the Federal Republic of Germany was certainly satisfied with the success which was achieved in this area (there have been about 100 000 cases of family reunion between East and West since Helsinki).

In the field of information exchange the Community countries also shared identical interests, although they had no illusions about any improvements that might be achieved. Naturally, the West could not and will not accept the demands which the East raised again in Belgrade, namely to allow only 'peaceloving' information to cross fontiers. This carried with it the assumption that responsibility for the content of such information – newspaper articles, television and radio programmes, books and magazines – would be left in the hands of the state. Instead the West insisted, and is still insisting, on the agreement reached in the Final Document, namely the facilitation of a freer and more comprehensive distribution of any kind of information. Another common concern of all EEC states was the improvement of the working conditions of journalists in Eastern Europe. The text in the Final Document referring to this matter is very clear, and since Helsinki there have indeed been some improvements.

In the area of *culture and education*, which in East–West relations is mainly dealt with bilaterally, France, as the country with the most extensive experience in this area, drafted papers on the position of the Nine. They all had a common interest in transferring certain multilateral topics to UNESCO in Paris, although they were aware that this UN organization, in contrast to the Economic Commission of the UN in Geneva, is inevitably more interested in considering the interests of developing countries, and that it has only marginal interest in dealing with 'European' topics.

Mediterranean questions were introduced into the CSCE mainly on the basis of proposals by the neutral and non-aligned countries with a Mediterranean coastline; these questions provoked considerable interest on the part of the Nine. Two of the most important EEC countries have themselves a Mediterranean coastline, the Euro–Arab Dialogue was then already on the agenda of EPC, there has been and still is a good working relationship with Israel and almost all Mediterranean countries were already connected to the EEC by preferential treaties. Thus in Geneva the Nine formulated the text for the Mediterranean Declaration, in which economic cooperation and protection of the environment are of central importance. The Nine used their influence to enable those Mediterranean countries who were not part of the CSCE (Algeria, Egypt, Israel, Lebanon, Morocco, Syria and Tunisia) to have a say at Geneva and Belgrade. In addition, the Nine reserved their position towards the controversial clause on security in the Mediterranean that was written in by Malta.

As an institutional consequence of the conference the Warsaw Pact countries suggested an institution for the supervision of the Principles included in the Final Document. This sounded very much like the previous plans to create an 'all-European system of collective security' which was intended to dissolve NATO and to disrupt the process of Western European unification. Thus the Nine stipulated from the very beginning that only the results of the conference could determine whether and in which way the multilateral process initiated by the CSCE will be continued.

Thus the Nine also managed to postpone the concrete discussion of proposals concerning a follow-up conference until Spring 1975, i.e. not before the main results would begin to become apparent. They presented the 'Danish Draft', which ultimately became the basis for the conference-drafters. This draft reflected the concept of an 'interim period'. The decision whether there should be regular meetings was postponed until 1977, it being argued that real progress in the process of detente could not be identified until a reasonable period had lapsed.

5.2 The preparation of the Nine's coordinated position

In November 1970 the cooperation of the then six countries in preparation for the CSCE began with a resolution of the foreign ministers in Munich, following a Belgian proposal to make the CSCE one of the first two topics of EPC. The Political Committee was asked to set up a working group for this purpose.

During its session in Paris in February 1971 the Political Committee established a brief very general mandate, which required the CSCE working group to meet on 1 March in Paris. This group was commissioned to investigate 'all relevant aspects' of the conference project that might be of interest to the Community. The governments of the member-states appointed to this working group the East European and/or NATO experts of their political departments who, in most cases, knew each other from the six-monthly meetings of the NATO East European experts. Out of this group of experts there gradually arose a real community of interests, which proved to be most effective during the conference itself and also continued to be so at Belgrade. In order to avoid any overlapping of work with NATO, the CSCE working group at first investigated CSCE problems with an exclusive emphasis on matters affecting the EEC. These were:

(1) The attitude of East European countries to the EEC;
(2) The possibility of improved East–West cooperation;
(3) The role of the UN Economic Commission for Europe (ECE) in East–West cooperation;
(4) An assessment of Eastern bloc positions concerning the conference (in particular, border issues, the question of EEC trade 'discrimination' and various institutional problems).

As these were topics which were within the competence of the Community it turned out to be necessary and useful to involve the EEC Commission in Brussels in this work. For this purpose, in May 1971 the six foreign ministers decided in Paris to establish a special *ad hoc* CSCE working group within the framework of EPC, which consisted of the CSCE working group plus representatives from the EEC Commission. When dealing with CSCE material in the Political Committee, the Director-General for Foreign Affairs of the Commission was coopted, as was the President of the Commission at ministerial and summit meetings. For issues such as the relationship between EEC and COMECON, both groups had joint meetings. The chair in the CSCE working group and in the *ad hoc* group was usually held by the same officials.

Before and after the sessions of the CSCE the two groups met roughly every two months in the capital of the respective presidency. During the conference itself, especially during its second phase in Geneva (September 1973 to July 1975), they were more or less permanently in session. The CSCE working group always met at the same time as the leaders of the Nine's individual delegations. The CSCE *ad hoc* group was divided up into special groups according to the conference topic. At times there were about fifteen special committees of the Nine meeting every week in Geneva, one committee for each subcommittee of the conference as well as the leaders of delegation with the CSCE *ad hoc* group providing overall coordination. Political questions which were of special interest to the Community in Brussels (e.g. trade policy, questions of status) were submitted to the Committee of Permanent Representatives (COREPER). In case of differences of opinion between this body and the Political Committee, the ministers had to make decisions in their dual capacity as members of the Council of Ministers of the Community and of the Foreign Ministers Conference of EPC. The important declaration of the heads of governments of the EEC states relating to the CSCE of 17 July 1975 was passed by the European Council; the latter can probably be described as the only genuine institutional 'umbrella' covering EPC and the Community[1].

During the second phase of the CSCE the national delegations were responsible for liaison between Geneva and the capitals of the Nine. The delegation of each presidency (Denmark during September to December 1973, the Federal Republic of Germany during the first half, France during the second half of 1974, Ireland during the first half of 1975, Italy from July to August 1975) took over the responsibility for informing the committees in Brussels. The guidelines of the conference were established by the delegations in Geneva in the autumn of 1973 and approved by the Political Committee and the Conference of Ministers of EPC in November of the same year in Copenhagen. Text proposals for the Final Document were usually put together from the drafts of the individual delegations on the basis of instructions from their capitals. The final versions were submitted for approval to the capitals or the Political Committee before putting them to the negotiation committee of the CSCE.

During the CSCE summit meeting in Helsinki in August 1975 the political directors of the EEC agreed to continue their cooperation on CSCE matters after the end of the actual conference in order to consider the results and to comment on the extensive text of the Final Document. Until the summer of 1976 the CSCE Working Group was mainly concerned with producing this commentary, the preparation of which was shared by several subgroups. The draft commentary to 'Basket III' remained the responsibility of the delegations in Geneva. The EEC Commission was to a large degree involved in the commentary to 'Basket III'. This extensive commentary (about 450 pages) enabled the EEC member-states and the Commission to act largely in cooperation with one another in bilateral and multilateral East–West talks. The Nine also agreed to the form in which the Final Document was to be quoted in bilateral agreements and declarations.

In the UN Economic Commission for Europe (ECE) in Geneva, to which the Final Document had allocated numerous tasks belonging to 'Basket II', the Nine have been increasingly acting as one since Helsinki. They introduced a proposal to transfer CSCE material to the working programme of ECE and took a joint position on proposals for high-level conferences involving issues of the environment, energy and transport which were submitted by the Soviet Union during the Annual Main Conference of the ECE in April 1976. Through this, a group of the Nine was also established in Geneva, and it is not very clear whether this should be counted as belonging to EPC or to the Brussels COREPER structure. The Nine took the leading role in the Western Caucus, to which all Western, neutral and non-aligned ECE members (including Yugoslavia) belong.

The Final Document of the CSCE allocated several tasks in the field of culture and education to UNESCO in Paris. There the cooperation of the Nine has been increased, although in a somewhat more modest way than in Geneva. UNESCO is a worldwide body, and the differences of opinion of the Nine concerning the North–South relationship influence their ability to present a common position. Finally, cooperation increased considerably between the embassies of the Nine in the Eastern European countries.

However, the greatest structural difference between Helsinki and Belgrade was probably the establishment of a CSCE committee within the COREPER framework in Brussels, which from autumn 1976 onwards took on the preparation of the EEC position in 'Basket II' for the session in Belgrade. While the previous CSCE *ad hoc* group of EPC, which stopped working in Geneva in July 1975, had consisted of government officials delegated from the capitals, the Brussels CSCE group has recruited from members of the Permanent Representations to the EEC, who receive instructions from the capitals. The work, therefore, was somewhat cumbersome, and the presidency had the difficult task of coordinating it with the work of the EPC CSCE working group; in the end this was achieved quite satisfactorily, mainly thanks to the cooperation of the highly qualified representatives of the EEC Commission, most of whom had CSCE experience and were working in both groups.

In Belgrade, similar structures were developed to the second CSCE phase in Geneva: representatives of the EEC Commission were members of the delegation of the presidency and always spoke in the name of the Community when the subject demanded it. In Belgrade, the Nine, as in Geneva, were more or less permanently in session. This was made possible by the conference programme, which was not too heavily overloaded. During the Belgrade preparatory meeting the Nine took part in setting up the conference programme and influenced its nature in a decisive way.

5.3   Conclusions: The Nine's leadership role in the CSCE

The Nine acted as a united body for the first time when on 15 January 1973 at the CSCE Preparatory Meeting in Helsinki they submitted their drafts of mandates for the Main Conference. This was not anticipated by the Eastern bloc states, and it took them some time to come to terms with it. Eventually they did get used to it, and at times in Helsinki and in Geneva one even had the impression that this constellation was welcomed, especially by the Soviet Union. With the USA content in Helsinki and Geneva with the role of observer, the Nine took the negotiating lead in a conference essentially concerned with non-security issues.

Consultation of the Nine with the USA took place mainly in the context of NATO, which, apart from Ireland, all the EEC countries belong to. Originally NATO had a start over EPC at the preparations of CSCE; the proposal already made in spring 1968 in Reykjavik to negotiate a 'mutual balanced force reduction' (MBFR) had been conceived as a counter-programme to the Soviet conference programme. The USA was not particularly interested in CSCE and was thus content to leave the leading role in this area of non-military East–West relations to the Nine. In contrast to this, the interest in CSCE of those NATO countries which did not belong to the Nine, especially Norway, which had taken part in EPC during enlargement negotiations, and Canada was considerable, and by and large identical with the interests of the Nine.

From the beginning of the preparatory meeting, voting with the neutral and non-aligned countries took place *in situ*, i.e. in Helsinki and Geneva as well as in bilateral meetings. After CSCE, multilateral voting with these countries also took place in the context of the Council of Europe in Strasbourg. In many areas, there are now and have been identical interests with these countries, especially economic and humanitarian questions.

In military matters these countries would demand much more extensive stipulations, i.e. a greater exchange of information on (and probably also a say in) MBFR, in which only about half of the CSCE participants are taking part. Also they had much more far-reaching ideas on the institutionalization of the CSCE process, because they thought that if there were frequent meetings they could participate more effectively in important decisions by relying on the participants' needs to obtain their continuing agreement.

While the Nine acted jointly in Helsinki, Geneva and Belgrade in all important questions, certain special relationships obviously did play a part. The condominium of the superpowers, which the Soviet Union still tried to exploit during the preparatory meetings, did not materialize, because of the USA's disinterest in Helsinki and Geneva and their preference for the role of observer. In Belgrade, on the other hand, the USA tended to seek confrontation. The Federal Republic of Germany was not prepared to approach Eastern bloc delegations singlehanded, because in this conference it was above all interested in the maintenance of the unity of the West. Denmark became active within the Scandinavian group, explaining the position of the Nine and bringing Scandinavian interests to bear in relation to the Nine. France, and especially Italy, tried to develop contacts with the Mediterranean countries; here they played a similar role to the Danes in the North. The Dutch and Romanians had similar interest with regard to confidence-building measures, whilst a special role was played by the unofficial 'German language group', which was necessary, since as well as English, French, Russian, Italian and Spanish, German was an official conference language of the CSCE. It was within this framework that the two German states, Austria, Switzerland and Lichtenstein met. If they saw that English and Russian texts did not agree (and this was the case more often than one would expect) they forced the conference to reformulate the text.

On the whole the Nine were able to realize their basic aims during the CSCE. The objectives of the Eastern bloc, as exemplified by the Prague Declaration of January 1972, were not regarded by the West as a reasonable basis for discussion. To achieve security and detente simply through the formulation of some basic principles which then were open to arbitrary interpretation could not satisfy the West, especially the Nine. They only agreed to the Conference when it was certain at the end of the preparatory meeting in Helsinki that there was a chance to discuss all the topics which the West had put on the agenda.

In Helsinki, the Nine had formulated their ideas concerning the agenda in the above-mentioned mandate drafts of 15 January 1973. The complete text appeared in what became known as the 'Blue Book' which became the basis of the main meeting, and it determined the structure and many of the important details of the Final Document.

It was from this point that the Nine took the initiative for the CSCE and they have retained it ever since. The framework suggested by the East was adjusted by the Nine to include the kind of content they thought was necessary and in this way they have actively contributed to the realization and the further development of their initial aims.

Instead of dividing the Nine, as some had feared, the CSCE managed to bring them together in one very important area of foreign policy. The signing of the Final Document of the CSCE by the Italian Prime Minister in his role as President of the Council of the European Community must also be considered to be the actual recognition of the Community by the East. Cooperation between the Nine and the USA has considerably revitalized the dialogue within the West. The Nine proved to be an attractive partner to smaller countries seeking to counterbalance the hegemony of the superpowers. This was aided by the fact that, within the Nine, there is no single superpower, and that jointly reached positions are already characterized by compromise. In the field of non-military East–West relations the Nine have established their community of interests. There were occasional temptations to go it alone, but these did not last long. By recognizing that 'together even the weak become strong' the Nine have succeeded together in an important field of politics, even if the preparatory internal discussions were often heated.

The special ambassadors of the thirty-five CSCE member-states met in Belgrade from 4 October 1977 to 9 March 1978 to study the interim results, though this meeting did not bring the desired improvements in the realization of certain conditions of the Final Document. This was due to certain tensions in the overall political climate, which the Nine can only influence marginally. However, one important aim of the conference was reached in Belgrade: all the questions dealt with in the Final Document, including human rights, could be discussed thoroughly and differing conceptions could be clarified. All delegations also had the opportunity to put proposals for the improvement of security and the development of cooperation in Europe and the development of the process of detente in the future, as was their intention in the Final Document. Because of the confrontation over human rights some suggestions could not be incorporated into the Final Document, but they will play an important part in bilateral and multilateral East–West relations over the next few years and in the second CSCE conference fixed for the autumn of 1980 in Madrid.

The Nine have also taken on an important role in ECE. The preparation and organization of the highly important conference on the environment, which was planned by ECE for 1977 as a direct result of the CSCE, gave the Nine and the EEC Commission the opportunity to continue their close cooperation within the East–West context. There is also further opportunity for this cooperation during the three expert meetings agreed on in Belgrade, and in a number of the forums, all of which owe their origins to the CSCE process.

The common front of the Nine on the international East–West stage, which began with the preparation of the CSCE, has proved to be part of a European reality today, and they will have ample opportunity to continue to play their role and to enlarge it after Belgrade.

Note

1 *Press and Information Office Federal Governments: European Political*   *Cooperation*, Bonn, 1978, pp. 122–125

Political cooperation and the Euro–Arab Dialogue

DAVID ALLEN

With the single exception of the activities of the Nine at the Conference on Security and Cooperation in Europe[1] the most obvious and public manifestation of the political cooperation machinery at work in recent years has been the establishment and pursuit of a 'European ' relationship with the twenty member-states of the Arab League that has come to be known as the 'Euro–Arab Dialogue'. However, whilst the 'Dialogue' can indeed be regarded as a success to date, albeit within somewhat limited parameters, it has also served to illustrate both the difficulties in practice of operating a procedure based on a theoretical distinction between politics and economics and the limitations of attempting much of substance in the field of common external policy without prior agreement on a number of internal policy concerns. More specifically, the Nine have been faced with the problem of creating and enhancing a relationship with the Arab states, of which the most notable are the oil-producers, having failed to agree amongst themselves either a common energy policy or (and this is perhaps more critical) a common and positive stance towards the Middle East conflict that weighs so heavily in Arab considerations.

Although the origins of the Dialogue are to be found mainly in the events of the autumn of 1973 and spring of 1974, when, following the Yom Kippur war, the Arab oil-producing states first selectively embargoed the supply and then quadrupled the price of oil, some credit must be given to the much-maligned European Commission for its pre-crisis anticipation of the eventual need for a new relationship with the Arab world. The EEC and the Nine are frequently and justifiably accused of merely reacting to events in the outside world in their formulation of external policies, and this was indeed predominantly the case in 1973–1974. However, in 1972 the European Commission, in a memorandum forwarded to the Council of Ministers[2], proposed, amongst other things, consultations with the oil-exporting countries on the basis of a complementarity of interest extending beyond the energy field, and went on to recommend agreements to promote the oil-exporters' economic and social development in exchange for certain guarantees of oil supply and price. However, despite the Commission's anticipation of these issues that were to form part of the basis of the Dialogue most observers have identified the Copenhagen Summit conference of December 1973 as its starting-point. Although doubts remain as to who, if anybody, actually invited them (some say the British, some say the French, some both) four Arab foreign ministers added to the confusion of the already divided Nine by presenting themselves at the Summit and suggesting that the relationship between the Community and the Arab world be placed on a new basis[3].

The Arab objectives, imprecise as to details as they were, seemed to be overtly political; recognizing the effects that their actions had had on the European states, they came seeking to exploit further their new-found power by persuading the Europeans to adopt a more sympathetic stance towards the Arab position in the Middle East conflict. There is also some evidence that the oil-producing Arab states were concerned by the fact that the oil weapon, which had been aimed primarily at the USA, had in reality created most havoc amongst European states at a time when Europe was beginning to emerge as an attractive alternative partner to the two super-powers. Thus there was a sense in which the Arab states were anxious to, if not make amends, at least repair the damage to the emergent relationship that their actions had caused. It may also have been the case (and this does seem to be borne out by the subsequent progress of the Dialogue) that the Arab countries saw in the European Community a model for integration that they would like to emulate in their own search for unity. To the extent that this was the case, the Europeans had an obvious interest in participating in a process which shifted Arab integrative forces away from an essentially negative attitude to Israel and the Middle East situation towards more positive issue areas. Nevertheless, in general the Europeans were less than delighted by this further intrusion on their privacy; already bitterly divided by their differing treatment during the embargo (the Netherlands was completely embargoed, like the USA; the UK and France were accorded friendly status and hence normal supplies, and the other Six faced phased reductions of 5 per cent per month), they now faced the problem of their collective response. There seemed to be three possible choices; first, they could attempt to formulate, as the Arabs at Copenhagen were demanding, a distinctively European line that distinguished itself from the more aggressive US position in recognition of Europe's special vulnerability; second, they could succumb to US demands for a collective and coordinated stance by all the major consumer-countries; and third, they could abandon all attempts at solidarity, either European or Atlantic, and seek national solutions by individual bilateral dealings with the producer-countries. In the event, all three courses of action were tried; the UK and France spearheaded the rush to conclude individual deals and the Nine as a whole attended the Washington Energy conference in January 974, where, despite a bitter confrontation betwen the French and West Germans, the Eight (i.e. minus France) decided to participate in the International Energy Agency that was set up as a manifestation of Atlantic solidarity. Finally, despite considerable internal disagreement, the member-states of the Community reluctantly agreed that a response was required to the Arab demands made at Copenhagen and thus agreed to talks about the establishment of a Euro–Arab Dialogue.

Whilst in retrospect it appears that the Europeans had very little choice in participating in the Dialogue their initial reluctance is understandable when one considers the problems that such a course of action raised. In the first place, the members of the Community had no real experience of a collective relationship with other state groupings other than in the context of Association agreements such as Yaounde/Lomé. Second, as with so many aspects of their external relations, they were divided and inhibited by the nature of their relationship with the USA, the state of which had reached a low ebb by the end of 1973, following the disastrous attempts to draw up a new 'Atlantic Charter' and the frictions that were generated by the refusal of a number of European countries to allow their NATO ally the use of European airfields for the resupply of Israel during the Yom Kippur war. Kissinger in particular was both suspicious of Arab motivations for proposing a Dialogue with the Europeans and concerned that any European reaction would undermine the solidarity amongst consumer-countries that he considered essential for successful dealings with the oil-producers. Furthermore, Kissinger was convinced that any independent action by the European states would have a detrimental effect on his own highly individual attempts to achieve a peaceful resolution of the Middle East conflict. Kissinger's firmly held belief that 'the Europeans will be unable to achieve anything in the Middle East in a million years'[4] combined with the knowledge that the main pressure for a distinctive European approach was coming from the French for traditional anti-USA reasons led to a series of outbursts against the Nine that only served to damage further the atmosphere in which Euro–American relations were conducted at the beginning of 1974. It was at this point that the political cooperation machinery entered onto the scene, for it rapidly became evident that, first, before any progress could be made with the Arabs the USA had to be squared, and second, that the substance of any Dialogue that emerged would require careful political handling and control if it was not to endanger further relations with Europe's most important partner. The major US grievance against the Europeans was a perception, on Kissinger's part in particular, that in determining their stance the Europeans were failing to consult with him in the way that he believed members of the Atlantic alliance should. The Europeans for their part tended to make matters worse by accusing Kissinger of behaving in exactly the same way over matters such as the US decision to call a worldwide 'nuclear alert' at a time when Soviet intervention in the Middle East war seemed likely. Matters came to a head in March 1974 when the Nine foreign ministers meeting in the context of political cooperation in Brussels announced their decision to begin a process that would eventually lead to the establishment of a large-scale economic cooperation with the Arabs[5]. The Nine had decided that despite the fact that the Dutch were still effectively embargoed and that several member-states were still concerned about the effect on the EEC–Israeli relationship, some sort of response to the Arab Copenhagen initiative was required. They proposed a threefold plan of action involving exploratory contacts with the twenty member-states of the Arab League, the establishment of a number of joint working groups and an eventual EEC–Arab conference at foreign-minister level. The timing of the announcement could not have been worse for, at the very moment that the foreign ministers were meeting in Brussels, Kissinger was arriving in Europe from his latest round of Middle East shuttle diplomacy to report developments both to the West Germans and the NATO Council. There then followed an embarrassing episode in which Kissinger refused to comment on the Nine's decision on the grounds that he had not been officially informed of it – an assertion that the West German government then proceeded to deny. However, it was when Kissinger returned to the USA that his reaction became most hostile. In a series of statements that the French Foreign Minister Jobert referred to as 'an inexact analysis of reality'[6] the US State Department accused the Europeans of deliberately subverting Atlantic solidarity, endangering Kissinger's peace mission and of adopting a 'take it or leave it approach' to consultation. It was, in fact, the issue of consultation that appeared to infuriate Kissinger most, for there was little evidence that his attempts to negotiate matters of substance with the Arabs had been in any way affected by the Europeans' decision. That this and other 'misunderstandings' were rapidly cleared up by mid-1974 was partly a triumph for the political cooperation machinery but primarily the result of fortuitous changes of leadership in the UK, France and West Germany. Despite the fact that at their informal meeting at Schloss Gymnich the Nine managed to devise an acceptable method for prior consultation with the USA over matters of political cooperation[7], the greatly improved atmosphere with the Americans that quickly developed hinged on the fact that a Europe presided over by Messrs Giscard, Schmidt and Wilson proved to be more pro-American than that of Pompidou, Brandt and Heath.

Thus by mid-1974 the Europeans had made good their relations with the USA and responded in part at least to the Arab request for a new relationship. There still remained, however, the difficult question of finding substantive issues that could be discussed with the Arabs without either further antagonising the Americans or exposing the fundamental disagreements that the Europeans still harboured within their own camp. The Nine decided on their stance by a circuitous route that involved the elimination of those matters that could not be discussed. The result was that discussion of either the oil problem or the Middle East conflict was rejected by the Europeans as being too potentially controversial and divisive, leaving the future economic development of the Arab countries as the only possible topic liable to be of interest to both sides. Having decided on a low-level (preferably apolitical) approach, the Nine, showing their customary confidence in the European Commission's ability to handle such matters, decided that the proper institutional framework for the European end of the Dialogue would be the political cooperation machinery. Thus an organ specifically set up to handle the delicate issues of 'high politics' was to be given the task of ensuring that such matters be kept out of a negotiation that was to be restricted to low-level technical deliberations. One of the reasons for this decision was presumably the fact that it was felt that the Dialogue would inevitably have political implications, even though the purpose of cooperation was not overtly political.

The political cooperation machinery had, of course, been concentrating its attention on the Middle East with varying degrees of success since its inception. There was a working group of Middle East experts from the Nine's foreign offices that met regularly to exhange information and prepare relevant agenda items for the Political Committee meetings. Indeed at the very first ministers' conference within the framework of political coopera-tion held in November 1970 there was 'the most detailed exchange of views' on the Middle East situation, whilst at the second meeting of May 1971 a whole day was devoted to the same subject[8]. At the height of the 1973 Middle East crisis the Nine had managed with some difficulty to issue a 'Declaration on the crisis in the Middle East'[9] despite the uneasiness of some member-states about what they perceived to be appeasement of the Arabs at the expense of Israel. This declaration, which did indeed lean towards the Arab interpretation of UN Resolution 242, formally recognized Palestinian rights and stressed the need for eventual Israeli withdrawal from 'occupied territory'. It was the same Middle East working group that was initially involved in the early 1974 preparations for the Dialogue. However, once the decision had been taken to restrict the items for discussion to economic and technical issues it was decided to maintain the distinction between these and more overtly political matters by creating a new and rather distinctive working group especially for the Dialogue. The need for such a new group was further underlined by the position of the European Commission, for whom a role in the Dialogue was envisaged, which did not at that time (nor indeed until fairly recently) participate in the established Middle East working group.

It was thus agreed to propose to the Arabs that the highest organ of the Dialogue should be a General Commission at ambassadorial level (with the possibility of future extension, as the Arabs wished, to foreign-minister level). To prepare for meetings of this General Commission a Coordinating Group was set up by the Europeans within the framework of EPC. This group differed slightly from other political cooperation working groups in that, because of the possibility of overlap with matters that come under the jurisdiction of the Community treaties, both the Commission and COREP-ER had to be involved as well. It was decided that the Coordinating Group would report via the presidency to COREPER as well as to the Political

Committee, and that the Commission was to be always represented. Furthermore, the possibility was envisaged (and has indeed become the case) that the normal political cooperation practice of meeting only in the capital of the presidency would be broken and that a number of the meetings would be held for practical reasons in Brussels. With the single exception of occasional French stubborness, the Dialogue, as it has progressed under political cooperation, has remained remarkably free of theological arguments. Indeed, as we shall see, a new and relatively unique relationship has developed between the two European institutional frameworks.

At meetings in both Cairo and Paris during the early period of the French presidency the Arab states accepted most of the European proposals for getting the Dialogue under way. It was decided to establish a number of joint Working Commissions below the General Commission to deal with a number of the different issue-areas that the Europeans had envisaged back in March (these were industrialization, infrastructure, agriculture, financial cooperation and cultural and scientific cooperation). The Arabs eventually persuaded the Europeans to add a sixth group on trade and eventually a seventh much later dealing with 'political' matters. On the Arab side the institutional framework that evolved was essentially a mirror-image of European procedures, lending further weight to the argument that in the European Communities the Arabs perceive a model for their own integrative ideals. The Dialogue was to be between the Nine and the twenty members of the Arab League. The organizing concept of a bicephalous presidency was adopted by both sides, with the Secretariat of the Arab League and the Arab state holding the presidency of that body relating to the European Commission and the European presidency. The only real problem that has arisen from this arrangement has been the difficulty that the European side has experienced in anticipating changes in and future holders of the Arab presidency. On the other hand, the Europeans, already beset with the problems of a grossly overloaded presidency, have found that the rapid expansion of the Dialogue has served once again to focus internal attention on the nature of that particular institution[10]. From the start, the problem of alternative forums – one that always dogged the Europeans with their disparate membership and enthusiasm for organizations like NATO, OECD and recently the IEA – was apparent, given the nature of the membership of the Arab League. Three of the states (Algeria, Morocco and Tunisia) are first-group Associates of the EEC, three (Somalia, Sudan and Mauretania) are ACP countries within the Lomé framework and four (Egypt, Syria, Jordan and eventually Lebanon) are Mediterranean Associates. Despite the fact that the main stimulus for the Dialogue had arisen at the time of the oil crisis, eleven of the member-states of the Arab League are non-oil-producers (Egypt, Syria, Lebanon, Jordan, Somalia, Sudan, Mauretania, Morocco, Tunisia and the Yemen), and this introduced a new element for the Europeans in the Dialogue. It was never possible, even if the oil-producers had been prepared to accept it, that the Dialogue would be simply a means of producer and consumer working out a satisfactory relationship. Given the presence of so many non-oil-producers on the Arab side, particularly states like Egypt and Syria so intimately involved in the Middle East political situation, there was never any real chance that political matters could be kept out of the Dialogue, however hard the Europeans strove to prevent them being discussed.

The political situation in the Middle East was, in fact, to be raised before the Dialogue even got off the ground and was to hold up any formal substantive meetings until mid-1975. Just as agreement had been reached as to the institutional arrangements and the topics to be covered by the various working groups and shortly before the anticipated first meeting of the General Commission, the Arab states, following the success of this tactic at the UN, demanded observer status for the Palestinian Liberation Organization as the recognized legitimate representatives of the Palestinian people[11] on the General Commission. The subsequent European refusal to comply with this request led to the Dialogue being frozen for several months whilst a solution was sought. That such a solution was found, and that it became known as the 'Dublin Formula', is to the credit of the Irish, in particular their Foreign Minister Garret Fitzgerald, who held the Community presidency during the first six months of 1975. At a meeting in Dublin in February the foreign ministers of the EEC decided to propose to the Arab states that even if the General Commission could not meet it might be possible for the proposed Working Groups to get down to work. Furthermore it was suggested that one possible solution to the Palestinian problem might be found if the General Commission were to meet, not on the basis of country delegations but simply as European and Arab delegations, thus avoiding the necessity of formally recognizing who made up the delegation and allowing the PLO to participate. Much credit must go to the skilful handling of this proposal by the Irish presidency and the personal diplomacy of Fitzgerald, who managed, after a number of visits to Middle East leaders, to persuade the Arab side to accept the compromise. As far as political cooperation was concerned, the success of the Irish on this issue tends to refute the suggestion that is often heard that only the larger states of the Nine, with their greater experience of international affairs, can successfully handle the arduous task of running foreign policy coordination. Political cooperation was here capably handled by the Irish, and they in turn found themselves playing a part in external affairs that would have been unimaginable outside the Community context. The success of the 'Dublin Formula' meant that, despite the untimely signing of a Community trade agreement with Israel in May 1975, the first meeting of experts was held in Cairo in June of the same year.

At the Cairo meeting the proposed working groups were set up and a joint Memorandum issued setting out in detail the areas to be covered by these working groups (see above, page 74). Furthermore, the success of this first meeting was highlighted by the fact that agreement was quickly reached to meet again in Rome the next month. At the end of the Cairo meeting Eamonn Gallagher, the Irish representative of the European presidency, stated that the meeting 'was unique of its kind' and that it had been 'a great success'[12]. At the second meeting that was held in Rome from 22 July to 24 July the working groups got down to substantive work and their reports contained a number of fairly precise suggestions, such as recommended areas for priority in industrial cooperation, an inventory of food-requirements and prospects and a plan to work out uniform rules for investment. Both sides seemed well satisfied with the meetings, even Arab participants like Algeria and Tunisia, who had adopted an extremely critical attitude at the opening meeting. Although it was once again agreed to set a date for the next meeting (to be held in Abu Dhabi) the Arab delegation also raised the question of arranging a first meeting of the General Commission at which they obviously hoped that political issues could be raised. Not surprisingly, the European delegation was not able to commit itself on this point[13]. At the third meeting in Abu Dhabi the Arab side was to get its way. Although the work that had been started in Cairo and Rome was continued, more projects defined and further specialist groups envisaged, the final communique[14] concluded that the preparatory work was now completed and that therefore the convening of the General Commission in order to define the mandates of the specialist groups was now essential. Of the substantive issues discussed there was general agreement in all but two areas. First, with regard to the question of financial cooperation the Arab states maintained a firm stand on the strict conditions they impose on European access to their capital markets, and second, the Europeans were not prepared to consider Arab demands for a generalized free trade agreement, partly because of the precedent that it would create and partly because of the fact that several Arab countries are already linked to the EEC, either by the Lomé Convention or the Mediterranean framework.

In pushing for a meeting of the General Commission the Arab strategy had been a patient one; they contented themselves with expert discussions to maintain the momentum of the Dialogue but constantly pressed for a raising of the level of representation, first to ambassadorial level, which they achieved when the General Commission was convened for the first time in Luxembourg in May 1976, and then they demanded that the foreign ministers meet with a view to preparing for their ultimate organizational objective – a summit meeting between heads of government.

As with so many other aspects of political cooperation, the progress of the Dialogue to date is of much greater interest in terms of the evolving procedure of foreign policy cooperation than it is for the actual substance of the deliberations. Nevertheless, when the General Commission met in Luxembourg a number of new issues were raised. First, and fairly predictably, the Arab side raised in its opening speech at the plenary session both the question of the European stance on the Middle East conflict (which the Arabs felt had been essentially static since the November 1973 Declaration) and the need for a foreign ministers' conference as soon as possible. The Europeans for their part reiterated the November 1973 position and pointed out that the Nine at the UN were now supporting consideration of the rights of the Palestinian people, most particularly the right to express a national identity. Second, the Arab side succeeded in stalling specific discussion of projects in order both to highlight the political context of the Dialogue and to ensure the need for further meetings of the General Commission. More specifically, the crucial question of finance was not discussed. It was, however, agreed to 'institutionalize' the General Commission as the 'Supreme Co-ordination Body', and it was decided that in this role it would meet twice a year at ambassadorial level and whenever else at higher levels that proved either desirable or essential. Finally, it was agreed that the General Commission would be convened again in Tunis in February 1977. The Tunis meeting yielded only meagre results and failed to resolve differences between the two sides on either economic or political matters. The Communique that was issued after the meeting[15] reflected this state of affairs whereby each side contented itself with a series of 'expressions of conviction' and 'reiterations of concern' but with few 'common agreements'. However, in reviewing the work of the specialist groups and working parties, the General Commission did manage to lay down a number of guidelines for the future. Most significantly, they decided to establish an *ad hoc* group to be responsible for the working-out of procedures to deal with the financial contributions that would be required if the various projects were to be advanced. Since then this issue has been resolved, for the present at least, by the European Council of Ministers' decision in May 1977 to match the Arab contribution of $15 million with a credit of $3.5 million from the current Community budget. The European Commission had initially proposed $5 million, but the reluctance of a number of member-states to give approval for such a sum (that would be spent in its entirety on projects in Arab states) led to the lower compromise figure being adopted. The initial finance is to go towards a number of as yet unspecified pre-feasability studies ($1.2 million has already been requested from the General Council by the 'agricultural and rural development' working party for the Juba Valley development project in Somalia[16]).

The Tunis Communique also dealt with such issues as the transfer of technology, commercial cooperation (specifically an Arab request for the establishment of a 'Euro–Arab Trade Cooperation Centre'), the protection and encouragement of investment, a number of agricultural projects such as the above-mentioned Juba Valley development, the Iraq potato development and the Sudanese meat project, the question of general terms of industrial contracts, cultural cooperation and finally the living and working conditions of migrant workers. At the time of writing the two sides are preparing for the third meeting of the General Commission to be held in Brussels at the end of October 1977. The working groups and specialist groups that have been meeting since the Tunis meeting have by all accounts made very little progress on the various topics entrusted to them; it seems likely that once again 'political' issues will be foremost in the Arab mind, although the recent positions adopted by the Nine on the Middle East problem may go some way to alleviating these difficulties. The speech of M. Simonet at the UN General Assembly went a long way towards satisfying the Arabs about progress in the European position. Whilst reaffirming the need for the Arab states to 'be ready to recognize Israel's right to live in peace within secure, recognized frontiers', Simonet, on behalf of the Nine, also described as 'illegal' the installation of Israeli columns on occupied territory and reaffirmed the 'Palestinian People's legitimate right to effective expression of their national identity'[17].

The balance-sheet to date of activities within the framework of the Dialogue, to which must be added a number of 'parliamentary' contacts between the two sides and a growing relationship between the European Commission and OAPEC, is not as yet particularly impressive. As always with political cooperation on the European side, problems begin to arise as soon as the delicate question of finance is raised; if the numerous projects noted above are ever to get past the feasability stage, fairly large injections of capital will be required. Here the Europeans and the Arab non-oil-producers have an interest in common in that they both seek to extract such capital from the wealthy oil-producers. The Europeans in particular would prefer to see oil funds being directed towards the development of industry in the Middle East rather than being invested in European companies in Europe because of the delicate questions of control that have recently tended to excite the attention of European domestic opinion. If this capital can be directed towards new industry in the Middle East then there are possibilities both for an initial export of European technology and capital goods, and in the long term the advantages of new consumer-oriented markets. The trend towards a closer connection between the two economic systems would seem to be quite clear. A report issued by the European Commission in September 1976 dealing with Euro–Arab trade developments showed that between 1970 and 1975 there was a 314 per cent increase in the volume of EEC exports to the Arab world, whilst the Arab share in total EEC trade with the world advanced from 6.2 per cent to 12.6 per cent. However, despite the above trend and despite the great amount of economic and technical activity in the working groups of the Dialogue there is evidence of a certain lack of enthusiasm on both sides, adding weight to the argument that the Dialogue is of essence political, that both sides have a greater interest in 'atmosphere' than in the actual projects under discussion. For the Europeans – the British and French in particular but also the West Germans

– tend to see the sort of projects currently under discussion as being ultimately more desirably handled by the private sector than by inter-governmental negotiations; other European countries, of course, are more interested in seeing further progress along integrated Community lines. For the Arabs – some of whom, as we have noted, have much to gain from these projects – there has been a marked desire to be guided by the Europeans. Many of the proposals have been put forward by the European delegation and the Arabs have experienced difficulty in ordering priorities or providing the stimulus to get past the feasibility stage. It is undoubtedly the case that, despite the relative degree of unity that the Arab League has been able to enforce, the Arab side is experiencing great difficulty in managing such a complex multilateral negotiation. The only matter on which Arab unity can be assured is the Middle East conflict, and it is thus hardly surprising that they attach greater significance to what they see as progress with the Europeans on this front than the nominal content of the Dialogue, namely economic and technical questions.

Thus once again, when discussing political cooperation we find little of any great substance; attempts at cooperation that are stimulated primarily by the need to react to pressure from outside the Community and to take into account countervailing pressures from the USA and an institutional framework (designed essentially to compromise internal EEC theological discussions) experiencing certain difficulties in its encounters with an external environment that increasingly refuses to be slotted conveniently into Community categories. However, as was noted earlier, the Nine, having allocated the Euro–Arab Dialogue to the political cooperation machinery, has managed to adapt that machinery in a pragmatic fashion to handle the content of the Dialogue. The practice of the country holding the presidency chairing all meetings during its six-months' tenure of office has been abandoned in the experts' working groups, such leadership being shared by several countries plus, more significantly, the Commission. Thus at the start of the Dialogue Britain chaired the Finance Group, West Germany the Industrial Group, France the Infrastructure Group, Belgium the Cultural Group and the European Commission, in recognition of the inevitable overlap with Treaty business, was given charge of both the Agriculture and Trade Groups. Whilst the Coordinating Group still con-tinues to meet in the capital of the presidency, many of the experts' working groups have chosen to meet in Brussels, using the Commission's facilities. Indeed, the role of the Commission, as in other aspects of political cooperation, would seem to be expanding. Increasingly within the context of the Dialogue, the Secretariat-General, with its detailed knowledge of activities at both Community and Political Cooperation levels, seems to be taking over some of the tasks that one would normally expect the presidency to perform, most obviously the preparation of technical papers for prepara-tory meetings within the Nine. It can, of course, be argued that this is a development that had to come, given that the substance of the Dialogue at this point in time so clearly lies within the traditional area of Community competence; some have indeed gone on to suggest that all responsibility for running the Dialogue should now be shifted to the Community institutions, away from Political Cooperation. Such a move would in probability be resisted by the member-states, not just because of the fact that the Dialogue has tended to take over from the CSCE as the main motor of political cooperation but also because of its inherently political nature. The point of the Dialogue is not so much the resolution of the problems of economic and technical cooperation – these probably could be (indeed are being) just as easily solved by the Commission working with COREPER – but the laying of the grounds for possible future political consultation as well. At a minimum, the Dialogue is an exercise in self-interest for the Nine, an attempt to manage delicately the growing demands of an emergent force; as such it is probably best kept within the framework of political cooperation under political guidance, whilst still making use of Community machinery where possible. Nevertheless, if the Dialogue continues to expand at the rate suggested by the lengthy list of topics in the Tunis Communique, the problem of management and the attendant strain on the presidency, particularly when it is held by one of the smaller countries, will begin to tell. Once again the arguments for either a longer term of presidency or indeed for some sort of secretariat for political cooperation are raised.

To date, the problem of management does not seem to be any worse in the Dialogue than in other aspects of political cooperation, thanks in part to the coordinating task that the Commission is able to take on. However, some participants on the European side have commented that, whilst the Arab states still look to the Europeans for initiating ideas, the Arab League delegations at recent meetings have appeared to be better prepared than the Europeans. Whilst the Arab side tends to meet for a quite lengthy period before Dialogue meetings to harmonize and prepare its positions, the Europeans have tended to find themselves, because of the great pressure of work on those participating, having to hold hastily organized *ad hoc* meetings on the fringes of the negotiations in order to brief themselves. One thing that does stand out from the experience of the Dialogue to date is the relative ease with which the Arab delegation has been able to assume the working methods that Europeans are so experienced in. Participants have been surprised by the quality of many of the Arab officials that they have dealt with (many of whom, of course, are Palestinians who have made their careers in the foreign services of other Arab states) and the discipline that the Arabs have been able to maintain in putting forward common negotiating stances. To the extent that this discipline is probably at the moment limited to the Dialogue (with the Arab states still divided on many issues), then the comparison with the Nine's own rather delicate agreements can be made.

What, then, can be said about the success of the Dialogue to date and where might it lead us? For the Europeans it must represent a partial success, although one that needs much qualification. If one assumes that the Nine wanted primarily to ensure future oil-supplies and to establish profitable markets for European technology without making significant political moves towards actively supporting the Arab cause in the Middle East, then they have gone some way towards creating the right sort of atmosphere, most notably in showing the Arabs that, to a certain extent, they are capable of international dealings as a European unit rather than merely as an appendage of the USA. However, as was noted above, this European position has still been constructed with a watchful eye on US sensitivities and in the face of growing Israeli hostility. That is why the Nine have as yet made no real contribution towards the efforts at a Middle East settlement; that is why they have conducted no exclusively European dealings with the Arabs over oil; and that is why they have been unable to answer Arab demands either for an extension of their preferential trade area beyond the Mediterranean to include the Arabian peninsula or for guarantees of the security of Arab investments that would attract oil funds away from the USA towards Europe. In terms of political cooperation, the most significant fact is that the machinery still remains one of reaction rather than action at any other than the lowest levels. Although the Nine have got over the nightmare of Arab political demands (when they were made more as a gesture than anything else at the General Commission Meetings) by finding them up to now fairly manageable, little or no real progress has been made towards the adoption of a common foreign policy towards the Arab world. One still fears the effect of another Middle East war both on the fragile unity that the Nine have constructed and on their collective relationship both with the Arab world and the USA. Sooner or later both the Arabs and the USA are quite likely to put further pressure on the Europeans to play an active role in Middle East high politics once again. It is difficult to see at this stage how the experience of jointly working together under political cooperation in the working-out of the Dialogue is going to ease the difficult task for the Nine.

The Arab states must, on the other hand, be well satisfied with progress to date. Perhaps fundamental for them at the start of the Dialogue was the concept of sitting around the negotiating table with the Nine (their ex-colonial masters in some cases) on an equal basis; this, at any rate, has been achieved, and its significance for the Arabs should not be underestimated. Furthermore, they can point to a shift, however cautious, in European attitudes towards the Palestinians and the Arab cause in general. To the extent that all the states have some interest in consolidating Arab unity, the experience of dealing with a partially integrated EEC has been a useful learning process, particularly for the wealthier and less radical Arab states, who see in multilateral negotiations of this type a chance to use the excuse of a united bargaining position to control their more hot-headed and potentially unstable brethren. The question of where the Dialogue is leading must remain unanswered: the suspicion remains that little of substance will emerge from a process which is notable mainly for its novel and unique procedural developments. Currently, and one suspects for some time to come, neither partner has the internal cohesion or decision-making capacity to achieve the organized relationship with one another that their growing independence and expectations demand.

Notes

1 See Chapter 5, p. 60, of this volume
2 'Necessary Progress in Community Energy Policy', 13 October 1972, *Bulletin of the European Communities* (Supplement), 11/72
3 See Annette Morgan, *From Summit to Council: Evolution in the EEC*, Chatham House/PEP, pp. 17–19
4 *Daily Telegraph*, 8 March 1974
5 *Agence Europe*, No. 1470, 4 March 1974
6 *International Herald Tribune*, 7 March 1974
7 See Chapter 3, p. 33, for an evaluation of the Gymnich Agreement
8 *Bulletin of the European Communities*, 6/1971
9 Declaration of the Nine Foreign Ministers of 6 November 1973 in Brussels on the Situation in the Middle East. *See Bulletin of the European Communities*, 10/1973
10 H. Wallace and G. Edwards, 'European Community: The Evolving Role of the Presidency', *International Affairs*, October 1976, for an examination of this problem
11 The Arabs had granted this recognition to the PLO at the Rabat Summit held in October 1974
12 *Agence Europe*, 1769, p. 5
13 *Agence Europe*, 1797, p. 5
14 *Agence Europe*, 1869, p. 6
15 Europe Documents, 933, *Agence Europe*, 5.2.77
16 *Agence Europe*, 5.4.77
17 *Agence Europe*, 2315, p. 5

Euro–American relations and European Political Cooperation

BEATE KOHLER

7.1   From the formation of the Community to the Nixon era

> The assumption that a United Europe and the United States would inevitably conduct parallel policies and have similar views about appropriate tactics runs counter to historical experience. A separate unity has usually been established by opposition to a dominant power: The European sense of identity is unlikely to be an exception to this general rule – its motives could well be to insist on a specifically European view of the world . . . which is another way of saying that it will challenge American hegemony in Atlantic policy[1].

This interpretation of European integration and its consequences for Atlantic cooperation has certainly influenced American politics in recent years. Nevertheless it remains necessary to examine the validity of this analysis. None of the West European organizations has been established in opposition to the USA although, of course, the European Economic Community has contributed to the economic strengthening of the Western European countries, and thus changed their position *vis-à-vis* the USA. This shifting of balance inevitably led to an intensification of arguments on controversial questions in the field of Atlantic relations. Already in the 1960s this became markedly apparent in questions of security and in the area of trade policy. The USA's global policy of security certainly did not meet with the unconditional agreement of their Western European allies and controversies about the distribution of burdens and the right of codetermination in, among other things, the field of nuclear policy, were additional strains on relations within the Alliance. The Kennedy Round led to frequent disputes about the reduction of protectionist trade barriers, whilst the unsatisfactory results of the negotiations on the 'sensitive' products of uncompetitive industries and about agricultural products became a source of new conflicts.

Tensions within the European–American relationship did not only stem from divergencies within bilateral relations, they were also the result of changes in the international system. The growing predominance of the North–South question over the East–West conflict, the general shift in the international balance of power and the weakening of established regulatory mechanisms necessitated a realignment of international relations. The reforms which now became necessary meant that the USA had to secure its economic and security interests on a long-term basis and that it had to maintain its role as the leading power within the Western camp. On both counts, the USA felt challenged by the EEC states who tended to pursue opposing interests and question the USA's claim to hegemony in the short term with regard to the realization of the reforms mentioned above and in the long term as far as the future position of the USA within the international system was concerned.

The stubbornness with which the two parties pursued their interests is only partially explained by existing structural divergencies. If such differences in the past have been contained by overriding common interests of security, the internal economic, social and political difficulties which the individual states now have to combat are increasingly narrowing the leeway for concessions in the field of foreign policy. Although all Western industrialized states face similar problems, they set themselves different priorities and often seek different solutions. In addition, the increasing importance of international economic relations for the overcoming of internal crises means that the fight to realize individual conceptions of the necessary reforms of the international system becomes fiercer. Each state tries to promote the use of those principles and rules of behaviour which best fit its own national needs.

The EEC states are, in comparison with the USA, much less able to overcome their own internal difficulties by transforming their international environment. At the same time they are much harder hit by international crises. This became clear during the dollar crisis of the early 1970s and in the later energy and raw material crises. The sort of conflicts that will now arise in the relationship with the USA became apparent mainly during the confrontation over the distribution of costs with regard to the solving of the currency crisis. As the Americans are themselves vulnerable 'they cannot afford to put common interests first. As they are, on the other hand, less vulnerable than their partners, they can enforce their own wishes more easily'[2].

Not least because of the realization of their own vulnerability the EEC states have attempted to strengthen their negotiating position by closer cooperation. Thus they laid particular emphasis on the development of a common foreign currency policy in the first stage of economic and monetary union. This increased American fears that the planned economic and currency union had been conceived as a defensive alliance by the Europeans against the hegemony of the American dollar. This policy seemed to comply with further endeavours by the Europeans to strengthen their international importance. The expansion of the EEC from six to nine member-states, the establishment of a large European free trade area with the remaining member-states of the European Free Trade Association (EFTA) the extension of association agreements with more than fifty states in Africa, the Caribbean and the Pacific, the notion of a global Mediterranean policy, the inclusion of more states of the Third World into a system of concessionary relations – all these are signs of the EEC's growing international importance since the beginning of the 1970s, a development which is viewed by the USA with a certain degree of apprehension. For the American observer, the impression of a developing EEC foreign policy orientation was reinforced by the institutionalization of the cooperation of the Nine on questions of foreign policy. During the summit meeting in The Hague, the mandate requesting the foreign ministers of the Community to demonstrate progress towards political union did not lead to deeper and closer relations within the EEC itself but rather to this particular initiative in the field of foreign policy. After certain initial difficulties, EPC seemed to the USA to develop into an efficient instrument of European foreign policy[3].

7.2 The Year of Europe

A situation characterized by the fundamental reconstitution of relations, where old partners are divided by considerable divergencies of interests and where the changing power relationships are still unsettled, will inevitably lead to conflict. It was not so much the accumulation of difficulties in the specific field of economics, money and security which led to the crisis in Atlantic relations but the constellation of internal and external conditions which surrounded them at the time. At the beginning of 1973 the US government took the initiative by proposing a reconsideration of European –American relations. In the speech at which he referred to the notion of the 'Year of Europe' Henry Kissinger suggested the preparation of a new Atlantic Charter and, at the same time, formulated the guidelines for it[4].

The EEC countries could hardly accept the differentiation that Kissinger seemed to be making between global and regional interests and obligations, since this would have meant stressing the American claim to hegemony in the Western world at a time when American action in world politics was meeting with harsh opposition from the European partners. Nevertheless, the desire for a unitary framework of action seemed obvious. European –American negotiations had run, until then, largely in parallel on different levels; they were conducted within numerous contexts all of which had reached differing degrees of institutionalization. Questions of security were discussed within the framework of NATO, currency problems within IMF and the 'Committee of Twenty', trade relations within GATT or in the 'bi-annual meetings' between members of Congress and the European Parliament. The kind of 'comprehensive approach' now suggested by the Nixon administration was received by the Europeans with great apprehension. They were concerned that the USA might exploit its strong military position to force economic concessions, especially in the area of trade. Apart from this, organizationally they did not feel strong enough to contest American claims. The production of a common policy on foreign trade is the concern of the EEC, which is also the desirable forum for agreements on currency matters, whilst the Euro Group of NATO proved to be only partially satisfactory for the coordination of European security interests. Harmonization of other questions of foreign policy within EPC was at this time still at an early stage of experimentation.

The consultations following Kissinger's initiative showed that there were considerable differences among the Europeans concerning their interpretation of American intentions as well as their readiness to commit themselves[5]. The form of the new 'Atlantic Charter' was also controversial and even the Americans had dropped references to the concept by the end of 1973. At no time were the Europeans prepared to consider Canada and Japan as participants in the negotiations, as the USA had initially suggested.

During the summit meeting in Copenhagen in December 1973, the Nine agreed on the preparation of three draft positions for negotiations with Washington:

(1) A declaration concerning European–American security relations within NATO;
(2) A declaration of basic principles concerning relations between the USA and the EEC;
(3) A declaration on 'European identity' in order to define the future role of European union in Euro–American relations.

The texts which were produced by EPC in close consultation with the Committee of Permanent Representatives in Brussels and after consultation with representatives of the US administration reflected the fact that the Nine (and not just France) were concerned that the USA might use consultations as an instrument of increased leverage over European politics[6]. The USA for their part were angered by what they thought to be the anti-American tenor of the draft. They criticized it mainly on the grounds that it had been produced without a sufficient contribution by the representatives of the US government. If the Community text stressed the independence of Western Europe, the US counterdraft emphasized interdependence and the need for a more substantial common approach. In October 1973, the Yom Kippur war and the subsequent energy crisis reinforced the profound differences of opinion between Western Europe and the USA. The American government believed that the Middle East war directly challenged the global balance between the USA and the Soviet Union and they were anxious to prevent any shift of power in favour of Moscow. For the Europeans, the war had a different significance: it was seen as being merely the most recent chapter in the long history of the Arab–Israeli conflict. They were primarily concerned about their oil supply, which they considered to be the greatest threat to their vulnerable national economies[7].

At the beginningof November 1973 the foreign ministers of the Nine published a declaration concerning the situation in the Middle East in which they took up a more pro-Arab instead of a pro-Israeli position. At the same time, the EEC member-states tried to start contacts with the oil-producing countries on a bilateral as well as a European level. France, who had opposed the US proposal for closer cooperation between the oil-consuming countries, took the initiative in calling for a world energy conference under the aegis of the UN. The EEC worked at its global policy for the Mediterranean, and sought to gain closer ties with the Eastern and Southern Mediterranean countries.

When, at the beginning of March 1974, the European foreign ministers announced their intention of developing a Euro–Arab Dialogue, the USA reacted angrily. The US government accused the Europeans of not having consulted them and of obstructing American foreign policy. During his Bonn visit immediately before the beginning of the Brussels EPC meeting in question Kissinger already knew about forthcoming European decisions concerning the Euro–Arab Dialogue. He was frustrated and annoyed that the Federal Republic of Germany, which at the time held the presidency of EPC, did not feel able to pass on this information in its capacity as spokesman for the Community.

Although the public impression suggested that the Nine did not consider it necessary to inform their American partners about such an important matter, the facts suggest that the USA expected the right to veto such decisions. The Americans insisted on consultation before decisions were made in EPC to ensure that they were able to influence any matters that the Europeans might choose to discuss, which they felt impinged on their own interests.

This event led to a further intensification of the confrontation. President Nixon declared that the Europeans could not expect any cooperation in the field of security policy from the USA if, at the same time, they retained a negative attitude in political and economic questions or even steered a confrontation course. He stated, among other things, that he was not prepared to sign an American–European declaration which concealed such grave differences of opinion[8].

The question thus arises as to whether the escalation of the conflict was not simply a pretext to avoid having to sign an unsatisfactory declaration. This becomes even more plausible if one takes into account that, in the meantime, the USA had succeeded in strengthening its position of hegemony by founding the International Energy Agency.

7.3   The Gymnich Agreement

Following exchanges of letters between Nixon and Brandt and intensive consultations among the Nine and between them and the USA, the controversy was settled by the European foreign ministers during an informal meeting at Gymnich on the weekend of 20–21 April 1974. The so-called Gymnich Agreement was a compromise, which made it possible to bring the USA into EPC consultations. It became clear that this compromise was also acceptable to the US administration[9]. It was agreed that whenever one of the Nine wished to initiate consultations on a certain topic, provided the other states agreed, the presidency would begin consultations with the USA before political decisions were finalized. If no unanimity concerning the commencement of consultations existed they would only take place at the bilateral level[10].

Since then, European–American relations have continued relatively smoothly. The US administration has made it its practice to inform the presidency of the Nine before regular EPC meeings about the US attitude towards international problems. The presidency of the Nine, in turn, has taken care to inform the USA after each EPC meeting about the nature and results of their deliberations. Normally, quite a lively exchange of information takes place, and the US administration is kept up-to-date on events at all levels of EPC. To a large extent, the flow of information goes through bilateral channels, but the formal process of information and consultation between the US State Department or embassies in Europe and the presidency representing the Nine has increased in significance.

Normally, the USA is aware of the items on the agenda of EPC meetings in advance despite an agreement among the Nine not to pass on any information to outside countries. When at the beginning of 1977 it became known that the agenda of a forthcoming EPC session had been passed on to the US administration by the British embassy in Washington, the French government in particular reacted very strongly.

The Gymnich Agreement has been applied in a relatively flexible manner. During some EPC meetings discussions arose on whether the presidency should contact the USA in relation to a specific topic. Here the official position of the French representative was generally more restrictive than that of his colleagues from other countries[11]. Even in cases where no official contacts were to be established, agreement existed that the country holding the presidency would consult the USA on a bilateral basis.

7.4   The relationship between US and European diplomacy

It is difficult to identify a consistent pattern in the relationship between the USA and EPC. Individual cases of conflict show that different kinds of relationships do not develop in a completely arbitrary way but are determined by certain conditions. Frequently the Nine has tried, with varying degrees of success, to use EPC as an instrument to develop and maintain an independent European position.

With regard to the Middle East conflict, the EEC countries did not succeed in achieving a clear-cut independent stand enabling them to become a potential political partner in the negotiations. Since the crisis in Atlantic relations was caused by the Nine's Middle East declarations, and was aggravated by their initiative for the Euro–Arab Dialogue, it is not surprising that this item proved to be a tricky question in the European –American relationship.

The Americans' sensitivity was one of the reasons why the Nine hesitated to adapt the content of their declaration on the Middle East conflict of November 1973 to further developments. At the end of 1976 the West German Foreign Minister took the initiative in this matter and the Nine succeeded in producing a draft which was submitted to the Conference of the Foreign Ministers at the end of January 1977 in London. Although the ministers agreed on the content of the draft, no declaration was published. They were pressured by the Americans to show this restraint, and the European partners were told in no uncertain terms that, at this point in time, a declaration concerning this delicate question would be inopportune. US opinion that such a publication could jeopardize the success of the forth-coming diplomatic attempts by Cyrus Vance to improve the situation was shared by the UK, the Netherlands and the Federal Republic of Germany[12].

If in this situation the Europeans reacted with dismay this was not so much a product of the American intervention itself but more the way it was done. As one European representative stated, it was not easy to make the Americans understand that the Nine were not prepared to have their willingness to cooperate exploited by the USA. It was believed that to take American interests into consideration would be detrimental to the image of European foreign policy. The Europeans said that their reason for not publishing the declaration was that it was enough to have come to an agreement about the Middle East problem and this agreement was by now public knowledge anyway. In contrast, the Arab states were of a completely different opinion, and in their opening speech at the meeting of the General Commission of the Euro–Arab Dialogue in Tunis they sharply criticized the Nine for not having publicly enforced those principles set up in previous meetings of the Euro–Arab Dialogue.

The Nine did not commit themselves publicly on this matter before the next European Council at the end of July 1977 in London. When they finally did so, it was only after close consultation with the USA. Yet even then coordination was not absolutely perfectly timed. The State Department published its new document concerning the question of Palestine two days before the Nine publicly announced their own position. This forced the Europeans to reformulate their declaration so that it corresponded largely with the American version. All this shows that the Europeans are only prepared to make a clear statement on certain issues *after* the USA has committed itself in public on them.

The apprehension against any sort of European policy in the Middle East, which the Nixon and Ford administrations (and especially Henry Kissinger) had already expressed, was based on the suspicion that the French attitude, considered to be too pro-Arab, might determine the attitude of the Nine. This caused less of a problem for the Carter administration, since their own new policy towards Israel was much more like the French position. This also meant that countries like the Federal Republic of Germany or the Netherlands, who hold a position which is more friendly towards Israel, could no longer refer to the interests of the American allies in their attempts to prevail in intra-European deliberations.

This episode suggests that the intervention of the USA in the European decision-making process can be effective when the Nine are not united and find it difficult to agree on a common strategy. In such a case it is difficult to judge to what extent a member-state's readiness to support American interests is used as a tactic in order to achieve objectives *vis-à-vis* the other members of the Nine.

Repeatedly, American attempts to gain the support of the Nine for American foreign policy have been met by a defensive European reaction. France was not the only country which strongly resisted the American appeals to strengthen their negotiating position in certain conflict situations by publishing a suitable EPC declaration. Thus, for instance, the American initiative on Vietnam was met by the Nine with united opposition. The Europeans refused in particular to put the main blame for the crisis on the North Vietnamese. Therefore the EPC presidency (in this case the Irish government) informed the US ambassador in Dublin that the Nine's analysis of the political situation differed from that of the US government[13].

The same fear of being viewed by the world as merely implementing US decisions is considered a major reason for France's rush to recognize the new government of Angola[14]. As the French saw it, their declared willingness to recognize the Angolan government in the near future prompted the US Secretary of State to send a message to all nine member-states, stressing the American point of view that recognition at this point in time would be 'premature'. Attempts during the Franco–German consultations and within the framework of the Nine to coordinate the timing for the general recognition of Angola failed because of the partner-states' hesitant attitude; the French claimed that the hesitation was largely out of respect for the American wishes[15].

In the case of the recognition of Angola, American intervention succeeded in dividing the European partners, but this does not apply to other areas of African politics. Moreover, there is hardly any cause for conflict, since the Europeans do not have common African policies, while the Americans try to avoid direct involvement in Africa. In the case of Rhodesia, this led to a situation where both sides willingly emphasized and supported the special role of the UK. It became especially clear in the context of Kissinger's tour of Africa, and later during the Rhodesia Conference in Geneva, that the UK government, to a certain extent, let itself be used by the Americans for this purpose. Thus the UK Foreign Office published for a long time a much more optimistic view of the situation than was justified by its its own assessment[16]. Moreover, Kissinger, in his negotiations with the Rhodesian Prime Minister, was prepared to modify Callaghan's proposals without giving London the opportunity to comment, whilst at the same time continuing to talk of a British–American initiative[17]. This meant that declarations of the Nine, made in the context of EPC, in support of British policies[18] seemed to support indirectly American initiatives in the Rhodesian conflict. This impression is strengthened by the fact that both the UK and the Nine as a whole lack the necessary means for implementing agreed policies. This applies particularly to the use of troops. In this special case, the close and direct cooperation of the USA and the UK was based on London's special responsibility for Rhodesia, so that one can hardly speak of bypassing the presidency of the Council[19] (in any case, during the decisive months of 1977 the UK itself held that presidency).

There is nevertheless a tendency on the part of the USA towards a closer cooperation with the 'Big Three' of the Community – the UK, France and the Federal Republic of Germany. In the case of Namibia, this special cooperation is assisted by the fact that the Europeans also recognize the special responsibility of the UN in this area. This fact is reflected in the composition of the 'contact group', which consists of the Western members of the Security Council: the USA, France, the Federal Republic of Germany and Canada.

As long as EPC activity is limited to the politics of declarations its capacity to intervene in international crises will also remain limited. If the Nine, in the search for solutions of international conflicts, content themselves more or less with the role of observer, European–American consultations become meaningless. Capacity for action lies, if anywhere, with the USA as it alone possesses the necessary set of instruments for intervention. The European countries can verbally support US policies but they run the risk of appearing to do no more than follow the US lead. If the Europeans represent a deviant position they can perhaps provoke a certain amount of attention and short-term uneasiness in the USA. But this disruptive effect wears off the more a conflict moves from the phase of arguing about the justification of divergent attitudes towards the phase of concrete negotiations, where economic and security measures are required[20].

In the contest between the USA and the European states for influence in the way international conflicts are solved, the latter are at a disadvantage. EPC and its formalized process of consultation certainly allows the Nine to ward off pressure of US intervention. But this again only applies to those areas of European foreign policy where the instruments at the disposal of EPC (and this includes instruments within the EEC) are potentially effective. The treatment of the crisis in Portugal is one example; another is the use of EPC in relation to CSCE.

EPC saw its greatest success during the preparation and realization of CSCE and its follow-up conference in Belgrade. This was partly because the objectives of that conference could be attained with those instruments which EPC has at its disposal. Coordination with the USA was on the whole relatively smooth, but was not necessarily the result of special efficiency on the part of the Europeans. The Americans for a long time did not consider CSCE as particularly important and thus left the leadership role of the West as a whole to the Europeans. NATO was used as an additional coordinating body. Thanks to the intensive exchange of information, all working papers of the Nine were automatically sent on to the respective NATO committees, and it was possible to regulate all differences of opinion immediately and to reduce any danger of misunderstanding about the partners' intentions and actions. Apart from the rare exceptions like CSCE, the cooperation of the Nine in the field of foreign policy is burdened by internal differences, which the USA can sometimes exploit to their own advantage. On the other hand, individual member-states of the Community will always try to mobilize the USA in support of their own positions. One can hardly object to this, but the constellations which exist in such cases are invariably the same, i.e. they are always predetermined by structural economic and socio–political conditions. The similarity of interests and the resulting tendency towards a particular kind of relations between the USA and a country like the Federal Republic of Germany are a great strain on relations between the European partners themselves. The spectre of a German–American hegemony which the French so often conjure up indicates the unease with which the other European countries view such developments[21].

Nevertheless the system of consultation has a certain protective function in so far as it enables the individual European countries to refer to their obligations to European cooperation whenever they reject US proposals. This protective function is appreciated by the US administration, which perhaps explains their strong reaction to the Tindemans Proposal suggestion that one member-state should be appointed to represent the Nine in relation to the USA[22].

In conclusion, it must be stated that the cohesion of the Nine *vis-à-vis* the USA cannot be guaranteed just by a consultation mechanism. The relationship can only positively develop to the extent that it is based on a recognition of mutual interests and on a realistic appreciation of the reasons for occasionally differing perceptions of those interests.

Notes

1 Henry A. Kissinger, *The Troubled Partnership. A Reappraisal of the Atlantic Alliance*, New York/London/Toronto, 1965, p. 39f.

2 Pierre Hassner, 'Security Problems in the Euro–American System', Ernst-Otto Czempiel and Dankwart A. Rustow (Eds.), *The Euro–American System*.

Economic and Political Relations between North American and Western Europe, Frankfurt, 1976, p. 162

3 See David Allen and William Wallace, Chapter 2

4 *Department of State Bulletin*. Vol. LXVIII No. 1768, 14 May 1973, pp. 593–598

5 The negotiation of the Atlantic Declaration is described in Dieter Dettke, *Allianz im Wandel. Amerikanische–europäische Sicherheitsbeziehungen im Zeichen des Bilateralismus der Supermätchte*, Frankfurt, 1976, p. 158ff.

6 The EPC draft was published in *The New York Times*, 24 September 1973; the American counterdraft was published in the same paper, on 9 November 1973. Cf. also Götz Roth, *Zur Europapolitik der Regierung Nixon – Eine Untersuchung struktureller Spannungen im amerikanisch–europäischen Verhältnis*, SWP-S Ebenhausen, May 1975

7 These contrasting concepts were developed by Henry Kissinger in his speech given before the Pilgrims' Society, 12 December 1973, in London

8 The crisis reached its height with President Nixon's speech in Chicago, 15 March 1974, where he accused the Europeans of ganging up against the USA

9 During the meeting between the West German Foreign Minister Genscher and the US Secretary of State Kissinger on 11 June 1974 in Bad Reichenhall, Kissinger expressed the full agreement of his administration to the solution that had been reached. He also ceased to raise any objections to the Euro–Arab Dialogue

10 The fullest description of the Gymnich Agreement was given by the German Foreign Minister Genscher in a press statement (*Europäische Politische Zusammenarbeit (EPZ)*, Bonn, 1978, p. 94ff.)

11 The period of the French presidency was a notable exception to this. It was characterized by (as the Gaullists called it) a certain 'atlanticism' on the part of the newly elected French Giscard d'Estaing

12 Press reports on the London meeting, e.g. in *Le Monde*, 2 February 1977: *Neue Zürcher Zeitung*, 1, 2 and 3 February 1977. The declaration was later published in *Al-Ahram*: cf. *Neue Zürcher Zeitung*, 23 February 1977

13 *Le Monde*, 17 April 1974, 'Les Neufs refusent de s'aligner sur les Etats-Unis'

14 See Nicholas van Praag, Chapter 10

15 *Le Monde*, 20/21 February and 25 February 1976, as well as *The Times*, 19 February 1976 and *Frankfurter Allgemeine Zeitung*, 24 February 1976

16 *Neue Zürcher Zeitung*, 27 January 1977

17 *Observer*, 19 September 1976 and *The Times*, 20 September 1976. The American representative, Andrew Young, declared during his short stop in London after his Africa trip that the Americans had treated their British partners 'not quite fairly' during the whole affair. Cf. *Neue Zürcher Zeitung*, 15 February 1977

18 The two EPC declarations on Rhodesia of October 1976 and January/February 1977

19 See Nicholas van Praag, Chapter 10

20 The dwindling influence of EPC in the Cyprus conflict is an important indication of this. Another indication is the reaction of the Israelis to the Middle East Declaration of the Nine. The Israelis acknowledged the changed position with great reluctance, but emphasized at the same time that the behaviour of the Nine was of no great significance, as neither EPC nor one of its member-states could act as a mediator in the Middle East. Cf. *Neue Zürcher Zeitung*, 9 July 1977

21 E.g. *Le Monde Diplomatique*, No. 273, December 1976, Jean Pierre Vigier, 'L'Europe sous une hégémonie Germano–américaine?'

22 Cf. *Neue Zürcher Zeitung*, 27 January 1976

CHAPTER EIGHT

Political cooperation and Southern Europe: case studies in crisis management

NICHOLAS VAN PRAAG

When European political cooperation began in 1970 the South European countries were not seen as a priority concern for the deliberation of the political cooperation structure outlined in the first Davignon Report. Indeed throughout its first three years the only mention of Southern Europe was as part of the long drawn-out discussion of an 'overall' approach to the Mediterranean, which dragged on until it was handed over to the Commission in November 1972.

The context in which Southern Europe has entered the mainstream of political cooperation over the succeeding years has been crucial. Two factors stand out. First, its geographical proximity linked to its economic, political and strategic significance had already made it a major focus of the Community's common external relations. By September 1973 every state from Portugal in the West to Greece and Turkey in the East (with the exception of Albania) were linked to the EEC by some form of trade accord or association agreement. These links had clear political significance; undemocratic Spain had to wait eight years for a very limited preferential trade agreement, having initially called for association. The Colonels' coup in April 1967 led to the partial 'freezing' of the Greek Association.

Political cooperation was thus presented with an area in which the distinction between 'high' and 'low' politics was already obscure. The rule-of-thumb definition for 'high' politics being those areas not covered by Treaties, the brief conferred upon political cooperation in Southern Europe was a particularly limited one, excluding all questions relating to agreements established under the common commercial policy and the enlargement of the Community.

Equally important in shaping the character and pattern of political cooperation in South Europe is that, while paying lip-service to medium- and long-term goals, the Copenhagen Report[1] in July 1973 laid down that consultation should essentially be concerned with establishing common positions in 'concrete cases'. G. Ducci, one of the main architects of political cooperation with Davignon and de Beaumarchais, had emphasized this topicality as one of the most innovatory features of political cooperation, allowing practical discussion in hard and fast terms with the aim of getting common European decisions[2]. This has given an essentially reactive nature to foreign policy cooperation in Southern Europe, awaiting as it must the existence of a crisis before it can contemplate cooperation.

Political cooperation has 'reacted' to three issues in Southern Europe:

(1) The Portuguese revolution of April 1974 and its aftermath;
(2) The Sampson coup in Cyprus in July 1974 and the partition of the island following Turkish intervention;
(3) The Spanish executions and succession in late 1975.

What do these cases tell us about the working of political cooperation in what one might term the 'wild' as distinct from the 'civilized' or institutional environment of the UN or CSCE with which the successes of EPC are usually associated? Is a coordinated European 'reaction' to a foreign-policy issue likely to be less effective than separate national ones? When and in what circumstances are the Nine likely to be spurred into joint action? How far-reaching and effective is such action likely to be? What constraints are posed by the instruments available to the Nine and how do they affect the character of foreign policy initiatives within the political cooperation framework? What is the connection, if any, between EPC and Community actions in Southern Europe? Before attempting to answer these questions it is necessary to examine Europe's foreign-policy record with regard to the three issues mentioned above.

8.1   The Portuguese revolution and its aftermath

The Portuguese question was first raised by the Dutch at a political cooperation meeting in Bonn on 10 June 1974, during a general exchange of views[3]. The nine ministers recognized the special importance of developments in Portugal, yet the result was a bland statement that asserted the Nine's hope for political evolution leading to democracy, and affirmed the importance of this for Africa and Europe. The Communique ended with a vague offer to help the Portuguese end their colonial wars and to foster social and economic development on the mainland.

The erratic character of the first stage of the Portuguese revolution and the developments in Cyprus during the summer of 1974 led the Nine to a more coherent approach. A South European working group was set up and the foreign ministers instructed their political directors to see what kind of action might be taken to 'promote democracy' in Portugal. While the political directors and their specialist subcommittee mulled over this question, the foreign ministers continued to exchange views and impressions, as they did following the Soames visit to Lisbon in January 1975, although without coming to any decision on joint action. The Nine's position was restated, though hardly clarified, at the July 1975 European Council, where the following 'conclusions' were reached. 'The European Council reaffirms that the European Community is ready to open discussions leading to closer economic and financial cooperation with Portugal.' This was to depend, conforming with the 'political and historic traditions of the Community', on evolution towards 'pluralistic democracy'[4]. Hardly a scrupulously defined policy! The ambiguous nature of the offer reflected the lack of consensus amongst members. France was against what she regarded as an inopportune and hasty action, while her partners wanted the offer repeated in more explicit terms. At the Political Cooperation meeting in September in Venice, Callaghan expressed his impatience at the lack of progress following the July summit and called for joint talks with the Portuguese to work out what form the promised emergency aid should take[5].

On 7 October 1975 the same foreign ministers, meeting as the EEC Council of Ministers, decided to accord extraordinary financial aid of 150 million units of account to Portugal from the European Investment Bank. The Sixth Provisional Government under Admiral Azevedo established in September, purged of radical officers and including the two main democratic parties had evidently gone some way towards satisfying the Nine that their conditions were being fulfilled. Arriving in Luxembourg to meet the ministers, the Portuguese Foreign Minister Antunes described the Nine's offer as an 'encouraging political gesture', adding that although Portugal needed far more substantial financial aid, 'for this year it is the proof that the European Community has confidence in the new course of events in Portugal'[6]. Rumor, as Council President, was equally anxious to emphasize the political significance rather than the size of the package[7].

Such a political gesture was clearly in line with the statement which followed the first political cooperation session at which Portugal was discussed in June 1974. Yet how relevant is this link? Much of the running seems to have been made by the Community structures independently, and without the guidance of political cooperation.

Portugal has been linked to the Community since the preferential trade agreement came into effect in January 1973 and Brussels was the major focus of Soares's rapid private trip around European capitals in early May 1974, where the Portuguese Foreign Minister discussed the post-revolutionary situation with the Commission and sought European support for the democratic and economic revitalization of his country. The Commission's position was equivocal. It went no further than the implication that the establishment of a democratic government in Portugal could but have a positive effect on relations with the Community.

Nevertheless, the emphasis on the European Community implicit in Soares's visit to Brussels deserves comment. The niceties of traditional diplomacy were little understood by the new Portuguese rulers that took over on 25 April. While the diplomatic missions of the previous regime were recalled and reorganized[8], other channels of communication with outsiders were needed. The Commission provided such an alternative, one with the additional advantage of being, as it were, above politics[9]. Most of the democratic political forces that emerged after the April revolution were agreed on the need to renew relations with the Community. Thus Soares could take advantage of existing channels to Brussels and deal with the suitably neutral Commission, rather than, for example, with the country holding the presidency, with its national and party implications[10].

On 26 June 1974 Soares, accompanied by the Prime Minister, paid a second visit to Brussels which resulted in the Portuguese request for the development of the agreement signed in 1972 together with a call for economic assistance and cooperation. The Commission's response reflected Soames's cautious attitude towards the Portuguese situation. Replying to a question put to him by the European Parliament at its October 1974 sitting, the Commissioner for external relations emphasized that the Commission could not make any 'concrete provisions' before the Portuguese government made more precise demands of the Community. The lack of effective government in Portugal was important in this apparently truculent stance. The general climate of revolutionary turmoil, especially after the departure of Spinola in September 1974, prevented the succession of provisional governments from either elaborating or activating coherent policies.

Extenuating though these circumstances may have been, the Community was nonetheless slow in formulating its own position, even given the absence of concrete Portuguese demands. Speaking to journalists in Brussels, Van Elslande, the Belgian Foreign Minister, had emphasized the lack of specific proposals as to how the Community might support democratic development in Portugal[11]. This job had been entrusted to the Political Committee which was to report in September 1974, yet progress was tortuously slow.

The Portuguese position was clarified somewhat at the EEC/Portugal Joint Committee meeting at the end of November 1974. The Nine agreed, at Soames's suggestion, to drop any legalistic insistence upon restricting the meeting to a discussion of the functioning of the 1973 agreement, enabling the Portuguese to outline their desire to develop relations with the Community in line with the provisions of the preferential trade agreement for its eventual extension[12].

Further clarification came at a subsequent meeting of the Joint Committee on 28 May 1975, following the victory of the moderate forces in the April elections to the Constituent Assembly. Two days earlier in Dublin there had been disagreement at the European Council as to how to consolidate the position of the Portuguese moderates. On the one hand, the Belgians pressed for the swift dispatch of loans, while on the other the Italians urged caution[13]. Genscher managed to persuade both camps to take up the suggestion by Antunes (who had been lobbying hard in both Bonn and The Hague) to call a joint ministerial meeting in July.

The July meeting was cancelled due to political upheavals in Lisbon, but the impasse had already been largely overcome by the Commission's note to the Council on 11 June, based on the Joint Committee's recommendations, suggesting the concession to Portugal of exceptional finance ($350 million over five years) together with some of the improvements the Portuguese had asked for on the 1972 trade agreement. Prompted by the Commission's note, at the subsequent meeting on 24 June, the Council directed the COREPER to examine ways of making available adequate financial assistance to Portugal[14]. The result was the July summit's declaration, followed by the Council's October decision to make 150 million units of account available to the Portuguese from the European Investment Bank[15] and to open discussions on the improvement of the trade agreement[16]. The loan represented a new departure as a common diplomatic tool. Article 130 of the Treaty of Rome sets out that the Bank is a development fund whose services are normally reserved for member- and 'associate' states. The requirement of a special financial protocol to give legal cover for the exceptional treatment of Portugal was waived under pressure from the UK, the Netherlands and Denmark. The French and West Germans were less happy at setting the precedent of backing EIB loans with community funds[17].

8.2   The Cyprus crisis of 1974

On 31 July 1974 Callaghan, then UK Foreign Secretary, announced to the House of Commons: 'I have been proud of Britain during the last week. If there is one thing that has pleased me, it has been the influence this country has had'[18]. This was at once an overoptimistic and rather uncharitable remark for, although on the whole British advice (on Cyprus) had been accepted by the Nine, he might have reserved at least some pride and a little pleasure for the system of political cooperation which had played a significant role in dealing with the crisis. While EPC did not achieve a solution (perhaps an almost impossible task given the intractable problem), the Cyprus crisis demonstrated clearly that political cooperation could work (and has helped convince the member-states of their potential to coordinate their stands), as well as starkly illustrating its shortcomings.

   As guarantor power and one with forces on the island, the UK was at once drawn into the crisis initiated on 15 July 1974 by Nikos Sampson's Greek-backed coup. Having decided on continued recognition of Makarios, flown him to London and begun talks with Ecevit, Callaghan and Wilson held discussions on the Cyprus question in Paris (19–21 July), where the UK Foreign Secretary expressed his desire for a strengthening of European political cooperation. Intense cooperation and coordination of the Nine's position ensued. France, holding the presidency of the Council and EPC, at once called a meeting of all EEC ambassadors and made diplomatic *démarches* in the name of the Nine in Athens and Ankara, coordinating the

Community's formal support for the UK's initiative to get Greeks and Turks to the negotiating table.

Meanwhile, on 20 July, the Turks had landed on the north coast of Cyprus and established a beach-head. Frenetic diplomatic activity, trans-atlantic as well as inter-European, brought an ill-observed ceasefire on 23 July which Sauvagnargues maintained had been brought about 'through the convergence of the effort of the Nine, of that of the British, who have a special responsibility in Cyprus, and of the US, who have the particularly effective means of economic pressure at their disposal'. This convergence with the USA was particularly significant in demonstrating the effectiveness of the compromise that had been worked out at Schloss Gymnich in April 1974, on the closer association of the Americans with EPC consultations. Sauvagnargues was particularly keen to underline the 'parallel and convergent' character of diplomatic action taken by the USA and Europe[19].

The Nine were kept informed of the numerous diplomatic *démarches* and the development of the situation by effective presidential briefing, backed up by constant contact between political directors, as well as through the deliberations of the working group who established an *ad hoc* committee to deal with Cyprus.

Meeting on the evening of 22 July in Paris, the Nine issued a statement, delivered by the French ambassadors in Ankara and Athens to their accredited governments the next morning, in which they appealed for a cease-fire and the reestablishment of the constitutional order on Cyprus (a call, which according to the Parliamentary Select Committee's Report, had little credibility for the UK government); recorded their fullest support for the UK initiative; and, emphasizing the 'association' connection, called upon Turkey and Greece to join the Geneva talks. The Nine ministers stressed the firmness of their position, declaring that they were determined to follow the diplomatic strategy outlined in their joint statement.

The establishment of a new Greek government under Karamanlis (24 July), the collapse of the second round of the Geneva talks (14 August) and the subsequent advance of Turkish forces in Cyprus to occupy 40 per cent of the island deepened the crisis and altered the nature of EPC's contribution. The optimism that had pervaded political cooperation's handling of the crisis began to evaporate. Once the UK initiative was dead, despite the Nine's last-ditch *dèmarche* early on 15 August calling on Greeks and Turks to resume negotiations, it became difficult to base European policy on supporting it. The Nine were further compromised by the repeated Greek pronouncements during August of their intention to apply for membership of the Community. The Turks no longer saw them as impartial, while the consensus of thinking amongst the Nine was affected by the new range of interests and loyalties that were brought into play.

Meeting in Paris on 16 September the foreign ministers and political directors heard a detailed and pessimistic report from Hattersley, UK

Under-Secretary of State at the Foreign Office, in which he emphasized the necessity of some form of joint action. But the Nine's views were no longer precise; they lacked the previous convergence. This made it virtually impossible for the political directors to establish a text, let alone propose action, reconciling their differences. The meeting ended with a general call for negotiations, respect for the territorial integrity of the island and the offer of aid on 'humanitarian' grounds to the Cypriot people.

Unable to move from 'declaration' to 'operation', the Nine gradually distanced themselves from the whole affair. While Cyprus continued to occupy most of the South European working group's time, by February 1975 the foreign ministers had announced that they no longer saw their role as being that of 'intermediary', but that of 'adviser'. By September 1975 this had been diluted to the offer of 'friendly action'. The series of inter-community talks which began in Vienna in April 1975 under United Nations auspices and the shuttle undertaken in February 1977 by President Carter's special envoy Clark Clifford have met with mere exhortations to succeed. (Plus lots of advice: something the Political Committee is never short on.)

The attitude of the various parties in the Cyprus affair towards EPC's role has evolved somewhat from initial Turkish disappointment with what she interpreted as European partiality in Greece's favour, and Greek willingness for the Turks to interpret the situation this way. Following the meeting between Makarios and Denktash on 12 February 1977 and the agreement to resume the Vienna talks at the end of March, the Nine issued a joint communiqué to all parties in the dispute, noting with satisfaction the results of the Nicosia meeting. They would continue to follow developments closely and looked forward to progress soon. Reactions were interesting. While Denktash continued with the line that if the Nine really felt they had to say something, the communiqué was acceptable, Ankara privately welcomed the Nine's moderate and balanced tone, fearing Soviet interference should the issue become too open to outsiders. Athens, with accession negotiations underway, welcomed the Nine's interest, while Makarios opposed the Europeanization of the problem, stressing that the Nine must work closely with the USA. This position was widened in April 1977 with Makarios's endorsement of the Soviet Union's call for an international conference on the island's future. This proposal had been rejected by the political directors at their meeting on 2 July 1976.

Action to underpin the Nine's repeated call for the territorial integrity of the island eventually came not from the EPC but from the Commission. In March 1976 the Commission put forward proposals for the opening of negotiations for the second stage of the Association Agreement. The first phase expires on 30 June 1977, and Article 2 of the Agreement stipulates that negotiations with a view to defining the provisions of the second phase shall take place during the eighteen months prior to expiry. The proposals caused little stir. No progress was expected until the problems of the relations between the two communities on the island had been settled[20].

The new Commission has adopted a more forward stance, arguing that, given Community obligations under Article 2, it would be a serious rebuff for negotiations to be turned down. The completion of the post-enlargement transition period at the end of June 1977 was additional juridical grounds for negotation. Economically, it was argued, there was no justification for delay.

The Council referred the matter to the Political Committee for its view of the political implications of the Commission's proposals, particularly in the light of the intercommunal talks that were about to restart in Vienna after a year's interruption. Following the political directors' deliberations on 2 March 1977 (and painstaking explanations from the Commission), the arrangements were accepted on the basis that they provided equal benefits to both sides. This recommendation was completely in line with Community policy. Indeed the Commission reprimanded the Political Committee for exceeding its brief in including in its note to the Council two paragraphs recommending what it considered as necessary contents of the second stage.

At its meeting on 3 May 1977 the Council gave the Commission directives to enable it to enter into negotiations with Cyprus to determine trade arrangements between the Community and Cyprus beyond 30 June 1977, and to determine the substance of the economic and financial cooperation to be added to the areas covered by the Association Agreement. Negotiations opened in Brussels on 16 May.

8.3 Troubles in Spain: the Burgos trial and the Franco succession

The trial and summary execution at the end of September 1975 of the five Basques accused under the anti-terrorist laws induced a muddled reaction from political cooperation. Preliminary exchanges between foreign ministries via the COREU network[21] and in the increasingly frequent meetings of the South European working group (every six weeks or so by the end of 1975) seemed to imply that a joint European protest might be effective given the well-known European ambitions of the Spanish and their likely sensitivity to such criticism. However, it was not until three days before the executions that the Nine agreed in principle to joint action. Nevertheless, domestic pressures for protest in the majority of member-states were strong. The result was that while the Italian government, at that time holding the presidency and thus political cooperation spokesman, eventually made several strong condemnations of the sentences and appealed to the Spanish authorities for clemency, it felt compelled by the separate protests that the British, West Germans, Dutch, Danes and Belgians had made, to make its *démarches* in both its own name and that of the Nine collectively.

More successful, in terms of political cooperation, was the secret appeal from the Nine delivered to the Spanish government on 25 September 1975. The appeal was worked out by the Community's foreign ministers while in New York for the thirtieth session of the UN General Assembly. The message, while emphasizing that the Nine did not intend to interfere in Spain's internal affairs, expressed the hope that the Spanish government might find it possible to review the terrorists' sentences as a gesture of mercy. The blandness of the statement provoked considerable controversy within the Nine member-states, but it appears that France, the UK and the Federal Republic of Germany used their weight to convince their partners that the appeal should be limited to humanitarian consideration. Other member-states, notably Denmark and the Netherlands, were pressing for reference to the character of the military trials carried out under the anti-terrorist laws.

Such disagreements had meant a delay in bringing about concerted action until the last moment. Although the Dutch had called for a joint initiative at the political cooperation meeting on 11 September in Venice, no action could be taken until there was agreement in principle to diplomatic protest. This did not come until the French finally agreed three days before the executions.

If protest was slow off the mark and fairly mild, joint diplomatic action proved chaotic. Acting as President, the Italian Foreign Minister, Rumor, asked the Nine to let him know their positions concerning their intentions to withdraw ambassadors so as to make possible the coordination of such a gesture. However, following the precipitate withdrawal of the Netherlands' ambassador, the Italians withdrew theirs without awaiting the response to their question, and were at once followed by the British, West Germans and Danes. The Irish, with their traditionally close ties with Spain and fear perhaps of parallels with political violence in Ireland, left their ambassador in Madrid. M. Robert Gillet, the French ambassador, was already in Paris, but no formal 'recall' was made. Rather than his ambassador, Sauvagnargues preferred to recall Talleyrand: *Ce'est pire qu'un crime, c'est une faute.*

A coordinated recall of ambassadors having been a failure, the Dutch and Danes suggested that at least their return might be a joint gesture. This was not be be, as Rumor made clear at the press conference after the Council meeting on 7 October. He announced that the ministers had agreed to leave each member free to decide the opportune moment to return his ambassador to Madrid. This conclusion was reached for two reasons. On the one hand member-states felt too constrained by domestic political circumstances to adopt a common stand, while on the other hand it would have given the Netherlands and Denmark too much say in how long the ambassadorial boycott was to last.

Joint action was to come on the initiative of the Commission. As early as 10 September the Commission had informed the Spanish government that it hoped the sentences would be commuted on humanitarian grounds. On the day of the executions, 27 September, the Commission put out a rather timid statement of protest, the restrained tenor of which was largely dictated by Ortoli (the President of the Commission) under pressure from Paris. Encouraged perhaps by the European Parliament's searing criticisms and vote for the freezing of commercial relations with Spain until the establishment of a democratic regime (25 September) the Commission announced on 1 October that it considered it impossible to go ahead with the negotiations with the Spanish (part of the Community's global Mediterranean policy), which were about to restart after having broken down in December 1974. It was on the basis of this that the Council declared that it was not possible 'at that time' to take up the negotiations between the Community and Spain, thus accepting the recommendation of the Commission to mark their protest at the actions of the Franco regime with a concrete political act.

The moderate tone of the Council's declaration (the Commission had suggested 'suspension' of negotiations) was a compromise between those member-states, such as the Netherlands and Denmark, wishing to show clearly the Community's contempt for the behaviour of the Madrid government and those such as the West Germans, British and above all the French, whose major proccupations lay in not poisoning relations between Spain and Europe of the Nine.

The British position was essentially practical. She was anxious not to have to comply with the 1970 preferential trade agreement from which she had been exempt pending the negotiation of new terms taking the enlarged Community into account. She feared that if negotiations were suspended indefinitely she would be forced to comply in the meantime with the 1970 package.

The French had long sought to cultivate relations with Spain so as to strengthen the Latin axis of the Community. Sauvagnargues strongly criticized the Commission for having, in his opinion, exceeded its competences. It had presented the Council with a *fait accompli* which he had felt compelled to accept (rather uncharacteristically) in view of the wishes of the majority. Ortoli had replied that it was ridiculous of Sauvagnargues to view the political competences of the Commission in such abstract terms. According to various sources, the President of the Commission even threatened his resignation.

The Nine's stance was not compromised by its inelegance alone. After all, trade negotiations were halted, and seven ambassadors 'withdrawn'. But the Spaniards had already declared themselves thoroughly dissatisfied with the package the Community was offering and were able to pass off the political rebuff as something of a mixed blessing. This was reinforced by the particular paranoia towards outside criticism that resulted from thirty years of diplomatic quarantine. The regime could thus draw a certain amount of domestic political capital from its foreign critics.

The increasing political tension preceding Franco's death on 21 November and the uncertainty that followed provided EPC with a more clearly diplomatic subject, yet one with tremendous implications for Europe. The Southern Europe working group of the Political Committee provided a useful forum for exchanges about thinking in the various capitals as to Spanish developments.

Meeting in Rome on 30 September 1975, the Political Committee expressed the Nine's desire to adopt a concerted stance towards Spain. A gesture of confidence in Franco's successor was seen as the best prelude to the hoped-for new era of relations with Spain. This did not mean that the Nine had yet thought out what the possibilities were of making a concrete and precise gesture. It had not been resolved by 21 November; indeed the Nine had not even managed to decide amongst themselves on the protocol to be adopted either for the funeral of the Caudillo or for the coronation of Prince Juan Carlos. The result was, fortuitously, a uniformly low level of representation at the funeral and a rather more imbalanced one at the coronation on 26 November. By the December European Council the gesture of confidence no longer seemed to rate high on the Nine's collective list of priorities and no mention was made in Rome of post-Franco Euro–Spanish relations.

8.4   Conclusions: the limited potential for crisis management

Unlike the workings of political cooperation within what one might term the 'civilized' or institutionalized environment of the UN, the Euro–Arab Dialogue and CSCE, with which the success of the EPC system are most often associated, this study has focused on the 'wild' or institutionally unstructured.

The Nines' attempts, through the political cooperation machinery, to exert influence on an area renowned for the rapidity and unpredictability with which events develop, whose chronic political–institutional problems have direct implications for the rest of Europe, highlight both the potential and shortcomings of the EPC system faced with the particular demands of crisis management. The reactive nature of the EPC system is confirmed by the case studies. Of course, all foreign policy is reactive to a certain extent, but EPC is perhaps less prepared and thus less able to play a role in shaping events than foreign policy-makers at the national level. The need for greater medium- and long-term planning was suggested by the Italians at the Copenhagen Summit in 1973. This proposal has not so far been taken up for fear that the EPC might overreach itself. It is not so much technical as political constraints that account for this.

A minimum of coordinated forward planning is not, practically speaking, beyond Community members, yet even the most rudimentary of contingency planning seems to be absent. There is little or no pooling of national intelligence information; indeed it appears to be closely guarded until the crisis breaks, as was the case in Cyprus. The UK Parliamentary Select Committee Report suggests that the British intelligence service had been in possession of information that a coup was in the offing, for at least a month, but at no time made this available to their Community partners.

In the absence of clearly defined common objectives, when is an issue likely to become the object of the deliberations of EPC? A general desire for stability in Southern Europe does not automatically predicate involvement or lead to the issue being taken up by political cooperation. The case studies suggest there are two situations where this is likely.

The first is where broad common interests are at stake or threatened. This was the case in Portugal, where the Nine were united by the vague concern for the development of 'pluralistic democracy', and in Spain, where their stance sprang from the desire to condemn an unacceptable act and provide the basis for new and improved relations with post-Franco Spain. Where such general common interests are involved it has proved difficult to contain the divergent currents that exist beneath them with decisive coordinated manoeuvering, or achieve anything more than a rather disorganized exercise in collective loss-cutting.

The second situation where political cooperation seems appropriate, and more likely to be successful while conditions hold, was illustrated by the Cyprus crisis and the threat it posed to stability in the Eastern Mediterranean. There was, of course, a common interest in that all three local actors were associate-members of the Community, though this in itself is hardly reason enough to bring an automatic Community reaction, either for fear of potential trade loss or due to special ties with associate partners. Crucial in Cyprus was the special interest of one of the Nine. While British interests did not clash with the wider general interest of the Community in the area, it allowed the other Eight to back the British position collectively at very little cost to themselves, with the bonus of winning the favour of the USA during a period of distinctly sour relations. This explains not merely EPC's reaction but accounts for its early success. So long as the UK gave the lead, political cooperation, under the skilful French presidency, was extremely effective in coordinating joint *dèmarches* and keeping members informed. The moment that leadership faltered the Nine's joint stance could no longer be 'accepted', but had to be 'made'. EPC's strategy disintegrated.

Once the Nine have decided to react one can discern a diminishing scale of effectiveness. Passive political cooperation is one thing, active cooperation quite another. Thus on the level of exchange of information and mutual consultation the EPC system is reasonably effective with channels established (presidential briefings, political directors, special committees) and growing mutual confidence amongst the European foreign policy fraternity, although the Nine can, and have, excluded topics from their conversations. This pooling of information and ideas obviously represents a basis for coordinated action, but it is not enough in itself.

Beyond mere consultation come joint declarations and diplomatic *démarches*. In all three case studies, political cooperation has used these traditional tools. These were seen at their most effective in Cyprus, with both broad appeals to the actors and joint ambassadorial *démarches* in Athens and Ankara, which played a useful if limited role. Here the Nine benefited from UK leadership. Portugal, too, presented the Nine with a situation in which thinking was similar enough to accommodate a series of 'European' declarations. Spain proved more difficult. Although the Nine shared a general overview, there was not the consensus or perhaps the presidential management that had been present in previous cases, with the result that the Nine's diplomatic strategy was both muddled and incoherent. Yet, whatever its shortcomings, one must not underestimate the usefulness of traditional diplomacy. What we might call declaration and *démarche* diplomacy has given a certain concreteness fo Europe's common identity in the eyes of third parties, and has undoubtedly been the fruit of political cooperation.

While the confusion over Spain illustrated EPC's difficulties in getting agreement on passive and limited gestures, where the threshold has been reached beyond which positive *action* is required, political cooperation has registered no success whatsoever in Southern Europe. What, then, are the instruments that EPC might have used, or could be placed at its disposal, in Southern Europe?

First, there are numerous instruments in the hands of the individual member-states which might be used on behalf of the Nine – for example, a military presence or special treaty rights, as was the case with the British in Cyprus; special trading or economic relationships such as West Germany's with Turkey, Greece and Spain; or France's arms-dealing in the area. Whether this national influence can be converted into a collective instrument depends on various factors. First, as in Cyprus, is an instrument that has already proved unsuccessful when used by a single state (in this case the UK) likely to prove more successful (or to be more wholeheartedly employed) with the collective backing of the Community? Second, would the member-states be willing to give *carte blanche* to one (or more) of their number to act as Community agent with the status this implies? Conversely, would a state allow its national assets to be put to collective use? The case studies give no clear answers.

More suited to collective action are a series of instruments in the hands of the Community as a whole. Europe is the major trading partner for every country in Southern Europe with the exception of Albania. This implies a major source of economic leverage. However, given the reactive nature of political cooperation and its consequently short-term view, trade sanctions and incentives provide a rather ponderous and unsatisfactory instrument.

Nevertheless they can and (in the case of Spain) have been used for political ends. A major drawback is that trade diplomacy in Southern Europe is likely to have an uneven effect on the Community, with its Mediterranean members being harder hit than those in the North. The difficulty of agreeing on the allocation of marginal sacrifices when it comes to offering a concrete economic package was particularly clear over Portugal in the months preceding the July 1975 Summit[22]. This makes consensus difficult. Added to this is the attitude in Community circles that trade should, as far as possible, be divorced from politics. Thus while the Greek Association Agreement was frozen in 1967 its trading aspects continued to apply.

Association agreements, although potentially a course of political leverage, did not enable the Nine to breach the 'operation' threshold in the Cyprus crisis. Local factors were so endemic and dissatisfaction with the existing agreements so high (especially in Turkey) that the association link was of little use to EPC other than as 'padding' for the Nine's declarations. Again, these are not a subtle diplomatic option for the Nine, especially when relations have been allowed to deteriorate to such an extent within the association agreements.

The carrot of accession to the Community is too full of implications to be used as a bargaining counter in crisis management, though obviously the general desire for membership of most of the countries of Southern Europe does exert a powerful, though not explicit, influence on the political climate of the area. In the sole situation where it has become an explicit factor, after Greece announced its intention to apply for full membership of the Community on 17 August 1974, it had a damaging effect on Europe's management capability, for it changed completely the parameters of the crisis. European, and especially French, support for the entry of a democratic Greece came to the fore, the Turks took umbrage and the EPC stance based on impartiality amongst three associate-states was severely weakened. The would-be manager became the managed.

Finance is probably the strongest political lever at the Nine's collective disposal. All the countries of Southern Europe are eager to attract loans and foreign investments. Thus the European Investment Bank provides a fairly useful tool of political cooperation capable of being used selectively and easily withdrawn, as was the EIB loan to Greece in 1967. It is, of course, the 150 million units of account loan to Portugal that is often seen as EPC's greatest success in Southern Europe. Money does nevertheless have its limitations, and there is not much reason to believe that European finance would have been any more effective in solving the Cyprus crisis than was Sisco's attempt to pacify Ecevit on 19 July with an offer of $30 million. Financial grants and loans can only be effective when they cease to be an insult and become an inducement.

So instruments for collective action do exist (although of a unidimensional character and thus lacking the flexibility of a wider variety of instruments) and Community instruments have been used in both Portugal (the EIB loan), Spain (the postponement of trade talks) and, most recently, Cyprus (the mandate to develop the Association Agreement). What then has been the link between EPC reaction and the employment of these Community instruments?

One of the major preoccupations of the study of political cooperation has been the coordination of EPC and the Community sector[23]. Over the last few years the potential for coordination has grown enormously. At the top, of course, the political cooperation ministerial meetings are identical in composition to the Council (give or take the Council secretariat, depending on the presidency). In addition to the formal (and informal), if episodic, presidential coordination, there is a small group within the Commission's Secretarial-General that sits in on and liaises with EPC. In some cases there is cross-membership of specialist committees. Thus despite the jealousies that exist within the separate structures (a separation nourished by many foreign ministries) there is scope for EPC policy to be executed with Community instruments, having been transmitted across the increasingly sophisticated, if still largely *ad hoc*, coordination network.

The case studies suggest that this has not been so. Where a crisis that has been dealt with in political cooperation has resulted in anything more than declarations or *démarches* the connection between the EPC's general stance and the Community's action has been, if not merely circumstantial, at least tenuous. The studies would seem to suggest, then, that in what have been hailed as EPC's greater successes action has been initiated, lobbied abd executed by Community organs. EPC seems to have been almost superfluous. The Community has kept broadly within its own competence. It has drawn its initiative from and has acted in accordance with its own constitutive principles of pluralistic democracy and civil liberty.

Political cooperation in Southern Europe illustrates the general convergence of the Nine's interests in the area, which has led on several occasions to the preliminaries of a 'European' policy being developed as well as establishing closer ties between foreign ministries. Undoubtedly, EPC has played an important role in the preliminary steps towards a more coordinated European foreign policy, yet the lack of any decision-making initiative, matched by the far from absolute character of European unity, has meant that EPC has not been able to conduct a coherent policy, or to act as the political rudder behind those actions successfully taken by the Community.

Notes

1 The Copenhagen Report, often known as the second Davignon Report, was commissioned by the foreign ministers immediately following the first Report of 1970 in an effort to deepen and maintain the momentum of political cooperation. See Chapter 2

2 *L'Europa*, 25 July 1975
3 *Agence Europe*, No. 1536, June 1974
4 *Agence Europe*, No. 1792, July 1975
5 *Agence Europe*, No. 1817, September 1975
6 *Le Monde*, 7 October 1975
7 The West Germans had earlier insisted on a maximum Community contribution of

100 million units of account. See *Financial Times*, 2 October 1975

8 *L'Unità*, 14 August 1974

9 Another option for the new Portuguese leaders was through transnational party relationships. Western European parties provided considerable financial aid to their Portuguese counterparts, lobbied their own foreign ministries to bring pressure to bear on the Portuguese government and acted as an open and informal international channel of communication. Brandt's visit to Lisbon in October 1974 at the invitation of the PSP is illustrative. He was travelling not merely as a representative of the SPD but on behalf of a wider ambit of social democratic parties. See *The Times*, 21 October 1974

10 This state of affairs weakened the role that EPC, based as it largely is on traditional diplomatic practice, might have played. Indeed it appears that the Political Committee was aware early on of its limitations as far as Portugal was concerned. It played a rather marginal role, occasionally checking whether the Council's conditions were being fulfilled. This tended to annoy the COREPER over what it felt was EPC interference

11 See *Financial Times*, 24 July 1974

12 Article 35 of the Preferential Trade Agreement

13 *The Times*, 27 May 1975

14 *Agence Europe*, No. 1776, June 1975

15 Funds to come from the EIB's own resources but to benefit from a 3% interest rebate (from 9½% to 6½%) to be paid directly from the Community budget. This is quite exceptional; but by avoiding the necessity for the sums to be entered separately in the Nine's national budgets the loans can be made available to the Portuguese more quickly

16 In June 1976, a month before the presidential elections, negotiations for the revision of the 1972 accord were completed. The Community made new concessions in the industrial, agricultural and migrant labour fields as well as concluding a financial protocol extending (to 200 million units of account for five years) and regularizing the emergency loan. See *Agence Europe*, No. 2012, June 1976

17 *Financial Times*, October 1975

18 *Hansard*, 31 July 1974

19 *Agence Europe*, No. 1566, 24 July 1974

20 Sir Christopher Soames made this point in his farewell address to the Brussels Press Corps (21 December 1976)

21 A direct communications system between the foreign ministries of the Nine established by the Copenhagen Report in July 1973

22 See J. Story, 'Portugal's Revolution of Carnations', *International Affairs*, July 1976

23 See Chapter 3

CHAPTER NINE

European Political Cooperation at the UN: a challenge for the Nine*

BEATE LINDEMANN

9.1 The UN – a challenge for European Political Cooperation

9.1.1 The special political situation in the General Assembly

Today the UN has become one of the most important areas for European political cooperation. Here 'speaking with one voice' on world politics is demonstrated in the clearest and most frequent way either by unitary voting behaviour or through joint contributions to debates or, finally, by a bloc-vote declaration. The Nine have 'to show their colours' almost daily, so that differing attitudes are immediately and clearly demonstrated. In New York synchronized diplomacy has become a fixed part of the UN policy of the Nine EEC governments as well as a political factor in the opinion-formation process of the UN.

When referring to EPC in the UN one normally thinks of cooperation within the General Assembly and its seven main committees. The EEC countries are all represented here, whilst in other UN organs and committees only a limited number of states are represented. Of the Nine, France and the UK are the only two states with universal representation in all UN activities along with one or, at most, two of the other EEC states. Consultation and harmonization of policies in the framework of EPC is therefore exclusively limited to the General Assembly (which takes place annually from September to December). On occasions the General Assembly by special resolution convenes Extraordinary Assemblies at which the Nine are also all represented.

During the period when the General Assembly is in session harmonization of the position of the Nine takes place in the weekly meetings of ambassadors and in a particularly intensive way within the main committees. When the General Assembly is not in session there are just the weekly meetings of ambassadors. These are intended to guarantee a regular and continuous process of harmonization between the General Assemblies. It is

---

*This chapter is based on a comprehensive study by the same author entitled 'EG-Staaten und Vereinte Nationen. Die Politische Zusammenarbeit der Neun in Den UN-Hauptorganen', *Schriften des Forschungsinstituts der Deutschen Gesellschaft Für Auswärtige Politik e.V.*, Bonn, Vol. 42, Munich 1978. Certain passages keep to the text of this study.

in this framework that the work of the other UN bodies with limited EEC representation is discussed. There are no consultations in these cases but the EEC members that are represented generally inform their colleagues about the work in these committees. However, away from the General Assembly the Nine does not attempt to put forward a concerted position.

In contrast to the other areas of international politics where EPC is practised, the General Assembly does present certain structural limitations. These are mainly a result of the fact that here political cooperation is confronted with the wide spectrum of international problems which are on the agenda of the UN. Over a period of several years, regular consultations on a wide variety of topics have been taking place within the framework of EPC in the capitals of the member-states as well as in New York; their objective is to produce common positions.

It is possible that EPC's work in New York could, in the long term, become a model for other areas of activity. It already shows signs of a certain independent development due partly to its particular internal structural conditions, partly to external political factors in the UN and finally to the geographical distance of New York from the different European capitals.

Since the admission of the Federal Republic of Germany on 18 September 1973[1] the Nine EEC countries are all represented in the UN. They represent a numerical minority in the General Assembly which consists of 149 member-states in all, but they provided in 1977 the largest contribution to the UN budget[2]. Nevertheless the amount of its financial contribution is in no relation to its real influence in the General Assembly. Here power and influence lie with the group of sixty-six members of the Third World who possess the majority to dominate voting procedures. They do not, of course, possess the financial, economic and political power necessary to actually carry out resolutions[3].

The Third World members decide alone which resolutions are passed, while the West carries the main burden of the financial implications of the resolutions, regardless of whether these have been passed against or with the votes of the West. The numerical domination of the developing countries is clearly reflected in the agendas of the different bodies and committees of the UN. These are dominated by the three major concerns of the Third World; development, Southern Africa and the Middle East. Traditional topics such as disarmament and human rights also remain, but they are subject to a specifically Third World interpretation.

The shift of power in the UN has led to a situation where the West today is no longer really interested in putting its own problems to the forum of the UN for discussion. The important political decisions in which the West is interested are not made in the General Assembly. They have become increasingly 'regionalized', i.e. they have been transferred to organizations made up of only countries who have an immediate interest in the special matter in question (OECD, GATT, IMF, IEA, NATO, etc.).

This is the political background for the West Europeans' attempt at cooperation within the General Assembly. The topics for discussion do not always touch the immediate interest of the Nine and so the cooperation of the Nine in New York is not exposed to the same amount of strain as elsewhere. Regional problems become less important when seen in the context of global problems. In a global community national feelings give way to a stronger feeling for common regional interests. The moment an individual state joins up with other states, its capacity to influence the political process increases[4].

A further challenge for EPC in New York arises in the pressure to unite which the Nine are exposed to by the outside world. The Third World countries expect a common front from the EEC countries in the North –South dialogue, for instance. In the UN the Nine are forced daily to prove how seriously they take their cooperation in matters of foreign policy. It is precisely the common challenge of the developing countries which forces the West Europeans in their turn to produce a united front and to confront the Third World proposals with proposals produced in the context of EPC.

Thus, in addition to the objectives of European integration there is a further motive for EPC in the UN, namely the bridging of the conflict between the West and the Third World. Here the aim is to revive multilateral diplomacy and, at the same time, to establish the Nine as a credible partner in negotiations in the Third World. The pressure to unite which the EEC states in New York are constantly exposed to from outside does create problems for EPC. They often fail to harmonize their positions in New York, in the Political Committee or at the foreign minister level. The Nine UN Delegations are in many cases more convinced of the necessity of joint action than their governments back home in the capitals of Europe. This discrepancy can, in the long run, become a negative factor in New York. Apart from this, if there is no possibility for joint action, individual EEC states tend increasingly to seek cooperation with non-member states who have parallel interests.

9.1.2   The Nine and the other Western countries

Only those states who have a seat and a vote in the UN committees can exert power and influence in the UN process. Candidates for seats and positions are put up by geographical groups which form a permanent part of the UN system[5]. With the exception of the General Assembly, committees and other bodies have only a limited number of members (between twenty-five and thirty). Therefore there is strong competition for representation in these bodies.

When it comes to distributing these seats the EEC states do not count as a separate group within the UN system but are part of the group of Western European and other states (WEOG), comprising twenty members. EPC does not yet cover questions of candidature, but every member of the EEC decides independently on applications for such positions[6]. However, as an unofficial subgroup on the WEOG, the Nine have a certain advantage. Because of the special position of France and the UK as permanent members of the Security Council, two of them are always represented on all UN committees. In the long run, this situation could disadvantage the other seven EEC states. It is possible that as the Nine's cooperation increases the rest of the WEOG members will become reluctant to give the EEC states additional representation to that of France and the UK.

There are consultations between the Western states on political questions at different levels and producing changing coalitions according to the different items on the agenda[7]. Since the intensification of the Nine's cooperation in the context of EPC several attempts have been made by outside states to strengthen Western cooperation as a whole. In particular, the smaller Western partners like Austria, Australia and New Zealand, who feel threatened by their isolation from EEC consultations, are increasingly seeking closer ties with the Nine.

In the wider Western context the EEC states take part in consultations within the so-called 'Vinci Group', consisting of the twenty WEOG members and Japan[8]. Normally, consultations do not go beyond a mutual exchange of opinion. The group is too large and the positions of its members too diverse to guarantee a common political basis for confidential talks. The EEC states are not very interested in consultations within the Vinci Group, since for them harmonization of policies in the context of EPC have a clear priority.

In the light of these unsuccessful attempts at Western cooperation in the UN the Nine's comparatively successful endeavours to act together have gained in significance. As the Nine's cooperation intensifies, coordination with the rest of the Western group will become harder. The stated objective of the Nine is to create a European Union, and the progress of West European cooperation in the whole field of foreign policy is theoretically meant to serve this purpose. For the more distant future, however, one cannot exclude the possibility that a united Nine may, one day, form the integrating nucleus for cooperation in the larger context of the West.

9.1.3   Special relations with outside states

The USA

Intensive political cooperation of the Nine West European States of necessity affects transatlantic relations. Therefore, with the EEC states' long-term endeavours to form a European Union and to take on an active role in world politics, a new phase in the European–American relationship was inevitable. Changed political realities in the Western Europe of the 1970s demanded a new definition of relations with the American partner.

Nevertheless European Union must not be seen as an alternative to transatlantic relations; partnership with the USA remains a basic precondition[9].

In the framework of the UN the relationship between the EEC states and the USA proved to be increasingly problematic as the Nine's cooperation grew. The more intensive EEC consultations became, the less frequent was the additional coordination of US and European positions. This development led to a situation where unification of the voting behaviour of the Nine increasingly isolated the USA. Former close allies of the USA, like the UK and the Federal Republic of Germany, increasingly aligned themselves in their voting behaviour to the attitudes of the Community. In the 30th General Assembly in 1975 contacts between the Nine and the Americans reached such a low point that even the exchange of information was severely restricted.

The reasons for this development were to be found on both sides. Through the unexpected successes of their concerted actions the Europeans received considerable encouragement for their cooperation, with the result that, for lack of time as well as interest, they appeared to attach less significance to relations with their American allies. The American UN delegation (led by Ambassador D. P. Moynihan) seemed not to be prepared to take the growing unification of the Western Europeans into account and unwilling to be forthcoming about planned American activities or tactics.

During the 30th General Assembly the isolation of the USA, apart from the field of economics, led to a political revaluation by the Nine. They were confronted with the objective challenge as well as the psychological responsibility of this difficult situation which had the effect of boosting their cooperation. More than ever before they appeared as one actor on the international diplomatic stage and tried, in the dialogue with the Third World, to take over the Western leadership role which the USA had temporarily vacated. Because of their disagreements with the Americans, the Nine appeared in the eyes of many developing countries to be relatively moderate, which was in no way detrimental to their policies[10]. As there was no formal Western position, the attitude of the Nine was taken by many delegations of the Third World to be representative of the West as such.

During the 31st and 32nd General Assemblies in 1976 and 1977 consultations between the Nine and the Permanent Representation of the USA at the UN in New York were increased. There was a lively exchange of opinion at ambassadorial level and the Dutch (1976) and Belgian (1977) presidency was in regular contact with the US mission. Here a problem arose because the American delegation, situated, as it was, so close to Washington, received voting directives at such a late state and in such detail that there was often neither time nor political leeway for consultations with friendly countries.

The activities of the Nine led, especially after 1976, to the USA taking more and more account of their positions in the planning of its own policies.

Yet the Europeans often reacted with surprise whenever US representatives acknowledged the growing unity of the Nine by informing the presidency alone before important votes rather than informing the Nine individual delegations. This is only one of the numerous examples which show that the Nine themselves are really not yet familiar with the consequences of their unity, especially when it means foregoing national privileges.

Relations with the Third World

The traditional special relations existing between individual EEC states and the Third World have already had a positive effect on the relationship between the EEC and a number of developing countries in the UN. The relations between the UK and the Commonwealth countries and France and francophone Africa and the Arab world are the best examples of this inheritance. The Netherlands also has good contacts with a number of developing countries, although the Dutch delegation often distance themselves from their European partners in order to give greater support to the position of the Third World.

The Dutch endeavour to compensate for disagreements with the other EEC states by increased cooperation with 'like-minded countries' of the West as well as with the Third World. Their attitude can be interpreted as a counteraction to Western economic summit conferences which are only attended by the larger countries of the EEC. The smaller EEC states, Belgium, Denmark, Ireland and the Netherlands, thus seek concerted action with other like-minded countries in the General Assembly. This may in the long term represent a serious danger for the EPC harmonization process.

In contrast to this, EPC can profit from good bilateral relations between the EEC and Third World countries. Thus some members of the Community receive timely information from friendly developing countries about planned actions or the intended voting behaviour of the Third World. They also often receive resolution drafts and position papers before these are officially circulated.

If important information received in this way is immediately brought into the EPC process, directives from the capitals can be received and coordinated in time, so that the Nine in New York are able to exert more influence on the formulation of the resolution texts. They are then also able to inform friendly states at an earlier period in time of their own position, which means that these will be more inclined to adopt the voting behaviour of the Nine. Finally, this procedure has the advantage that national attitudes can be discussed in the capitals and the Political Committee more intensively in time to make effective harmonization a possibility.

The confrontation over Israel in the 30th General Assembly in 1975 illustrates the Nine's attempt to exert influence on the basis of good bilateral relations. The Nine launched a concerted attempt, agreed on by the Political Committee in Rome in November 1975, to influence sixty-five states in

Africa, Asia and Latin America to change their attitude towards a resolution on Zionism. The target states were specifically selected because they had good bilateral relations with individual EEC states. Even if the action was not totally successful, partly because it was started too late and a number of states had already agreed to support Arab policies, it could nevertheless, in the context of EPC, be considered to be the beginning of a new strategy for exertion of political influence in international relations.

9.1.4   The Security Council

Together with the three superpowers (the USA, the Soviet Union and China) France and the UK have permanent representation in the Security Council, which is the only UN organ to make binding decisions[11]. The special status which these two states have, compared with their Western European partners, brings political influence and respect in the UN. Because of their permanent membership they have further important institutional advantages in the organization. Like the other three members, they have quasi-permanent seats in all other UN bodies and committees with a limited number of members. They also occupy influential posts in permanent succession, and this gives them a greater opportunity for regularly exerting political influence on the opinion- and decision-making process in the UN.

The special position of France and the UK leads to a situation where they both sometimes pursue interests which are not in harmony with those of the other EEC member-states. This can, for instance, be observed in questions relating to the general area of security, where their status as nuclear powers is of relevance. Here France, more than the UK, emphasizes its special role. Nevertheless, since the 30th General Assembly in 1975 and especially since the preparation of the 8th Special General Assembly on disarmament in 1978, unexpected progress has been made in the attempts to discuss disarmament in EPC and to reach a common Community position.

In the General Assembly, France and the UK place great emphasis on the main responsibility of the Security Council for the preservation of world peace and of international security by not assuming a definitive attitude when actions of the Security Council are voted on. Usually these are resolutions demanding action from the Security Council or commenting on the results of the Security Council's deliberations. The result of the British and French attitude is that the Nine are only able to vote together if the other seven members are prepared to join British and French abstention.

In the context of EPC there are no consultations on agenda items of the Security Council. Neither France nor the UK are at present prepared to have such consultations. However, if EPC is to be successful in the long term and is to lead to a common European foreign policy through concerted diplomacy, the two states will have eventually to relinquish their special status and submit their policies in the Security Council to the Nine's consultative process. They will lose credibility if they continue to insist on their special world political responsibility on the one hand, while on the other they continue to support the development of EPC. Therefore it should be in the interest of France and the UK to be guided by the consensus of the Nine in their voting behaviour in the Security Council.

The first attempt to express a concerted diplomacy of the Nine in the Security Council was made during the Namibia Debate in January 1976. The UK, France and Italy (which was at that time a non-permanent member of the Security Council) referred in their speeches[12] to the declaration of the Nine foreign ministers concerning Namibia, which had been circulated as a document of the Security Council on 27 January 1976[13]. They jointly supported the concluding resolution of the Security Council and thus acted within the context of an agreement that had been reached in EPC.

However, the representation of concerted EEC positions in the Security Council still remains problematical. If the reform of the structure of the Security Council demanded by the Third World were to take place, the West European states would, in all probability, not keep their two permanent seats. The pressure would be heightened if France and the UK were already giving the impression that they acted no longer as individual members but were pursuing the policy of the Nine in the Security Council. Both members are therefore anxious to keep security questions out of the harmonization process with the EEC partners and to continue to give priority to consultations with the USA and the other Western non-permanent members of the Security Council.

The differing political status of the EEC states in the UN will thus be a problem for the development of EPC. The presence of Italy (1975–1976) and the Federal Republic of Germany (1977–1978) in the Security Council increased the readiness to inform the remaining EEC partners of events in the Security Council. This readiness was particularly apparent when Italy, during its EEC presidency in the second half of 1975, was responsible for coordination of the cooperation of the Nine. The Italians raised the question of the work of the Security Council during consultations at the ambassadorial level. This occurred again when the Federal Republic of Germany took over the EEC presidency for the second part of 1978, the same time as it was represented in the Security Council.

The cooperation of the three large EEC countries – France, the UK and the Federal Republic of Germany – with the USA and Canada in the Security Council was especially close in the case of problems relating to South Africa and Namibia that arose in the spring of 1977. The 'Gang of Five', as the five Western partners were called in the UN, tried in 1977–1978 not only to take the role of mediator between the South African government, SWAPO (South West African People's Organization), the Front Line States and the UN, but also to produce a common position of their own with proposals for the solution of the problem.

In the long run a closer cooperation between the three large EEC partners could lead to new areas of friction with the smaller Community countries and become a serious strain on EPC.

9.2   The work of the Nine

9.2.1   Instruments of policy

EPC demonstrates that the Nine EEC states are willing to act jointly in matters of foreign policy. To manifest this, there are theoretically five possibilities in the UN:

(1) Raising of their own agenda items;
(2) Raising of their own draft resolutions on agenda items;
(3) Joint declarations on agenda items;
(4) Joint voting behaviour;
(5) Joint declarations concerning voting.

Until now, in practice the Nine have only made use of the last three options in the UN. Raising agenda items or draft resolutions is, in general, difficult for the West. There are hardly any problem areas in which the West shares common objectives with the Third World. Recent experience has shown that Western initiatives (amnesty for political prisoners) as well as Eastern initiatives (reduction of defence budgets, world disarmament conference) have always been altered by Third World amendments to suit their own interests. This led to a situation where the states who had raised the draft resolution either finally withdrew it or had to abstain from voting themselves because the text no longer suited their political interests. This had led to frustration within the Western camp and occasional suggestions that the UN should in effect be handed over to the Third World. However, if the West became more active by submitting thoroughly prepared initiatives and thus showed its interest in the work of the organization it could, in the long run, lead to a reactivation of multilateral diplomacy.

In the 31st General Assembly (1976) the Federal Republic of Germany submitted an agenda item concerning the 'Draft of an international Agreement against the taking of hostages'. This led to the acceptance of a resolution by consensus in the 6th Main Committee as well as later in the Plenary Session (General Assembly Resolution 31/103, 15 December 1976)[14]. Although this proposal was originally planned as an initiative of the Nine, some EEC states (especially France and the Netherlands) feared counter-reactions from the Arab states, and were therefore not very keen on a joint submission. The Federal Republic of Germany therefore decided to go it alone. In fact, the West Germans were able to attract the support of thirty-eight states, and it was thus possible to avoid a situation where the initiative was seen to have Western character directed against the interests of the Third World. This example shows that a common position of the Nine at present does not necessarily contribute to a strengthening of the Western position. It is possible that the political leeway of the EEC states and their credibility and attractiveness as a coalition partner of the Third World would increase if the Nine did not always act as one.

However, where there is already an agreed common position and particularly in economic questions which relate to the EEC Treaties, the Nine are seeking a more forceful demonstration of their concerted diplomacy. In future, this could include the joint submission of selected agenda items, draft resolutions or amendments to draft resolutions. The Nine's involvement in the coordinated preparation and advancement of positions in the capitals and in New York would no doubt strengthen the impression of their solidarity as a political group and would have an important psychological effect as far as the goal of European unification is concerned.

Apart from their voting behaviour, which is discussed below, the growth of cooperation between the Nine manifested itself particularly in the growing number of Community declarations in the plenary sessions and the committees. The united front of the Nine as a political group is most clearly demonstrated to the outside world whenever the EEC presidency makes declarations on behalf of the Nine in the plenary session and in the main committees of the General Assembly. The number of these joint declarations has grown from session to session. Thus:

Two declarations in the 28th General Assembly, 1973;
Fifteen declarations in the 29th General Assembly, 1974;
Thirty-six declarations in the 30th General Assembly, 1975;
Fifty declarations in the 31st General Assembly, 1976;
Sixty-one declarations in the 32nd General Assembly, 1977.

Since 1975 these declarations are no longer limited to explanations of a particular vote: they are often published at the negotiation stage as contributions to the debates in the Committees. There is a fundamental difference between these two types of declarations: those which are normally made immediately before voting reflect the Nine's interpretation of the resolution, and their tactical aim is to influence the voting behaviour of outside states. Thus while explanations of votes in the plenary session refer to the resolutions which have already been worked out, Community declarations in the committees refer to draft resolutions which are still under debate. The possibility of the Nine influencing the negotiations on texts increases if they can produce a united front and if they can establish their position within a reasonably short time-period.

The question remains as to whether joint declarations should be made on principle even if the Community states do not vote together. This was the case in the 30th and 31st General Assemblies when, in some cases, declarations on voting were read out by the presidency, even though the

Nine, after long negotiations, had not agreed on a common attitude[15]. It does not seem advisable to use Community declarations to cover up differences in the positions of the Nine.

As long as the concept of concerted diplomacy is the basis of the cooperation of the Nine and as long as the final target of a European foreign policy is not achieved, presidential declarations appear to have only a minimal effect in the UN because they represent the lowest common political denominator and the sole expression of the political will of the Nine. Declarations of the Nine may help the internal development of European unity, but they are not really effective or politically convincing contributions to the debate in the General Assembly. The work and time spent on preparing Community declarations often does not bear any relation to the substantive content of the declaration. With the present state of European cooperation it would, therefore, seem sensible if, in addition to Community declarations, individual member-states used their own declarations backed by their own strong political convictions. They could be used to support and intensify the joint declarations by expressly referring to the presidential declarations and they could emphasize individual points by stressing particular national interests. The speeches of the Nine foreign ministers in the general debate in each of the General Assemblies already manifest this combination of national and Community viewpoints.

9.2.2   The common approach and its limits: voting behaviour

The solidarity of the Nine and the coordination of the UN policies is manifested most clearly in the voting behaviour of the member-states. It was in the 30th General Assembly in 1975 that the EEC states appeared for the first time as a united group in a number of important votes. It often proved possible, after initially divergent voting in the main committees, to harmonize voting behaviour around the same resolutions in subsequent plenary sessions. The intensive consultations which had meanwhile taken place in New York and in the various European capitals helped to achieve the eventual harmonization of national positions. Smaller EEC states, whose political importance was increased by EPC, often appeared to tip the balance decisively. Thus they often adopted an initially divergent position and then fell in with the Community line after a period of high-level negotiation.

The survey in *Table 9.1* of the proportion of uniform votes by the Nine to the total number of all votes taken in the last five General Assemblies since 1973 does not contain any indications of the extent to which the resolutions approved unanimously by the Nine concerned issues of political substance and material significance. One diplomat from the Third World characterized the common voting behaviour of the Nine as being uniform on unimportant questions and divergent on important ones, whereas the opposite held for the countries of the Third World.

Table 9.1 *The uniform voting behaviour of the Nine in the General Assembly (1973–1977)*

Sessions of the General Assembly	Number of votes taken (excluding consensus resolutions)* (total = 100%)	Number of uniform votes	Proportion of uniform votes to total (%)
28 (1973)	77	36	46.8
29 (1974)	92	54	60.9
30 (1975)	101	66	65.3
31 (1976)	108	62	57.4
32 (1977)	113	71	62.8

*Number of consensus resolutions: 29th General Assembly, 89; 30th General Assembly, 110; 31st General Assembly, 158; 32nd General Assembly, 166.

There is a tendency these days for resolutions to be approved by a consensus procedure in the main committees and in the plenary meetings of the General Assembly as well as in the other UN bodies and at other international conferences[16]. As a rule the West only agrees to the acceptance of resolutions by acclamation on the condition that its interests are given sufficient consideration in the process of decision-making and are reflected in the texts of the resolutions. The common positions of the Nine are manifested more strongly in the general consensus resolutions, while actual votes (mainly on controversial political issues) tend to illustrate the Nine's disunity (*Table 9.2*).

There were 126 points on the agenda of the 31st General Assembly in 1976 (32nd General Assembly, 131 points), on which 108 votes were held (32nd General Assembly, 113 votes). Of these the voting of the Nine was split on forty-six occasions (32nd General Assembly, 42 times). The distribution of the split votes in 1976 was as follows:

Decolonization: 13 out of a total of 19 votes;
Namibia and Rhodesia: 6 out of a total of 9 votes;
Arms control: 7 out of a total of 18 votes;
Human rights: 6 out of a total of 15 votes;
Apartheid: 6 out of a total of 12 votes;
Budget questions: 4 out of a total of 19 votes;
Economics: 3 out of a total of 10 votes;
Cyprus: 1 out of a total of 1 vote;
Middle East: 2 out of a total of 10 votes;
International law: 2 out of a total of 2 votes;
Vietnam: 1 out of a total of 1 vote.

Table 9.2 *The divergent voting behaviour of the Nine in the General Assembly (1973–1977)*

Sessions of the General Assembly	Number of votes taken (excluding consensus resolutions) (total = 100%)	Number of differing votes	Number of opposed votes	Proportion of differing votes to total (%)
28 (1973)	77	41	6	53.2
29 (1974)	92	36	3	39.1
30 (1975)	101	35	2	34.7
31 (1976)	108	46	2	42.6
32 (1977)	113	42	1	37.2

The limits to a common approach by the Nine are found particularly in the following politically relevant areas:

(1) Middle East, including Palestine;
(2) Decolonization, including Southern Africa;
(3) Disarmament;
(4) Economics.

Middle East
The effects of the oil embargo on the West European economies demonstrated how central the Middle East has become to the interests of Western Europe. The need for the involvement of the European Community in the Arab world became more urgent than ever and the Euro–Arab Dialogue was introduced as an attempt at a 'new form of diplomacy', namely 'collective diplomacy'[17].

The effects of the Dialogue on Euro–Arab relations in the UN have been minimal. The Euro–Arab Dialogue and the Middle East debate in the General Assembly cover different themes and for the Arabs run on parallel but separate lines. The solution of the Palestinian problem which the Arabs are anxious to enforce was from the beginning rejected as subject-matter for the Dialogue by the Nine. Various spokesmen on the Arab side who, whilst moderate in the Dialogue were more radical in the Middle East debate of the UN, effectively prevented any simple translation of the atmosphere of cooperation developed in the Dialogue to the General Assembly.

It is not simply *inter*-regional cooperation which has foundered on the Middle East problem but *intra*-regional cooperation as well. The cooperation of the Nine in the Euro–Arab Dialogue has little influence on the shaping of Community attitudes to the central issues of the Middle East. The demands of the Arab states in the UN resolutions go substantively beyond the common basic position agreed upon by the governments in the EPC report of May 1971 as well as in later Middle East declarations.

The creation of a Community attitude in the UN has been impossible until now primarily because of the policy of the French. The latter achieved some degree of dominance within the Nine in the 31st General Assembly, when Belgium and Luxembourg partly allied themselves to the grouping around France, Italy and Ireland which was more friendly towards the Arabs. The Netherlands and Denmark found themselves in a minority position within the Nine. The UK and the Federal Republic of Germany tried to adopt a mediating position between the two groupings, but all the indications were that in the future there would be a majority for the French line. The first indication of this was the first united abstention by the Nine on the resolution concerning the situation in the Middle East in the 32nd General Assembly in 1977.

In the 29th General Assembly France was the only Community state to abstain on the resolution which granted the PLO observer status in the UN (the other eight voted against)[18]. France, Ireland and Italy supported the resolution of 14 October 1974, which invited the PLO to take part in the Palestine Debate in the plenary session of the General Assembly (the other six abstained)[19]. The French Foreign Minister had already declared the support of his government in discussions with the Egyptians prior to the opening of the Nine's discussions. Only Italy (as a state adjoining the Mediterranean) and Ireland, which had always been interested in good relations with the Arab states, adopted the French position. An opposed vote was only avoided because the UK shifted from its original plan to reject the resolution to a decision to abstain. The UK and the Federal Republic of Germany were closely involved in the coordination of their policy on this question.

So far, France has not supported the resolution on Palestine passed in the 29th General Assembly. In the 30th and 31st General Assemblies, France, Ireland and Italy abstained, while the other six rejected it after the resolution had become unbalanced in its political demands and went too far in its formulation.

It was in the 31st General Assembly that progress was made for the first time towards a common position of the Nine in the consultations on the Middle East debate in that all the EEC partners were prepared to amend their positions. Even France compromised on important questions, such as Palestinian participation in the Geneva Conference or the existence of a state for the Palestinian people, and thus facilitated the production of Community declarations. The two resolutions in which the Nine could not agree on a common vote concerned Palestine[20] and the situation in the Middle East[21].

In the seven controversial Middle East resolutions at the 32nd General Assembly the Nine voted disparately twice, namely on the two Palestine resolutions (there were a total of thirteen resolutions, on three of which the

Nine achieved a consensus and on another three achieved near-unanimous acceptance). All Nine delegations abstained for the first time as a block on the resolution concerning the situation in the Middle East (General Assembly Resolution 32/20, 30 November 1977; there were only two negative votes – the USA and Israel). The uniform vote became possible after the UK, the Federal Republic of Germany, Denmark and the Netherlands gave up their previously negative position on the Middle East resolution.

In the resolution on the Palestine question, France, Italy and Ireland abstained as in previous years, while the other EEC partners continued to reject it (General Assembly Resolution 32/40A, 2 December 1977). Apart from this, France was the only EEC state to abstain on the decision which was reintroduced in the 32nd General Assembly concerning the establishment of a special Department for the Rights of Palestinians in the UN Secretariat (General Assembly Resolution 32/40B, 2 December 1977). The fact that the French went it alone suggests that the French government had already made assurances to the Arab states in advance from which they could no longer retreat. Behind the negative vote of the other EEC governments there lay the fear of a further politicization of the UN Secretariat.

The Belgian presidency, on behalf of the Nine, submitted contributions to the debate concerning all five agenda items on the Middle East (Palestine, Middle East question, UNRWA, Israeli practices in the occupied territories and the latest illegal Israeli measures). With the exception of the items on Palestine and Israel, common voting declarations were also presented. In the Palestine Declaration of 1 December 1977 the presidency explained that the Nine could not agree to the resolutions for the same reasons as in previous General Assemblies. Their reservations concerned the lack of political balance in the work of the Committee for the Exercising of the Inalienable Rights of the Palestinian People, to which both the resolution texts in 1977 had related.

In the Middle East debate of the 32nd General Assembly it was once again shown that the attitude of the UK and the Federal Republic of Germany was decisive in producing uniform voting behaviour on the central resolutions concerning the Middle East and Palestine. The Netherlands and Denmark in particular (who held the most pro-Israeli position of all the member-states) shifted their positions towards British and West German policies. Denmark took on the role of mediator between the EEC and the Scandinavian group. The consequences of this for voting behaviour was that the Scandinavian states voted almost exclusivley with the Nine.

Cooperation with Ireland proved to be the most difficult problem in the Middle East debate in 1977. The pro-Arab attitude of the Irish, which manifested itself particularly in relation to problems in the area of human rights, has a historical background in the parallels between the PLO and the Irish liberation movement. Thus Ireland was the only state to publish a national declaration on its voting intentions on 2 December 1977 in addition to the Palestine declaration of the Nine. Belgium took up a noticeably harder line towards Israel in the 32nd General Assembly.

It was the British and West German governments that clearly achieved the greatest turnaround in the direction of a more balanced policy. They facilitated the unification of the Nine's position. The progress of EPC on the Middle East question, which had begun in the 31st General Assembly, was successfully consolidated a year later. It was the Middle East declaration of the European Council of 29 June 1977 which formed the basis of the Nine's consensus.

Decolonization

This issue-area has been dominated in recent years by developments in Southern Africa. The question of apartheid has also been linked to that of decolonization despite attempts by the West to keep the two issues separate. The African states have been encouraged by the political changes in Southern Africa to act more forcefully and to increase the pressure on the West to take action over South Africa. The official recognition of SWAPO as the sole authentic representative of the people of Namibia and its achievement of UN observer status[22] represent some measure of success for the African states. It is important to remember that for Africans, events in Southern Africa, particularly in the context of apartheid policies, assume the same political importance as the question of Israel does for the Arab states.

In the decolonization debate in the 31st General Assembly the Nine were divided over the issue of sanctions against South Africa. Denmark voted for a resolution on an arms embargo despite the fact that the text cited France, the UK and the Federal Republic of Germany as countries who had supplied weapons to South Africa that were used both for internal repression and external aggression[23]. Denmark has not been alone amongst the Nine in developing an independent position on issues of decolonization. Ireland has frequently demonstrated its opposition, partly for historical and partly for current domestic reasons, to UK policy in this area. Similarly the Netherlands and Italy, in reaction to internal parliamentary pressure, have exerted great pressure on the rest of the Nine in internal discussions.

In the 29th General Assembly in 1974 a notable change took place in the basic attitude of the two former colonial powers and permanent members of the Security Council, France and the UK, towards decolonization issues. This has assisted the cooperation of the Nine. Whilst in the 28th General Assembly in 1973 France and the UK had voted twelve and eighteen times respectively against the majority of EEC states, this happened on only two occasions in the 29th General Assembly in 1974[24]. However, when resolutions touched on the rights and duties of the two permanent Security Council members or on their overseas possessions they continued their practice of resisting the development of a Community position.

The progress in the cooperation of the Nine which was achieved in 1974 did not continue in the following years. Thus:

29th General Assembly, 36 resolutions: 19 consensus resolutions, 9 uniform votes, 8 differing votes;

30th General Assembly, 44 resolutions: 25 consensus resolutions, 8 uniform votes by the Nine, 11 differing votes (no opposed votes);

31st General Assembly, 45 resolutions: 18 consensus resolutions, 6 uniform votes, 21 differing votes (one opposed vote).

The negative development in the voting behaviour of the Nine can be explained mainly by the uncooperative attitude of Denmark. This led to the Netherlands and to a lesser extent Italy being prepared to deviate from the majority position by reacting more favourably to the demands of the Third World. The Federal Republic of Germany, on the other hand, found itself increasingly unwilling to agree to the radical demands of the Africans or even acknowledge them with a simple abstention. Whereas in the 30th General Assembly the Federal Republic of Germany produced only two rejections in 19 controversial votes, in the 31st General Assembly it was seven rejections out of a total of 27 controversial votes.

The Nine were only able to reach very limited agreement on common positions in the decolonization and South Africa debates in the 31st General Assembly. This did not provide a basis either for common voting or for initiating counter-proposals; only for issuing rather bland declarations.

In the 32nd General Assembly in 1977 the collapse of the Nine's position in four of the six resolutions on the Namibia question is explained by the policy of the three EEC members represented in the Security Council. The UK, France and Federal Republic of Germany coordinated their position most closely with the USA and Canada. The five Western Security Council members had been conducting exploratory talks with the parties involved (SWAPO, South African government, Front Line states and the UN) since April 1977 on the basis of the Security Council Resolution 385 of 30 January 1976.

The close cooperation of the five Security Council members meant that EPC produced only one common declaration as a contribution to the debate. It also led to a more marked disintegration of the Community attitude partly as a reaction to the lack of information provided by the three members of the Security Council.

In summary it can be seen that there were no essential changes in the attitude of the Nine towards the problems of decolonization, including Southern Africa and apartheid policies during the 32nd General assembly. As in previous years Denmark, the Netherlands and Ireland were more prepared than the other EEC states to agree to the demands of the developing countries. In the case of Italy in 1977 the tendency to support the Third World was reinforced by domestic political difficulties.

Disarmament

Cooperation between the Nine in the area of disarmament is a new phenomenon of EPC. Since the 30th General Assembly in 1975 consultations have been held in New York on questions of general disarmament (in contrast to regional and special negotiations like MBFR and SALT). In the disarmament debate of the 30th General Assembly in 1975 the cooperation of the EEC group proved to be the most successful consultation mechanism that the West as a whole possessed. The diminishing coordination within the framework of NATO assisted this development.

The cooperation of the Nine, which led to a common attitude on eight of a total of seventeen votes in 1975 and seven of a total of fourteen in 1976, was therefore more notable, given that the EEC governments often disagree on questions of security policy because of their differing military–political status. Ireland is not a member of NATO and Denmark tends towards the more progressive attitude of the Scandinavian states in the area of disarmament. The Netherlands supports the demands of the Third World in numerous cases whilst France has withdrawn from the military integration of NATO and is a non-signatory of the Non-proliferation Treaty. This leaves only the Federal Republic of Germany, Belgium, Italy and Luxembourg as a core-group of EEC states with largely identical security interests.

It is the policy of the two nuclear powers, in particular France, which has been responsible for the relative success of EPC since 1975. For some time France had taken on the role of an outsider because of its particular attitude to questions of disarmament and arms control as well as its pursuance of a 'policy of the empty chair' in the Geneva Disarmament Conference (CCD). The work of the CCD is at the centre of the disarmament debate in the UN. France's interest in the extension of EPC consultations to the area of disarmament and its correspondingly cooperative attitude can be seen as a move to avoid further isolation.

The Dutch at first expressed reservations in their attitude towards disarmament in EPC. They were encouraged, however, by members of the Third World who let it be known in personal conversations that they welcomed the development of a coordinated position by the Nine in the area of disarmament.

The Nine were also able to play a leadership role *vis-à-vis* other Western states. Thus during the UN disarmament debate in the winter of 1975 a Western grouping emerged, consisting of Spain, Portugal, Greece and Turkey, which sought to align its voting behaviour to that of the Nine. These were all states that had expressed their fundamental interest in joining the Community. Their tendency to orient themselves towards the position of the Nine weakened in the 31st General Assembly.

In the case of some other Western states there was a more negative reaction to increased European cooperation. Their behaviour was determined in part by a desire to achieve an independent profile and avoid being overshadowed by the Nine. Thus it was countries like Austria, Australia and New Zealand who felt excluded from Western consultations within EPC, cut off from the flow of information and increasingly forced into political isolation.

These varied reactions to the Nine's activities all demonstrated the need to improve communication. If information on the Nine's position could be passed on at an early stage and on a systematic basis then this could both contribute towards the coordination of Western policies and the strengthening of its position as well as securing the long-term influence of the Nine *vis-à-vis* the Third World.

A look at the statistics of the voting behaviour of the Nine in the area of disarmament in the 32nd General Assembly confirms the trend of the last few years towards the development of common positions. Of the sixteen resolutions where a vote was taken (there were eight consensus resolutions) the Nine voted together on ten occasions and differed on six.

Disagreement arose over the resolution on incendiary weapons and other conventional weapons (General Assembly Resolution 32/152, 19 December 1977). Denmark, Ireland and the Netherlands supported the proposal to convene a UN conference on the banning and limitation of the deployment of certain conventional weapons. The other six EEC partners abstained.

EPC represents an important framework of action for the Federal Republic of Germany as it enables that country to place its role as a military ally of the USA in perspective. The non-aligned states have up to now continued to view the Federal Republic as first and foremost a very close ally of the Americans whose attitude was practically identical to that of the USA and whose significance as a negotiating partner was thus limited. On the other hand, the USA has often taken the support of the Federal Republic for their positions too much for granted, which has led to a lack of timely information being passed on to the West German government. The increasing integration of the Federal Republic into the cooperation of the Nine stresses the greater independence of West German policies and thereby enables the Federal Republic to exert more effective influence in the framework of the EEC, in its relations to the USA and finally in negotiations with the Third World.

Economics

The development of a common approach by the Nine in economic affairs was reinforced by the granting of observer status to the European Community on 11 October 1974[25]. However, the differences between the various national positions often appeared greater than the common ground on international economic issues, even in those areas which had already been subject to Community agreement. France's particular sympathy for the Third World which was highlighted in the preparations for the North –South Dialogue in the Conference on International Economic Cooperation

(CIEC) presented a severe test for the Nine. In addition, whilst the Netherlands took on the role of a 'progressive' outsider in the group of Nine, the policies of the Federal Republic of Germany were characterized by a hardening of position.

In the 31st General Assembly in 1976 the relationship of tension between North and South, which had coloured the debate in economic affairs, continued unabated. The unanimity of the states of the European Community had in contrast diminished in comparison with the previous year. On the most important economic resolutions (General Assembly Resolution, 31/163, 21 December 1976: Industrial employment favouring the developing countries; General Assembly Resolution 31/174, 21 December 1976: Acceleration of the transfer of resources; General Assembly Resolution 31/178, 21 December 1976: Assessment of progress) the Nine were not able to vote together mainly because of the policies adopted by the Dutch.

The Dutch presidency delivered a total of eight Community declarations of which seven related to voting intentions. It was a considerable strain on EPC that the Nine on several occasions lacked a common leadership in negotiations. The Community became incapable of conducting negotiations on many important questions because of the refusal of the Dutch presidency to act as spokesman, illustrating the central role that the presidency plays in the process of coordination between the Nine.

In the 32nd General Assembly in 1977 the difficulties with the Dutch continued. The Dutch deviation from the majority of the Community states pushed Denmark into seeking greater solidarity with the Scandinavian states (this had also been manifested in the summer session of ECOSOC 1977). The diminishing common approach of the Nine could endanger the Nine's dialogue with the 'Group of 77'. The statistics show that 66 resolutions in the area of economics were approved, of which 50 were by consensus. The Nine voted unanimously on ten resolutions, and on six occasions their voting was divergent. The Belgian presidency delivered five common declarations in the name of the Nine on its unanimous vote and two on consensus resolutions.

In 1977 EPC functioned less harmoniously than in the previous year. Although the presidency at no time relinquished its leadership of common negotiations for the Nine, the conduct of the presidency was often too weak to promote actively the establishment of community attitudes.

9.3 Conclusions

Progress in political cooperation in New York is closely linked to the further development of the European Community. It tends to highlight the tension between Community interests and national interests and is thus dependent upon the European commitment of the member-states. If the discrepancy between the progress achieved in the process of harmonization in New York and the readiness of governments to produce uniform Community positions becomes too great, then EPC is in danger of regressing within the context of the UN.

Experience with cooperation in the recent General Assemblies has shown that every coordinated approach by the Nine has helped to strengthen its position internally and externally. Such success provided the incentive for the continuation of internal harmonization and the pursuit of a coordinated strategy. This became particularly apparent in the area of disarmament during the 32nd General Assembly; it was here that the first breakthrough was made by producing a unanimous vote and the delivery of a declaration of the Nine's voting intention in the case of the Mexican initiative on the definition of the concept of Nuclear-free Zones (General Assembly Resolution 3472B, 11 December 1975), which was achieved despite initially differing instructions from the capitals and which can be interpreted as a sign of this new spirit.

EPC influence at the UN is undoubtedly limited by internal differences, but that influence does certainly exist. Faced with the united front of the Third World, the Nine have had a measure of success in harmonizing their national positions via the consultation process. This often leads to an intensification of cooperation in the Political Committee and at foreign minister level.

Nevertheless this process has not so far promoted the development of a common foreign policy of the Nine. Rather it leads to successes on an *ad hoc* basis and from one case to another. The Nine still vote differently on certain issues despite a relative uniformity in their national positions. This is the result of a differing assessment of the significance of texts and resolutions, as well as of particular political tactics. Often the attempt to retain a national profile and to pursue particular political and economic interests weighs more heavily than the commitment to Europe.

The cooperation of the Nine in New York has confirmed a basic rule of international negotiations. The greater the unanimity in the approach of a group of states the greater their international value becomes as partners in discussions and the more they are regarded as significant actors in the considerations of outside states. EPC has in this respect achieved unexpected successes in the UN. Outside states, above all from the Third World, consult the Nine to a degree hitherto unknown. The Nine also influence the voting behaviour of outside states to the extent that they can adopt a harmonized position at an early date.

In terms of cooperation with Western partners there have been more problems than achievements. The Nine are so busy with their own consultations that they hardly have any time left for contacts with their Western allies. In the long term this could lead to a disadvantageous lack of cohesiveness that could affect the position and potential influence of the

West. Western states that are forced into isolation will be forced to react. In the area of disarmament, for example, they might increasingly support the views of non-aligned states like Sweden, Finland and Yugoslavia, or align themselves more closely to the positions of the Third World as an expression of their opposition to continuing European cooperation.

Thus it is important that EPC in the UN is seen not as an alternative but as a complement to a general Western harmonization.

EPC in the General Assembly has under present conditions reached its limits. During the 31st General Assembly from September to December 1976 a total of 190 meetings of the Nine took place in New York. The process of drawing the Nine delegations closer together is so advanced that from the technical point of view there is little room for improvement. EPC achieved its highest level of development hitherto in the 30th General Assembly under the Italian presidency. In the 31st General Assembly in 1976 under the Dutch presidency the diminishing discipline of the Nine, particularly on questions of decolonization including Rhodesia, South Africa and Namibia, made itself felt, despite certain progress in the creation of a uniform voting pattern on the politically controversial topics of the Middle East and disarmament. The fact that no Community position could be achieved concerning the two resolutions, where three EEC partners were sharply criticized for their relations with South Africa, signified a clear setback for the Nine's cooperation[26]. In the 31st General Assembly Denmark repeatedly sought a common position with its Scandinavian partners both in its terms of voting and in the presentation of declarations, at the cost of the solidarity of the Community.

Finally, the sympathy of the smaller EEC states for the Third World's concepts of economic and development policy as well as with their political demands in relation to Southern Africa led in the 31st General Assembly to a decline in the Nine's uniform voting behaviour. One reason for this is that the Third World resisted political propaganda issues, for instance on the question of Zionism in the 30th General Assembly, which had helped to promote the cohesiveness of the Nine in the past.

The achievement of common attitudes in matters of foreign policy will, in the long run, only materialize if the process of unification in Western Europe is further developed. This process should, above all, have an integrative effect on the behaviour of those states which at present divide their loyalty between two groups (Denmark) or which, in certain problem areas, identify more strongly with the attitude of the developing countries (the Netherlands, Ireland).

Even if substantial advances in European integration are made, questions will still remain as to the desirability of achieving harmonization on every issue. It may not always be the case that one bland common position, representing the lowest common denominator, is preferable to nine strongly held national positions. Here one has to take into account the fact that the

General Assembly is a forum for speech-making where flexible national declarations are often more appropriate than laborious compromise formulae.

These considerations lead us to the problem area of uniform voting behaviour. On several occasions members of a number of EEC governments have expressed the opinion that the position of the Nine could be strengthened by positive votes, even if they are not cast unanimously. In controversial questions, differing votes might be preferable to abstention. If the Nine, after intensive consultation and consideration of all political factors, finally agree on a positive uniform vote, then this vote may have more weight and may serve as a stronger example to other UN members than a policy of abstention designed to serve the purpose of covering up internal disunity.

Thus it may well be the case that in the UN, political cooperation pursued for its own sake may lead to behaviour that is, in the long term, counterproductive to the real interests of the Nine.

Notes

1 General Assembly Resolution 3050 (XXVIII), 18 September 1973

2 The Nine provided 25.2% of the UN budget; just a little more than the US contribution of 25%. West Germany is the fourth largest contributor after the USA, Soviet Union and Japan

3 See, for instance, the speech of the American ambassador to the UN before the 29th General Assembly (*New York Times*, 7 December 1974)

4 Johan Kaufmann, *Conference Diplomacy. An Introductory Analysis*, 2nd edn, Leyden, 1970, p. 149ff.: John G., Hadwen and Johan Kaufmann, *How United Nations Decisions are Made*, Leyden, 1960, p. 56ff.

5 For a full account see Beate Lindemann, 'Die Organisationsstruktur der Vereinten Nationen und die Mitarbeit der Bundesrepublik Deutschland', Ulrich Scheuner and Beate Lindemann (Eds.), *Die Vereinten Nationen und die Mitarbeit der Bundesrepublik Deutschland*, Munich, 1973, p. 220ff.: Christian Tomuschat, 'Tyrannei der Minderheit? Betrachtungen zur Verfassungsstruktur der Vereinten Nationen', *Jahrbuch für internationales Recht*, Vol. 19, Berlin, 1978, p. 278ff.: also Thomas Hovet, Jr. *Bloc Politics in the United Nations*, Cambridge, Mass., 1960, p. 32ff., p. 95; and Robert O. Keohane,

'The Study of Political Influence in the General Assembly', *International Organisation*, Vol. 21, 1967, p. 222ff.

6 The question of the coordination of questions of candidature has been discussed on a number of occasions in the Political Committee of EPC as well as in the Group of Experts (United Nations), without achieving any agreement on procedural steps

7 See, e.g., Walso Chamberlin, 'The North Atlantic Bloc in the UN General Assembly', *Orbis*, Vol. 1, 1957–1958, p. 459ff., and Leon Hyrwitz 'The EEC in the United Nations: The Voting Behaviour of Eight Countries, 1948–1973', *Journal of Common Market Studies*, Vol. 13, 1974–1975, p. 224ff.

8 The group which took its name from the Italian ambassador to the UN, Piero Vinci, began its work in 1969. The reason for its being convened was the agenda item proposed by the Soviet Union for the 24th General Assembly on the 'Strengthening of International Security', with which the East hoped to conduct a propaganda campaign against the West. The group later extended its consultations to other political issues. The meetings were stopped in 1973 but were taken up again in 1975. The meetings take place exclusively at ambassadorial level, but at irregular intervals

9 See Otto von der Gablentz, 'Wege zu einer europäischen Aussenpolitik', Heinrich Schneider and Wolfgang Wessels (Eds.), *Auf dem Wege zur Europäischen Union? Diskussionsbeiträge zum Tindemans-Bericht*, Bonn, 1977, p. 105. On the so-called 'Year of Europe' see, above all, Henry A. Kissinger, 'The Year of Europe', Gerhard Mally (Ed.), *The New Europe and the United States. Partners or Rivals?* Toronto, 1974, p. 29ff.: Martin J. Hillenbrand, 'Die USA und die EG: Spannungen und Möglichkeiten', Karl Kaiser and Hans-Peter Schwartz, *Amerika und Westeuropa. Gegenwarts und Zukunftsproblem*, Stuttgart, 1977, p. 290: and Andrew J. Pierre, 'America Faces Western Europe in the 1980's: Atlanticism Preserved, Disengagement or Devolution?' James Chace and Earl C. Ravenal, *Atlantis Lost. US–European Relations after the Cold War*, New York, 1976, p. 183ff.

10 See also Beate Lindemann, 'Das westliche Europa und die Dritte Welt. Die politische Zusammenarbeit der Neun in den Vereinten Nationen', *Europa-Archiv*, Series 13/1976, p. 436f. (English translation in *The World Today*, London, July 1976, p. 260–269)

11 See Beate Lindemann, 'Das westliche Europa und die Dritte Welt', p. 441ff.

12 Documents of the Security Council S/PV. 1881, 27 January 1976, and 1883, 1884, 29 January 1976

13 Security Council Document S/11945, 27 January 1976

14 See Rainer Lagoni, 'Die Vereinten Nationen und der internationale Terrorismus', *Europa-Archiv*, Series 6/1977, pp. 171–180

15 30th General Assembly: On the two Palestine Resolutions, 3375 and 3376 (XXX), 10 November 1975; 31st General Assembly: On the Palestine Resolution, 31/20, 24 November 1976

16 See Christian Tomuschat, 'Tyrannei der Minderheit?'

17 See Günther van Well, 'Die Entwicklung einer gemeinsamen Nahost-Politik der Neun', *Europa-Archiv*, Series 4/1976, p. 125

18 General Assembly Resolution 3237 (XXIX), 22 November 1974

19 General Assembly Resolution 3210 (XXIX), 14 October 1974

20 General Assembly Resolution 31/20, 24 November 1976

21 General Assembly Resolution 31/61, 9 December 1976

22 On the subject of the liberation movements see Christian Tomuschat, 'Die Befreiungsbewegung in den Vereinten Nationen', *Vereinte Nationen*, Jg. 22, 1974, pp. 65–72: and Eckart Klein, 'Nationale Befreiungskämpfe und Dekolonisierungspolitik der Vereinten nationen; Zu einigen völkerrechtlichen Tendenzen', *Zeitschrift für ausländisches Recht und Völkerrecht*, Vol. 36, 1976, pp. 618–653

23 General Assembly Resolution 31/6D, 9 November 1976

24 On the voting behaviour in the 28th and 29th General Assemblies see also Manfred Kulessa, 'Mehr Ja als Nein, doch meistens Schweigen. Das Abstimmungsverhalten der EG-Länder zum Südlichen Afrika', *Vereinte Nationen*, Jg. 22, p. 77ff.

25 General Assembly Resolution 3208 (XXIX), 11 October 1974

26 General Assembly Resolution 31/7, 5 November 1976: Economic Interests in South Africa

CHAPTER TEN

European Political Cooperation and Southern Africa

NICHOLAS VAN PRAAG

Until 1974 the whole of Southern Africa had been an area in which the Nine tacitly agreed to follow national policies rather than develop a common European strategy. When forced upon them at the UN, where political cooperation is increasingly successful on other issues[1], Southern Africa proved to be one of those subjects on which agreement was accepted as being difficult to achieve.

This is no longer the rule; since the mid 1970s there has been a development and intensification of political cooperation over Southern Africa. This change stems from the Portuguese revolution of 25 April 1974, which brought to an end a decade of increasingly bitter colonial wars and opened the way to the independence of Mozambique and Angola. Portugal's retreat changed decisively the balance of power in Southern Africa.

While previously it had seemed appropriate that the Europeans should conduct their affairs independently in the subcontinent, the overthrow of the Caetano regime introduced new elements of uncertainty and fluidity into a situation that, depending on one's point of view, had previously seemed either stubbornly rigid or reassuringly stable. Most members of the Community shared Washington's view, set out in the National Security Council Review of 1969, which asserted that 'the situation in the region is not likely to change appreciably in the foreseeable future, and in any event we cannot influence it'[2].

Following the Portuguese revolution such assessments needed to be radically revised. Wideranging reappraisals of policy towards Southern Africa were undertaken in the Community capitals as the implications of Angolan and Mozambican independence sunk in; Rhodesia's position became untenable with 300 miles of border exposed to hostile pressures from Mozambique; Namibia was exposed and South Africa's *cordon sanitaire* to the north had disappeared. If the Nine were to have any role in the evolution of events in Southern Africa some kind of cooperation seemed to be necessary.

This chapter traces European efforts through the EPC structure[3] to influence collectively the final stages of the 'unfinished African revolution' from the independence of the Portuguese colonies, to Rhodesia, Namibia and the Republic of South Africa itself. This leads on to a rather tenuous consideration of the potential and effectiveness of the Nine's political cooperation in Southern Africa.

The first collective move came over Mozambique. Portugal announced that Mozambique would become independent on 25 June 1975. Power was to be handed over to Frelimo, the only significant freedom movement in the colony. During the Irish presidency of the Council of Ministers in the first half of 1975, the African experts group of the Political Committee met only twice. Neither Mozambique nor the rest of Southern Africa were priorities.

On the eve of independence the Irish Foreign Minister, Garrett Fitz-gerald, addressed a message of congratulations to the new Mozambican government on behalf of the members of the EEC. Despite this joint declaration, only three of the Nine (the UK, the Netherlands and Denmark) were invited to the independence celebrations, reflecting Frelimo's desire to acknowledge a debt to those who in the past had refused to sell Portugal arms for use in her African wars and had turned down participation in the Cabora Bassa dam project.

What might be considered a minor issue of diplomatic protocol was an unexpected blow to the European image which political cooperation tries to project. It was not an auspicious beginning for EPC in Southern Africa.

Angola came next. With Portuguese withdrawal set for 11 November 1975 it was not until 31 October 1975 that the Community foreign ministers, meeting in Rome, squeezed in a brief exchange of views on Angola at the end of their political cooperation session. The Nine were apparently 'preoccupied' with the political climate in which the country was about to achieve its independence[4].

Other outsiders had not waited so long to take an interest. In July and August 1974, 125 Chinese military instructors had arrived in Zaire together with 450 tons of armaments destined to support the FNLA. By August 1975, South African troops had penetrated deep into Angola; far deeper than the ostensible object of their mission, the defence of the Cunene river scheme, demanded. The USA had been supplying the FNLA during the latter half of 1974 and 1975. Although this aid was pitched at a fairly low level at first, by March 1975 the 'pro-Western' FNLA was gaining ground against its rival, the Marxist-orientated MPLA. This triggered off Soviet involvement. US government estimates suggest that between March 1975 and January 1976 the Soviet Union supplied the MPLA with $100 million to $200 million of military equipment and 170 advisers, while Cuba supplied $70 million in military aid and more than 15 000 advisers[5]. Meanwhile in the south the smallest of the three main liberation groups, UNITA, was also receiving Western military support.

The transitional government that had been established in January 1975 after negotiations between the Portuguese and the three liberation movements (FNLA, MPLA, UNITA) disintegrated rapidly. By July 1975 intermittent clashes between rival groups had turned into open civil war.

Despite Soviet assistance, the MPLA fared badly at first. Having been driven out of Luanda in July, by August the FNLA had pushed back to within 32 km of the city. In the south, where the FNLA were fighting in loose alliance with UNITA forces, the MPLA was also under pressure. Here the FNLA–UNITA forces were strengthened by a South African motorized column.

So the almost disinterested attitude expressed by the Nine in Rome came at a time when the outlook for the MPLA seemed bleak. On Independence Day, 11 November 1975, the Portuguese handed over power to the 'Angolan people'. Both sides established governments. While the Soviet Union recognized the MPLA, Kissinger argued that US assistance had prevented an MPLA victory.

In December 1975 the situation was to change. Soviet and Cuban aid increased. The successful MPLA counter-attack began. Congressional fears of involvement in Angola led to an embargo on military aid to the pro-Western forces. US diplomatic pressure on the Soviet Union was weakened and South African forces pulled back to consolidate their position on the northern border of Namibia.

European capitals came under pressure from Washington, whose hands were now tied, to play a more active role. However, a European position was slow to develop. At the NATO foreign ministers meeting on 13 December 1975, Callaghan, the UK Foreign Secretary, raised the Angolan question[6]. Despite the fact that Angola is far outside the Alliance's area of interest, Callaghan urged members to use their influence through the Organization for African Unity to bring about the conciliation of the rival factions and the withdrawal of foreign troops. At the same time Callaghan underlined that the South African connection ruled out, as far as the UK was concerned, support for the FNLA–UNITA faction. France, Belgium the Netherlands, Denmark, Ireland and Italy hesitated. They shared British uncertainties as to developments in Angola. Only the West Germans accepted the US view that the war in Angola was crucial to Western security. A State Department official lamented that 'the difference in interpretation of what security is all about has been exposed here'[7].

It was not until 9 January 1976 that the Nine were able to come up with a formula to accommodate their differences of view and satisfy the Americans[8]. The technical details that had held up a declaration were apparently due to the need to reconcile the neutral tone on which the Dutch and Danes insisted, and the strong condemnation of the MPLA and its patrons called for by the French (and less energetically by others). The compromise that was accepted condemned all foreign military intervention and called for the OAU-backed tripartite solution. This joint position, announced in The Hague, was communicated to the OAU Secretary-General Eteki via the Dutch ambassador in Addis Ababa.

Such a position, albeit a common one, was a little late. The success of the MPLA counter-offensive was already becoming clear. By February it was beyond doubt. As the majority of OAU states swung round to recognition of the MPLA it became somewhat irrelevant for the Nine to argue in favour of the establishment of a three-party government of reconciliation which was no longer supported by its original sponsors. While continuing to condemn foreign intervention, reports from London and Paris indicated moves towards recognition of the MPLA[9]. The criteria on which recognition has traditionally been based appeared to have been met; the MPLA controlled not merely the majority of the territory but the majority of the population as well, and the prospects that it would continue to do so were reasonable. In addition the Europeans were anxious to break the monopoly of friendship that the Soviet Union and Cuba had been able to establish with the MPLA. On 13 February 1976 the British Foreign Office issued a statement stressing that 'whatever happens will be done in an orderly and coordinated way with our partners and obviously the US'[10].

A preliminary meeting of EEC ambassadors had been held in Brussels on 9 February 1976, where the recognition of the Peoples' Republic of Angola was discussed. A week later (16 February) the political directors met in Luxembourg to organize swift action to accord full diplomatic recognition to the MPLA as the legal government of Angola. A joint declaration following the Foreign Minister's Council on 23 February 1976 was suggested. However, the smoothness of the operation had already been threatened by the French. During the previous few days the Quai d'Orsay had not missed an opportunity to let black African states know of its intentions. The plan for simultaneous recognition collapsed on 17 February after the failure of top-level attempts in Luxembourg to prevent the French, in Harold Wilson's words, 'going off at half-cock'. The psychological and symbolic impact of a collective recognition to demonstrate the Community's political sovereignty was lost. While other members insisted on more time to confer with their capitals[11] and with the USA, the French declared on the morning of 17 February that they were to recognize Angola at midday[12]. The other eight were left with no choice but to accept that individual states would recognize the Peoples' Republic of Angola in time.

France wished to hasten recognition of Angola for several reasons. She was keen that her long flirt with the MPLA's rivals be forgotten. French policy towards Angola from the beginning had been dictated by the position of her ex-colonies in Africa. Once the francophone members of the OAU came round to recognition of the MPLA, tilting the balance within the Organization, the French were keen to realign their position. The situation in Djibouti was an added incentive, where France was under strong pressure to abandon her strategically placed colony. More simply, as a Brussels diplomat put it, 'when the French change horses they like to do it fast'. Despite criticism from her partners, the French remained unrepentant, insisting that their decision had permitted the Nine to recognize Angola in less than four days, while it would have taken at least a month had Kissinger's exhortations to delay been accepted.

The foreign ministers met shortly afterwards in Luxembourg. Recriminations against French actions of the previous week were strong, yet out of the chaotic recognition episode the Nine managed to salvage a degree of credibility. While expressing their hope that the people of Angola would henceforth be able to work out their own future and condemning all foreign intervention on Angolan territory, the text went further than mere *post-factum* position-taking. It emphasized the Nine's willingness to cooperate, both economically and politically, with the states of Southern Africa and rejected all attempts by outsiders to establish a zone of influence in Africa. In particular, the Nine stressed the right to self-determination and independence of the people of Rhodesia and Namibia and the unacceptability of the system of apartheid in Southern Africa[13].

The text of the declaration had been hotly contested. Genscher, the German Foreign Minister, supported by several colleagues (British, Danish and Dutch) had insisted that the declaration should not be limited to Angola, which would indeed have seemed extremely thin after the recognition performance. The French fought a rearguard action, protesting against the inclusion of references to other countries, especially South Africa, but eventually conceded to her partners. The exaggerated mood of accomplishment after the ministers' meeting owed a great deal, one might imagine, to the successful solution of these internal divisions. Van Eslande, the Belgian Foreign Minister, argued that 'for the first time the Nine have established a precise and coherent policy on a question of foreign policy'. Hattersley, deputizing for Callaghan, was perhaps more realistic. He saw the joint declaration as a useful way of impressing upon Ian Smith how untenable was his position.

Rhodesia is recognized as a special British concern. Since Rhodesia's unilateral declaration of independence in 1965 the Eight have backed British policy towards the Rhodesian rebels and have been happy to continue to do so.

From early 1976 Anglo-American cooperation became the dominant feature of policy towards Rhodesia. The European role has been marginal. Although the British kept the Nine informed of developments in Rhodesia through the political committee and its specialist African subcommittee, it was the 'special relationship' that appeared for a while to have broken new ground. A somewhat euphoric Dr Owen, then British Foreign Secretary, commented on his return from his first African shuttle in April 1977 that 'very rarely in diplomatic history has there been quite such a concerted and coordinated attempt by two democratic nations to work together'[14].

In October 1976 the Nine were able to support and follow closely the British chairmanship of the unsuccessful Geneva Conference charged with the job of straightening out Rhodesia's confused route to majority rule, through the daily briefings of Community diplomats in Geneva. The ill-fated African tour in January 1977 of the conference chairman, Ivor

Richard, inspired a joint call by the Nine to all parties to use the opportunity to achieve a just and lasting solution[15]. The Eight still felt fairly closely involved.

Such illusions faded fast. In April 1977 Dr Owen attempted to sell the Africans the idea that the issue of the transfer of power, which had been such a sticking-point in Geneva, should be temporarily left aside in favour of an attempt to draw up an independent constitution. During Owen's shuttle, all dispatches to London were immediately forwarded to Washington. Community members had to await the Political Cooperation meeting on Owen's return.

In August–September 1977, Owen and Andrew Young, the US representative to the UN, presented a joint Rhodesia Settlement plan to the Front Line presidents and, finally, to Ian Smith on 1 September. The plan proposed to established a limited period of direct British rule, backed up by a UN peacekeeping force prior to general elections and independence in 1978[16]. The main point to note here is that the proposals were never thoroughly discussed by the Nine. Indeed, until their publication details had been kept a closely guarded secret.

A common stance on the most longstanding and controversial issue, the Republic of South Africa, has always been recognized as extremely difficult. Individual national positions have been moulded by a kaleidoscope of factors on which it is hard to base a 'European' position. The differences that exist amongst the Nine were illustrated at the 31st United Nations General Assembly. The Nine split on various issues, including trade, arms sales, investment and sports exchanges with South Africa. Denmark, Ireland and the Netherlands and, at times, Italy, tended to vote with the Third World group. The UK, France and West Germany, who were singled out in some of the resolutions as collaborators with South Africa, voted as a block throughout[17]. Of greater significance perhaps was Italy's abstention in the Security Council vote on 19 October 1976 in the face of a British/French/US veto on a resolution for a binding arms embargo on South Africa[18].

This lack of togetherness on South Africa has meant that the Nine have tended to hedge their position in their joint declarations. Where member-states can agree is in their criticism of the apartheid system. Speaking at the World Conference against Apartheid held in Lagos in August 1977, Mr Simonet, the Belgian Foreign Minister and President of the Council of Ministers, spoke of apartheid's 'failure, not only morally, but also in terms of it practical applications'[19].

Nevertheless, Simonet's speech in Lagos reflected the growing realization within the Nine that to retain credibility in black Africa it was high time to move beyond simple declarations of principle. At their political cooperation meeting on 12 July 1977 foreign ministers decided to study measures to accelerate the transition towards a system of equality for both blacks and whites using the European economic inheritance in South Africa as a catalyst for change. A working group was set up to examine the possibility of drawing up a code of conduct for European companies operating in South Africa, as well as economic and trade sanctions.

Despite such progress, the technical and legal difficulties involved remain considerable. Anti-apartheid rumblings continue to predominate. But the Nine have been more decisive on issues closely linked to the Republic. It would seem that it is easier for member-states to establish obliquely substantive common positions towards South Africa. Over both the recognition of the Transkei and the Namibia question, the Nine coordinated their position through the political cooperation structure.

Transkei became 'independent' on 26 Octobr 1976: not a single black African state was represented at the celebrations. It was ignored by both the OAU and the UN and there were no representatives from any of the major powers East or West, the Nine included – hardly a shattering example of European unity.

Transkei had long been the showpiece of South Africa's Bantustan policy which itself is a lynchpin of separate development. The unanimous decision not to recognize the Transkei came because the independence of the territory set the seal on apartheid in an important symbolic, if not final, sense. The Dutch Foreign Minister Stoel's declaration that the Nine had no intention of recognizing Transkei 'on the occasion of her supposed independence'[20] was a move towards more active European condemnation of the ideology of separate development.

A common policy towards Namiba would not appear to be any more difficult. All member-states have long affirmed UN responsibility for the territory. Community members on the Security Council, supported by the rest of the Nine, voted for Resolution No. 385 on 30 January 1976 condemning South Africa's 'illegal occupation' of Namibia and its 'discriminatory and repressive laws and practices' in that territory. The Security Council demanded free elections under UN supervision and the withdrawal of the South African administration, failing which it would reconsider the question at the end of August 1976.

The MPLA's victory in Angola gave added urgency to the need to find a solution to the Namibian question. Yet despite the unity shown at the UN, when Namibia was discussed by the Political Committee on 11 May 1976, in an attempt to work out an agreed line to be adopted by the foreign ministers at their forthcoming meeting at Senningen, the attempt was unsuccessful. Member-states were divided. The majority wanted some kind of joint European declaration while the UK and France refused to recognize the urgency of such a move.

In June the Nine came under attack from the South-West African Peoples Organization (recognized by the UN and OAU as the main political group in Namibia) over the UK's proposal that a Community fact-finding mission be sent to Namibia to talk to the 'relevant population groups'. SWAPO protested that not only was this contrary to Security Council Resolution 385, but that it gave implicit legitimacy to South African Bantustan-oriented policies[21]. The idea of the mission was abandoned.

By the end of August 1976, in an attempt to contain growing pressures within the Community, the foreign ministers managed to agree on a stance towards the South African-sponsored Windhoek Constitutional Conference and its attempts to establish a multiracial interim government that was to administer the country until the end of 1978, the provisional date for Namibian independence. Time was short. Both the Netherlands and Denmark were threatening to break off diplomatic relations with South Africa over Namibia, should such a move be recommended by the UN Security Council. Van der Stoel, as President of the Council, explained in a letter to Waldheim, Secretary-General of the UN, the European view that the Windhoek proposals came nowhere near meeting the requirements for genuine self-determination and independence laid down by the UN. The Nine insisted that the Windhoek Conference could not be a substitute for a meeting at which all groups, including SWAPO, were represented. They were determined, the Dutch Foreign Minister stressed, to continue to exert pressure through the UN on South Africa for the independence of Namibia[22].

While all members of the Community recognize that vital strategic and commercial interests are at stake in Southern Africa in some way or another, such a realization has not provided the basis for a clearly defined consensus on which to act. The situation is further complicated by the confusion that exists amongst the Europeans as to their role between the vying of the superpowers and the demands of the black liberation movements for majority rule.

Given this lack of clarity in European thinking it is hardly surprising that Genscher's repeated calls for an overall European strategy[23] and the European Parliament's pointed criticism of the absence of comprehensive policies for the subcontinent as a whole[24] have met with little success. The Nine's cooperation in Southern Africa confirms the lessons of EPC's performance in Southern Europe. The EPC structure is limited to reacting to individual issues as they arise, even if the logic of the links from one to the next are as obvious as they are to the foreign ministries of the Nine in Southern Africa.

While the Political Committee and the increasingly frequent meetings (every six weeks or so) of the African experts group (made up of the heads of the Africa Departments of the Nine foreign ministries) provide flexible and efficient channels for sharing information and views, reaction has tended to follow the chronology of events. The result has been that the Nine have to develop their policy within a framework established without their participation. This, of course, weakens the role they are able to play.

Joint reaction presupposes consensus. Such convergence is easy enough where one of the Nine has, and is accepted as having, a special responsibility. This is the case as far as the UK and Rhodesia are concerned. UK policy over Rhodesia has long been accepted by her Community partners and they have been willing to follow the UK lead. The UK position is thus strengthened and European unity demonstrated with little effort. Whether the UK and the Eight is a formula likely to be any more successful than the UK alone is not yet clear.

Even without a leader to follow, issues as uncontroversial as the condemnation of apartheid in South Africa and the refusal to recognize Transkei (along with most of the rest of the world) make 'speaking with one voice' a reasonably simple matter. The other side to this case of position-taking was illustrated by the slightly humiliating response to the joint recognition (again an uncontroversial issue) of Mozambique. Here the Nine agreed on and executed a routine diplomatic manoeuvre only to have it thrown back at them. A common move is only effective if its object recognizes the Nine as an entity. Frelimo was unwilling to allow what it regarded as the duplicities of the past disguised behind a united European front. This illustrates a more general problem. Unless the Euorpeans can act together regularly in international affairs they risk either being ignored or, worse, split when they do manage to agree.

Consensus is relative. In Namibia national interests complicate the situation. For example, the UK (through Rio Tinto Zinc) has important interests in uranium-extraction. The West Germans have the residual problem of 10 000 German passport-holders. Nevertheless in Namibia the Nine are lucky. Without having to define exactly what they mean (and the UK suggestion of a Community fact-finding mission would suggest they do not all mean the same thing) they can safeguard their credentials with black Africa behind UN resolutions for Namibian self-determination and independence with which they can all agree.

Angola was more difficult. As members of NATO (Ireland aside), the Nine had ignored Portugal's colonial wars. Although there had been no major contradictions in the past, the rivalry amongst the freedom movements, whose divisions were matched within the Community countries by conflicting allegiances, make it particularly difficult for the Nine governments to adopt a common position when the Portuguese withdrew in November 1975. Perhaps they hoped for a quick FNLA–UNITA victory (it looked possible in November) which would have allowed them to ignore the issue. With the success of the MPLA counter-attack in December–January 1975, the Nine turned to collective support for the OAU tripartite solution[25]. The recognition of Angola, 'un chapitre quelque peu controverse' according to van der Stoel, showed the fragile nature of the European stand. With the die cast, member-states rushed forward individually (the Italians in the lead), to establish diplomatic relations with Angola.

External factors complicate consensus-formation. The Nine agreed on informal consultations between themselves and the US on EPC topics at the Gymnich meeting in April 1974[26]. In Southern Africa, European policy has all along been broadly aligned with that of the USA. This was the case over the National Security Council report of 1969, and it has continued to be so since the Portuguese Revolution. Nevertheless, US influence on the EPC in Southern Africa (i.e. on those specific issues to which the EPC has reacted) has been ambiguous, either helping to unify European positions or splitting them hopelessly[27].

Where the Nine fall in with the practice of US policy it has had a coat-tail effect, whereby the Europeans are swept along together behind the Americans. Most obviously this has been true over Rhodesia, where the Eight's support for the UK position has been thinly disguised European support for the US position. The very opposite effect was true over Angolan recognition. Here the Nine could not agree amongst themselves on the US line, which was to delay, and their previously reasonably serried ranks were split. Indeed the precipitate nature of the French decision owes something at least to French resentment at having to wait for Kissinger's permission[28].

Even where consensus or convergence of individual positions is possible, it appears difficult to express to either the main actors or outsiders. While European diplomats working within the EPC structure may know each others' minds, expressing agreement (disagreements, of course, are ignored) is problematical. Joint declarations and *démarches* are the most common form of EPC instrument and have a certain symbolic weight, though their substance on Southern Africa issues has tended to be so diluted to accommodate all points of view that much of the potential impact is lost. The Angolan declaration of 23 February 1976 was perhaps an exception, setting out in four points the European position. However, it must be remembered that the declaration came after the fact; the MPLA had already been recognized individually by the Nine and the declaration appeared rather as an attempt to put the record straight than to influence actively the course of events.

The recognition of Angola demonstrated the shortcomings of the joint use of diplomatic instruments even over an issue where there were no differences of principle amongst the Nine. The way to Community decision-making is hardly to announce to your partners that you have reached a decision on your own and set a time-limit for every one else to fit in with it.

Accepting such limited and essentially passive diplomatic tools as the rump of those available to the Nine, what is available when circumstances suggest or require the continuation of political cooperation by other means?

Economic or 'civilian' options would appear to offer more scope to the Nine than the use or threat of military force. Money is a powerful weapon in the Third World. Financial inducements on a bilateral basis have been distributed to various Southern African states in support of the Nine's position, notably to Mozambique as compensation for the loss of revenue that resulted from the closing of her frontier with Rhodesia. Although vaguely coordinated, their bilateralness rather than their Europeanness have tended to be most obvious[29].

Sanctions are difficult. Even over Rhodesia, where there was consensus, sanctions-evasion was not unknown. Over South Africa a comprehensive sanctions policy could never be effective without its wider acceptance amongst the Nine. Limiting sanctions to military sales is only partially successful, despite the tightening of the French (one of the main offenders in the past) embargo early in 1977 to include all weapons. This is largely due to licensing agreements which allow South Africans to manufacture locally the arms that its previous suppliers no longer find it politic to provide. The EEC's modest plan, given the go-ahead by the Council in September 1977, to establish a code of conduct for European companies operating in South Africa is not the panacea.

The code is purely advisory and will have no statutory force, partly because of the difficulty of imposing external guidelines on companies subject to South African law. But it is hoped that it will create a psychological incentive to employers to improve the wages and working conditions of their black African staff. Companies will be asked to report periodically on how they have observed the code, so that its effectiveness can be monitored by the Nine.

In the view of most EEC governments there is little more that they can do to put pressure on South Africa economically in the immediate future. More radical measures such as special EEC tariffs on South African imports and the cutting of export credits to South Africa are generally considered impracticable, at least for the moment. It should not be forgotten that at least part of the appeal of a code to the Nine is the hope that it will head off more far-reaching demands from Black African governments at the UN.

The Lomé Convention provides EPC with a potentially useful collective instrument. Signed in April 1975, the Convention illustrated the Community's constructive interest in African affairs. Previous links with the EEC (Yaounde and Arusha Conventions) had been hangovers from the French African empire and were of little significance other than to continue French influence in her ex-colonies. Lomé was different. It reflected a new awareness of the interdependence of world economies, and the desire to develop a new 'post-imperial' role in the development of the associated states.

Following the Portuguese coup and the first moves towards winding up the overseas empire, the Commission saw its opportunity. In September 1974 Cheysson, the Commissioner responsible, announced that he hoped that Guinea Bissau, Mozambique and Angola (when the situation there clarified) would join the ACP states then negotiating the new trade and aid deal with the Community. While offering membership of the Lomé

Convention the Commission was extremely careful to retain a neutral stance. In January 1976 Cheysson was the first member of the Commission to comment on the Angolan civil war. He condemned foreign intervention and argued that it would be absolutely wrong for the Europeans to interfere in the internal affairs of an African country. In March the Commission's proposal for exceptional aid to states affected by the Angolan war, totalling 25 million units of account, was approved by the Council[30].

While Community instruments do exist (and European statements on Southern Africa have increasingly taken to emphasizing them), the ignorance of Community policies in political cooperation discussions has been a limitation. Community instruments are more likely to be successful as tools of the EPC the more the policies in the two areas complement and promote each other, and are not thrown together haphazardly to serve the moment. Meanwhile their effectiveness in Southern Africa has yet to be proved. So far, neither Mozambique nor Angola have taken up Cheysson's offer of membership of Lomé. Indeed on his visit to Rome in September in 1976 the Angolan Prime Minister, Lopo do Nascimento, emphasized the importance his country placed upon bilateral ties in preference to swift moves towards membership of the Lomé Convention[31].

What, then, in short, has been the EPC's policy record in Southern Africa? In Mozambique the Nine were snubbed; in Angola they managed to agree upon a policy (with what degree of good faith it is yet hard to assess), only to break ranks at the last moment; UK policy for Rhodesia required and received no more than token support ('sympathetic observation', to use Genscher's description); the Nine's Namibian policy lacked clarity of detail beneath the general call for the independence of the territory; fundamental divisions over South Africa have so far prevented more than the routine condemnation of the apartheid system. The only real coup has been the non-recognition of the Transkei[32].

However 'remarkable the degree of coherence' that European foreign policy-makers see in the EPC's role in Southern Africa, more objectively, the record is scarcely dazzling. The key perhaps is that the state of flux in Southern Africa that followed the Portuguese revolution drove the Nine together for essentially national reasons; the desire to have some sway on events that looked hard to achieve via the traditional channels.

Despite this tactical recourse to EPC, national interests have remained at the fore. Where they can be served by individual national initiatives these continue to take precedence.

Notes

1 See Beate Lindemann, Chapter 9
2 National Security Council interdepartmental group for African study in response to NSC memorandum 39: Southern Africa AF/NSL 1969
3 See David Allen and William Wallace, Chapter 2
4 *Le Monde*, 1 November 1977
5 *Le Monde*, 11 January 1977
6 *Guardian*, 13 December 1975

7 *International Herald Tribune*, 26 December 1975

8 See *Guardian*, 7 January 1976, for announcement of greater Anglo-American coordination in their diplomatic strategies for handling the fighting

9 *Financial Times*, 12 February 1976

10 *New York Times*, 14 February 1976. The British were willing to grant what, in normal circumstances, might have appeared premature recognition because having done so and exchanged ambassadors, Angola would become a friendly nation in terms of the Foreign Enlistment Act (1870). The exasperating problem of British mercenaries would thus be ended, as their recruitment would become illegal

11 The West Germans were expecting Zaire's Foreign Minister on 18 February and the Belgians, the Zambian Foreign Minister on 19 February. Both Zaire and Zambia had opposed the MPLA. Bonn and Brussels felt that it was not correct to recognize Angola during these officials visits. Other governments had to wait for cabinet meetings later in the week. See *The Economist*, 21 February 1976

12 The French offered another example of such precipitate action with the unilateral support extended 'in the name of Europe' to a Morrocan expeditionary force in Zaire, following the invasion of the southern Sheba province by Katangese ex-gendarmes exiled in Angola. The French government merely informed the British, who held the presidency of the Council of Ministers, of its intention to send aircraft to Zaire shortly before the planes left. See *Guardian*, 16 April 1977

13 *Agence Europe*, No. 1925, 23–24 February 1976

14 *Guardian*, 19 April 1977

15 *Bulletin d'Information EEC*, 1 February 1977

16 *Financial Times*, 2 September 1977

17 *European Report No. 371*, 13 November 1976

18 *European Report No. 364*, 23 October 1976. The British and French had informed other EEC members of their position and had gathered support for their states. They feared the resolution would damage negotiations with South Africa over Namibia. Italy argued that it could not oppose a motion designed to punish South Africa for defying a UN resolution (No. 385) demanding their withdrawal from Namibia by 31 August 1976

19 *The Times*, 24 August 1977

20 *Agence Europe*, No. 2062, 30 September 1976

21 *Anti-Apartheid News (London)*, June 1976

22 *European Report No. 351*, 4 September 1976

23 *Agence Europe*, No. 1974, 3–4 May 1976

24 *Agence Europe*, No. 2009, 24 June 1976

25 State Department officials have alleged (*New York Times*, 10 March 1976) that this was not to the exclusion of French, UK, West German and Belgian support for the FNLA–UNITA faction. In time (the French declared then–*Le Monde*, 12 March 1976) such allegations would suggest that the declared European position was a neutral front for more partisan involvement. UK diplomatic sources reject such a crucial interpretation without denying the possibility of 'diplomatic tightrope walking'

26 See Beate Kohler, Chapter 7

27 Institutionally the US's continuing disregard for the EPC structure was demonstrated in its bypassing of the presidency in favour of direct contacts with the leaders of the 'Big Three', the UK, France and West Germany

28 6 February 1976. Kissinger sent a message to all European foreign ministers informing them that recognition of the MPLA was premature. Sauvagnargues had immediately replied that this was not the view of the French government and simultaneously called a meeting of the ambassadors of the Nine in Luxembourg to discuss the question with her partners. See *Le Monde*, 25 February 1976

29 By April 1976 bilateral aid by Community members to Southern Africa amounted to more than £50 million. See *Financial Times*, 7 April 1976

30 *Daily Telegraph*, 18 March 1976. The aid went to Zaire, Zambia, Malawi and Botswana but *not* Angola or Mozambique, which are not members of the ACP group

31 *Relatione Internationale*, No. 41, October 1976, p. 171

32 Even here the Nine's position was equivocal. Having voted for the UN General Assembly resolution declaring Transkei's independence 'null and void', the Dutch, speaking on behalf of the Nine, said that the Community's support for the resolution did not prejudice the freedom of member-states to handle individually their relations over particular problems with the Transkei. See *Agence Europe*, No. 2082, 28 October 1976

The future of European Political Cooperation

REINHARDT RUMMEL

11.1 Introduction

The cooperation of the Nine in foreign affairs over the last seven years has not yet given rise to a common European foreign policy. However, in the years since its establishment in 1970 some progress has been made towards this goal. It is difficult to predict whether this development will continue as there are no reliable indicators on which to base a judgement. Nevertheless one can describe those factors which play a more or less significant part in this context. These include the identification of the likely future challenges to the politics of the Nine as well as an investigation of the adaptability of the EPC structure. Finally, it will be necessary to examine the internal European conditions governing the development of the Community as well as influential factors from the external environment[1].

A striking feature of EPC is the apparently continual extension of the Nine's consultations to more and more areas and problems of foreign affairs. The cooperation of the Nine is increasingly losing the selective character which it had at the beginning of the 1970s. Nevertheless, little seems to be changing in relation to the limitation of its work to certain sectors. EPC's area of activity continues to be diplomacy – where economic and military questions are excluded. Topics such as disarmament in the UN Conference of the Committee on Disarmament, although they come under the aegis of EPC, do still not rank highly in the overall context of discussions on defence and security policies between East and West. The same can be said with regard to international economic relations. Indeed, right from the beginning it was not envisaged that EPC would take over important functions in these areas; and despite its obvious desirability, no close coordination of EEC foreign economic policy and EPC activities has yet been achieved. The few cases of a pragmatic coordination of both strands of European foreign policy (in the CSCE and the Euro–Arab Dialogue) tend to be offset by an exaggerated demarcation in other situations (the EPC statement on the Cyprus conflict and the various declarations concerning the Middle East). On the other hand, it is becoming apparent that the gap is narrowing between some of the EEC's and NATO's fields of activity and those of EPC. No conclusions can yet be drawn regarding this development.

The continuing extension of its range of topics should not lead one to the false assumption that EPC has become the primary instrument of policy initiatives by the Nine in international relations. The defensive nature of the EPC system has not fundamentally changed. The central focus of its performance capability has remained that of reciprocal information and common analysis[2]. Similarly, the low degree of political obligation in EPC has remained unaltered. The accumulation of a fund of common views and harmonized positions in foreign affairs has so far achieved little; individual states still make active use of the possibilities for developing a national profile at the expense of the Nine's solidarity[3].

Apart from the extension of topics in EPC one can observe a second dynamic development, namely the tendency of EPC committees to widen their scope and occasionally to develop into relatively independent bodies. There is more to this than a mere proportional extension corresponding to the increase in problem areas. Expressed negatively, one could talk of an excessive growth in the EPC apparatus, which, as in the framework of the Euro–Arab Dialogue for example, produced an indeterminably large number of working groups, *ad hoc* groups of experts and sub-groups which were scarcely manageable and which in turn made it necessary at this early stage to establish a coordinating group. Within national administrations the recruiting area for participants is no longer limited to the officials of the foreign ministries but now extends to take in experts from many specialized ministries. At the same time there has been an increase in the degree of consultation and cooperation among the diplomats of the Nine in non-EEC states and in international organizations. In each case the tendencies towards independence are reinforced: measured against the official national position, experts (who are on the spot) frequently enjoy a greater and shared insight into that which needs to be done, so that national political decisions become subject to the pressure of suggestions which already bear the 'Nine's stamp'.

While EPC has up to now been in a phase of procedural development in some areas, the point seems now to have been reached where the whole structure could fall apart. The Political Committee, the central body of EPC and the connecting link between political and administrative levels, is faced with difficult tasks in this respect. This body has itself become excessively formalistic and is gradually turning into a technocratic club with no particular political impetus, especially now that M. Davignon and his fellow-innovators have, in the main, moved onto new positions. The call for Gymnich-style political directors' meetings such as the foreign ministers cultivate, within a less formal framework, is only a symptom of the stage of development which has been reached. In other words, there is a trend towards arterial sclerosis.

Without cataloguing further features of the present stage of EPC one can state provisionally that it has today reached a level of development where the capacity of the system has been largely exhausted. Thus, EPC is already coming up against its own self-imposed limits at certain points (the extension of topics, the exceeding of procedural limits).

11.2   The Nine's essential areas of operation

The central (geographical) areas in which EPC has up to now operated, and which have been the subject of individual case studies in this present volume, will in all probability remain much the same in the future: Eastern Europe, the Middle and Near East, the Mediterranean area, Africa, North America and the UN. Additional problem areas could include central and eastern Asia as well as South America and Latin America. Indeed, there have already been sporadic exchanges of opinion on questions relating to these regions within the framework of EPC; however, compared with the other regions of world politics the European have to date seen in these other areas no cause for coordinated diplomacy of any significance. At present there are also no reliable indications that would suggest any early change in this position[4].

Thus EPC activities in respect of relations with Eastern European countries have up to now been limited to producing a common position at the CSCE. In future, however, EPC could be viewed not simply as a form of management for preparing and sustaining East–West conferences but could also be used by the governments of the Nine to coordinate diplomatic relations with the East on a broader basis. This prognosis needs a certain amount of clarification. It is clearly desirable for the credibility of the Nine's position that, beyond the results of Helsinki and Belgrade, they can proceed from a common basis in other multilateral or bilateral East–West talks. If one adheres to this view then in future it will be not so much the preparation for CSCE follow-up meetings which will occupy the West Europeans as much as the variety of forums in which the Soviet Union chooses to test the Nine's unanimity. In this respect the topics for discussion extend beyond the competence of EPC but are reciprocally related to its area of operation: they include such issues as Moscow's relations with West European Communist parties, the MBFR negotiations, the retroactive effects of the SALT agreements, the demands for equal rights in relations between COMECON and the EEC, Brezhnev's proposals for pan-European conferences on questions of energy, the environment and transport, and Soviet attempts to initiate global disarmament discussions in the context of the UN.

Undoubtedly, the Eastern bloc's view on these themes is not always unequivocal but in the main it is ambivalent in its discussions with the West. For the West Europeans two things are important in this regard: first, not to allow themselves to be forced apart as Europeans or within the Atlantic Alliance (e.g. through pan-European action); second, to retain a general overall view in the face of the assortment of Eastern advances; to view often disparate issues in conjunction with one another; and, for example, not to isolate areas of cooperation from the background of antagonism just because on the Western side there are differing frameworks for action. The given limits of cooperation among the Nine exclude the possibility of producing a comprehensive view of East–West relations and subsequently of being able to provide wide-ranging proposals. However, the Nine could perhaps be forced by events to come to grips with these problems and in this regard a modest contribution could be expected from EPC. For example, the analytical power of EPC could fulfil a function which no other body could provide. Equally, it would not be out of the question that in this context more imagination and pragmatism could be deployed within EPC to overcome the sectorally limited approach to problems, since questions of security and defence policy are an integral element of all relations with the East. Undoubtedly internal European discussions concerning the breadth, the nature and the significance of a Western European common approach to integration policy would thereby gain in relevance. In view of the firmly established national positions (the French position on independence in defence policy, the Danish insistence on the notion of European civilian power) it will not be possible within EPC to achieve much more than a cautious exploration of positions regarding the handling of problems of security policy within the context of the Nine[5].

In contrast to East–West relations it is economic questions which provide the particular challenge to West Europeans, particularly with regard to North–South relations. Here the Nine will probably be increasingly unable to get by simply by pursuing a Third World policy which, viewed from an extreme, is directed solely at specifics such as the level of textiles imports from developing countries or the ways and means whereby Europeans can secure supplies of raw materials. Parallel to these goals much could depend on what the Europeans actually have to offer in terms of the much-vaunted 'new world economic order' and how, in the event, they behave towards national liberation movements, the transformation processes taking place in political and social systems as well as towards racial problems in the countries of the Third World. Here the Nine might in future have to tackle a number of awkward questions, which again, as in the case of the East–West problem, go far beyond the capabilities of European Political Cooperation but which could involve EPC in a useful subsidiary role. An example of this kind of role occurs within the context of the UN, where the Nine have developed a modest but successful tradition of adopting a concerted European approach. Here the Nine will have to go further than their present practice of merely concentrating on their voting pattern. The value of cooperation within the UN could come to depend on an ability not just to agree internally within the Nine but also to cooperate with other groupings of states. The UN is such a large forum that a voting bloc of just nine states does not have that great an impact[6].

As well as dealing with North–South problems at the global level the Nine are also likely to have deal with a number of specific issues in this context. Thus in future the Nine will hardly be able to avoid producing responses when, for instance, the Saudi Arabian Minister Yamani relates reservations with regard to an increase in oil prices to hopes for changes in the European attitude towards the Palestinian question. The Nine will also have to be prepared for new crises, such as the problem in the Horn of Africa, at least to the extent that they will be able to resist the pressure of the conflicting parties. Particularly in the Middle East and in Southern Africa, where the Nine have issued a whole series of public statements, it might be subsequently necessary to demonstrate flexibility and a willingness to produce new assessments in the face of rapid changes in conflict situations. It may be that the Nine will be in a position to offer their services as mediators, as, for example, the Namibia Contact group has done in relation to South Africa[7].

Apart from developing a constructive attitude in situations of crises and tension the Nine have had a more profound long-term interest in basing their relations with Third World states on structural interdependencies. The Euro–Arab Dialogue is a good example of this, where the Nine, in association with the Arab league, have sought pragmatic ways of developing a climate of understanding and cooperation between the regions[8]. Problems arose because the Euro–Arab Dialogue did not encompass a comprehensive European approach to the issues involved in European–Arab relations[9]. For a long while the Europeans resisted Arab attempts to introduce political and security issues into the Dialogue despite the obvious difficulties involved in separating them from the economic discussions. There was no precedent for a comprehensive approach, and so EPC in this area has been characterized by only gradual and hesitant extension and intensification. Recently, the Euro–Arab Dialogue has, to a limited extent, included aspects of security policy alongside the economic and cultural components and thus one could argue that, in one case at least, there is evidence that the framework of EPC allows the organizational integration of several sectoral policies. However, the problems of substantive progress remains; EPC like the EEC itself, frequently has difficulty in following up common declarations with significant action[10].

Another central area of concern for EPC has, of course, been Southern Europe[11]. Here the political scene has changed completely, and thus the Nine are going to be presented with many new and difficult challenges in the future. Initially there is the issue of how the process of enlargement of the Community should be managed; eventually there will be questions to be faced concerning new dimensions of the Community's foreign policy following enlargement.

In contrast to the EEC treaty, the agreements and rules of EPC contain no directions for entry negotiations. It will thus be initially important to ensure that the *acquis politique* among the Nine, achieved with the help of the EPC, is not jeopardized. This will be more difficult for those broader areas of agreement which have not been fixed in writing than for those areas where public declarations have been made. The entry of new members to the 'EPC club' will thus not be so easily negotiable in the traditional sense. The participation of EEC aspirants in the foreign policy cooperation of the Nine *before* entry, such as has been under consideration from time to time, seems to be problematic. The convergent approach of EEC and EPC would suffer as a result of any divergencies in the membership of the two bodies. The discipline of non-member-states would probably be less marked; the political commitment within EPC would be even less certain. Other Western states might want to invoke precedents of this kind, especially Turkey, although it should be pointed out that consideration was first given to the notion of early membership of EPC in the specific case of Turkey. In any event, it will still be necessary to acclimatize the new members to the EPC procedure and to the idea of consensus in foreign policy in a transitional phase. This will also include in all probability a new phase of adaptation for present members of the EPC circle, since the internal organization could be put under considerable strain by an expansion from nine to probably twelve participants. The process of harmonization could become even more ponderous, the number of COREU telegrams, at present at around 8000 a year, will probably shoot up to a level which national administrations will have problems in managing. The presidency could be faced by immense political technical problems of management.

Apart from these organizational problems, the Nine might in addition have to deal with problems that may arise from the potential instability of the 'new' democracies of Southern Europe. This could be primarily an economic and financial task, but one which will still generate additional political and diplomatic activity. In addition, it needs to be mentioned that the entry of new members to EPC will lead to a simultaneous 'internalization' of some special problems (Spain–Gibralter–UK; Greece –Cyprus–Turkey, among others). In contrast to the cooperation of the Nine in the UN, where one is dealing with worldwide topics which are often far removed from specific European interests, Southern Europe and the Mediterranean represent areas of immediate concern.

Furthermore, it will be necessary to take account of the foreign policy orientation of the new members. Spain and Greece have no diplomatic relations with Israel, a factor which could disturb the cautious steps of the Nine towards a common and balanced Middle East policy. Portugal and Spain have 'special relationships' with Latin American states, which might lead the Nine to modify some of their positions but which also might gain new potential for influencing North–South questions. As the Community expands geographically it may become more directly involved in individual regional conflicts (North Africa, Middle East, Cyprus, Canary Islands). Thereby the importance and responsibility of the Europeans in this area will probably increase. It is possible that they will find themselves increasingly unable to avoid being involved in stabilizing tasks relating to security policy. This would pave the way for a partial redefinition of the relationship with the superpowers, in particular to the USA and NATO. Nearly every question of European foreign policy touches on Euro–American relations. In this sense, the Nine's European Political Cooperation is also a further mechanism with which one can attempt to keep European Union compatible with Atlantic relations. Until now the Nine tend to see EPC more in terms of establishing its own identity *vis-à-vis* the USA than as an instrument for foreign policy discussions with Washington[12]. Against this background, Tindemans in his Report on European Union proposed that a member of the European Council should be given responsibility for a specific Euro –American dialogue. Meanwhile, however, on both sides of the Atlantic the centres of interest are beginning to shift. The arguments within the Atlantic context (EPC versus US diplomacy) have, at least in the short term, become less important. Increasing priority could thus be given to developing and implementing harmonized positions outside the Atlantic context. In Cyprus, in Southern Africa and the Middle East this has, in fact, become the case in varying degrees. The impression has been gained that the USA is far more prepared to be flanked by the Europeans in international conflicts. It also looks as if the Carter administration is actually encouraging this 'junior partnership' in questions of worldwide stabilization. It is not so much the structure of the partnership that they are concerned with but rather the consciousness of a responsibility which the West has to bear[13].

Washington is obviously seeking strong partners for 'burden sharing' as a part of the policy of worldwide stabilization, which could mean a role either for the Nine, or individual European states, or smaller European groupings. For this reason it may be less of a priority for Europe to achieve internal unanimity in its dealings with the USA with the aid of EPC; in this instance the function of European political cooperation could be different. It is not rendered superfluous but plays a more indirect role, serving mainly to harmonize those activities of some West European states, which are based on the Atlantic relationship, with the other partner-states. In the area of economics the summit meetings *à la* Rambouillet can be seen as a model for such an arrangement. Until now non-economic questions have only played a marginal (or at least an unofficial) role at these summit meetings. In view of the growing connection between economic questions and those of security policy and diplomacy, the future could witness certain changes in this area. The members of EPC will doubtless develop increased interest in broadly based contacts with all Western states because of their dependencies in foreign economic relations and in foreign policy. This would go far beyond the dialogue with the USA and would clearly include consultative relations between EPC and among others – Canada, Japan, Australia, Norway and Turkey[14]. The participants in EPC might be forced to develop new structures for this multiple dialogue with Western states.

11.3   Future functions of EPC

The future problem situations which will come under the aegis of EPC are characterized by three main features: first, the Nine will have to reckon with the consequences of its previous common declarations and *démarches* (e.g. in Southern Africa); second, there will be an ever-increasing connection between the substance of hitherto isolated activities of the Nine (e.g. connections between the CSCE and the Euro–Arab Dialogue, the overlapping of the North–South and East–West conflicts in the UN); third, the conjunction of aspects of economics, security policy and diplomacy seems to be becoming the typical shape that problems will take in the future (e.g. the international crisis area of the Mediterranean). Under these conditions it will not be sufficient to continue along the lines of 'business as usual'. Rather it will be necessary to consider a number of shifts in function, which should not overtax the present EPC system but which will allow it to deal more adequately with the probable intensification of tasks.

First and foremost it is necessary to consider whether the current central function of EPC as a coordinating mechanism for information and analysis should not change to one of analysis and action. There are good reasons for this: the Nine's foreign policy information pool is becoming increasingly less useful, since the more extensive accumulation of information is producing more of an administrative burden than any marked benefits. The only area within EPC which has not been exhaustively developed relates to cases where the Nine inform each other about individual contacts with outside states. Apart from this, it could in future be more a question of processing information in terms of its relevance to European politics before it is passed on to the Nine rather than simply transmitting that information unprocessed.

This task might place the smaller member-states in some difficulty regarding personnel whereas the larger EPC members would be required to continue to forego pressing their own national interests, especially during the period that they hold the presidency. Experience shows that this kind of development poses serious obstacles.

The situation regarding EPC's consultative tasks is no less complicated. In future the actual content of the consultations between the partner-states could become more important than the question of automatic agreement (coordination reflex). Any consultation on important questions of foreign policy presupposes a greater readiness to act flexibly in contrast to the straightforward passing on of information. Until now better results have clearly been achieved on a bilateral level (e.g. Franco–German consultations as personified by the relationship between Schmidt and Giscard d'Estaing). With the approach of the second enlargement it is unlikely that better consultative relations encompassing all the member-states will emerge. An increased trend towards bilateralism is more likely. This does not necessarily have to have negative consequences provided that a sufficiently strong channel back to the multilateral level is preserved. EPC could then be viewed as a collecting point for all these bilateral initiatives.

Along with the question of consultation between the EPC members there is also the question of future contact with states and organizations outside the EPC group. Here again it could become apparent that less and less can be achieved with mere information. The more firmly EPC specializes in 'classical' diplomacy the more it will be dependent on cooperation with other specialized bodies (EEC, OECD, NATO) and important states (USA, Canada, etc.), especially as problems increase in complexity. The question of how to organize these substantive and political consultations will be dealt with thoroughly below. At this point it is enough to point out that because of the necessities of consultation with outside bodies and states it will become desirable to consider shifting the emphasis of EPC from its current primary informative function to an increasingly consultative role.

It is impossible to foresee the extent to which this will happen. On the one hand, it will be important for Western Europe, as was suggested above, to take on a more active role in the management of international politics in order to overcome future problems of foreign policy; on the other hand, the limits of EPC's own capacity are real, the limited sphere of EPC activity being all too symptomatic of this state of affairs, so that the preconditions for a real change of function are hardly visible.

Nevertheless, with the continuing development of EPC it would be worth while giving priority to the analytical function of EPC over its consultative and informative functions. This would undoubtedly meet better the demands placed upon European foreign policy, since, in any event, the common production of positions and the continual discussions on 'European' criteria of assessment will be a precondition for the development of efficient procedures.

It is in this direction that the fund of common perspectives will most clearly gain both greater breadth and depth. At the same time the basis and the habit of seeking agreement with one another could develop in such a way that would help the internal supportive function of EPC in crises and other critical political situations. There are naturally some doubts regarding the realization of even these modest aims.

Until now 'analysis' within EPC has rarely led to conclusions regarding future action (and the means to be deployed). In cases where this was attempted there was frequent and varied dissent among the Nine. The qualitative leap from a common appraisal of the situation to concrete action was achieved relatively rarely, for the reasons given above. However, it is probable that in the future it will be increasingly difficult for Western Europe to assert itself firmly from such a defensive position. There is a danger that the Nine may be forced even more onto the defensive by such a policy (e.g. in Africa). In the East–West as well as the North–South discussions the Nine might thus be increasingly tempted and obliged to take the initiative in order to defend their positions adequately. For this purpose increasing use might be made of previous experiences with EPC conference diplomacy (CSCE, UN, EAD). The negotiating strength of the Nine could thus be improved by a policy mix of national and European approaches such as is already being practised to a limited extent in the General Assembly of the UN. Where a realistic opportunity presents itself, the Nine could also increasingly take up 'mediating' positions, something they have already attempted *vis-à-vis* the question of human rights at the second CSCE: here the Nine adopted a more moderate attitude in the arguments with the Soviet Union than did the USA. Naturally, the development and implementation of West European positions in a worldwide context will produce considerble problems of compatibility and adaptability. This is particularly the case in relation to the degree to which such a policy can be sustained on the domestic political front. It is possible that a stronger exposition of West European foreign policy will not be received with the same indifference by politically relevant groups within member-states as the previously more reserved activities of the Nine.

These considerations could be significant if the Nine were to develop the EPC system into their main instrument of international 'crisis management' with regard to 'security' issues. Until now it has been difficult to conceive of Western Europe in the role of 'global policeman', even though in the past, in a limited number of cases, the Nine have participated in the resolution of local conflicts with limited success (i.e. Cyprus, the Horn of Africa, Rhodesia, Namibia, Zaire, etc.). This tendency suggests that the Nine (or Twelve) could in future be much more heavily involved in crises than has appeared desirable up to now. On the one hand, it is possible to identify potential reserves in the EPC system, namely the ability of the Nine to get together directly at the point of crisis and in the respective capital cities; on the other hand, the Nine will also have to be prepared to take on substantial functions as mediators and guarantors. However, it is questionable whether the West Europeans can really muster sufficient material and political weight for such a role – even if they were prepared to take it on. In the recent case of European crisis aid to Portugal, during the period of instability brought about by the political transition from dictatorship to pluralistic democracy, the Nine did indeed demonstrate that they were able to deploy all available means – from EEC financial aid to contacts at the party level to the activation of special relationships and diplomatic *démarches*. However, this one example can hardly be made into a general paradigm[15]. Apart from conference diplomacy and the management of crises, the EPC system could in future be employed in harmony with EEC foreign trading relations. This relatively narrow task was, in fact, the original and main motive behind the idea of foreign policy cooperation between the Six. The fact that this most obvious task has up until now hardly been fulfilled can possibly be explained by the fact that at first EPC and the EEC approached each other with more reserve than sympathy. Meanwhile, however, two decisive factors have changed: first, the relationship between the EEC and EPC has relaxed; the participants in both bodies have learnt to live and work with each other. Second, the priority now, and in the future, is not so much the establishment of new areas for consultation as the overcoming of complex problems which arise. The Lomé Convention, the cooperation agreements with Canada and Iran, the drafting and implementation of the global policy on the Mediterranean, the treaty on trade with the People's Republic of China – all these have brought out very little parallel action from EPC. An exemplary beginning had been made in this respect in the case of direct relations between the EEC and Comecon. One might ask whether EPC should not provide a regular foreign policy view on all EEC projects in foreign economic affairs.

However, if there is a further consideration of EPC/EEC activity as well as an expansion of its present operative functions this will clearly alter the course of EPC development. A progressive variant would be conceivable (see Chapter 3) and would have clear consequences for the decision-making and operational structure of EPC. The system which has up to now been developed in its informative and consultative capacity would have to produce additional capabilities to deal with an expanded role such has been outlined above.

11.4   Possible adaptations of the EPC's structure

The EPC apparatus has up to now proved to be relatively adaptable; a clear example of the gradual improvement of cooperation between the Nine can be found in the negotiating rounds of the CSCE. The Euro–Arab Dialogue, on the other hand, demonstrates the absolute limits of the system's adaptability. A number of conclusions can be drawn from these and other experiences relating to several years now of EPC activitives; these conclusions could be used to assist the future development of the EPC system. Dealing with their own organization is by no means alien to the EPC participants as the production of the Luxembourg and Copenhagen Reports proves. The production of a third report of this nature has not been announced to date. Whether such a report could act as a means of preparing the Nine for some of the future new functions and shifts in their central aims is a question which has not yet been discussed. The first two reports at any rate tended simply to record modes of procedure which were already in practice. Thus it would not just be necessary to change the style of the report; rather it would be important to specifically refer to some of the weak points in the EPC system. This could include cataloguing the disadvantages that arise the fact that EPC does not have a permanent meeting-place nor its own permanent secretariat, and thus is subjected to upheavals every six months as the presidency revolves.

Whilst there are important political reasons of principle for preserving certain special features of the EPC system, some gradual changes ought to be considered in order to increase efficiency.

If, for example, the bulk of the meetings of EPC committees were held in Brussels instead of the capital cities this would not simply help to stabilize the procedures of cooperation but would reduce the increasing stresses and the extensive organizational expense relating to travel, communications and coordination.

To achieve this it might, for example, be worth considering setting up a technical clearing-point in Brussels, which could help the Nine and in particular the presidency, to keep the EPC machinery intact even under its approaching increased load. The administration of the presidency is clearly already suffering from excessive burdens, and this holds for both small and large countries. Most of the predominately technical/managerial functions of the presidency (the organization of hundreds of Nine meetings, the exchange and registration of thousands of telex communications, language and translation services, archival work) could be located in Brussels, where much of the technical infastructure of the EEC is already established.

This suggestion does not mean that a back-door would be opened for the introduction of an independent political secretariat of EPC, since this would involve the unnecessary reinforcement of the parallelism of the EEC and EPC as well as touching an issue that is politically tabu. A pragmatic solution is more feasible; the EPC staff from the respective country of the presidency could administer the permanent EPC service, which would be housed in the General Secretariat of the Council. Similar to the General-Secretariat of the EEC Commission, this would create an EPC service which, among other things, would be an important precondition for closer communication between the Council, the Commission and EPC. The essential part of this arrangement would be that the Brussels EPC service would be established as a technical unit, which would remain under alternating national control and would be a clearing point for relieving the presidency of some of its load. Ultimately the purpose would be to enable the presidency to concentrate on the political tasks of the temporary office, i.e. to handle the internal political management within the Nine as well as to look after external representation and operations.

The growing importance of the country of the presidency as the spokes-man for the Nine would justify any reforms aimed at relieving the presidency of some technical burdens. Here some revision of the biannual rotation of the presidency might be feasible, since this arrangement corresponds in no way to the actual conditions of operation in the field of international relations. It would be possible to implement a more systematic overlapping of the presidency in office with both its immediate predecessor and successor. The proposed EPC technical service in Brussels would in addition facilitate a smoother transition between chairmen, and would allow longer-term planning of technical operations, as well as providing informational and organizational aids for the transition from one presidency to another. Finally, a better coordination of EEC and EPC activities might be achieved this way.

As valuable as the system of the presidency is for bridging some of the structural gaps in EPC, its potential is nevertheless also limited. The supportive elements proposed above simply relieve the presidency in the organizational and technical fields. There would, however, also be a need for aid in the field of political action. In the absence of a Commission (as in the EEC system) the presidency in the EPC system finds itself being forced into an initiative role. The country holding the presidency is increasingly being expected to produce proposals for new areas for consultation as well as plans for solutions to pending problems. However, whoever holds the presidency is constantly facing problems of split allegiance, having to fulfil at one and the same time national and European functions[16].

But it is not simply for this reason that the function of making initiatives is so underfulfilled in the EPC system. In order to get away from the overemphasis on the defensive orientation of cooperation, the absence of any direction for operations and the tendency towards the politics of the *status quo*, the distribution of tasks will have to be more clearly structured. Here the conceptual power of initiative of all nine countries together should be tapped to as great a degree as possible, rather than being suppressed by the function of the presidency. This purpose would be served most effectively if the Nine could decide to establish their own 'initiative group' within the system of the various EPC committees; a group which would be composed of close associates of the Nine foreign ministers. The initiative group and the Political Committee would relate to each other reciprocally, supplementing each other's activity (resembling the relationship between the political section and the planning staff in the West German Foreign Office). The initiative group would not be just another working group in the technical sense but would have a motor function in EPC work with a real operative orientation. The group would thus be more comparable with a task force than with a planning staff. It would be concerned less with 'futurology' and more with stressing the substantive breadth of its proposals concerning current problems.

In contrast to the technical service of EPC in Brussels the initiative group would not be permanently in session but would still meet more frequently than the political directors who come together every four weeks. The 'proximity' of the members of the initiative group to their foreign ministers would underline the group's own political image of itself. Even then it could not be guaranteed that the emphasis of EPC work would shift from analysis to operation, thereby meeting the future qualitative demands made by the development of EPC tasks. It would at least, however, demonstrate the existence of a will to take the initiative, especially if this could be derived directly from the political level of decision-making.

11.5　The division of labour between the EEC and EPC

If one proceeds from the legal powers, the political duties and the respective 'strengths' of the EEC and EPC one can outline a hypothetical pattern for the division of labour and the interplay between the two institutions:

(1) Questions of the new world economic order as well as international trade and development come under the jurisdiction of the Community. Within this established framework these questions have to be handled, in the spirit of full responsibility, with a generous interpretation of the Treaty's latitude. The Community is relatively well equipped for this set of tasks: it has experienced negotiating teams and its own agencies in the most important centres of international debate on economic policy (Geneva, Paris, New York, Tokyo, Ottowa, Caracas).

(2) The daily representation of the Nine in bilateral and multilateral relations with outside states, at non-economic conferences and in international organizations would remain the domain of the EPC group. Experience shows that political cooperation is at present the best common instrument for adapting traditional national attitudes to new compatible interests of the Nine, and for representing common European positions in international relations. The domestic and worldwide diplomatic apparatus of the Nine is an indispensable precondition for this process, which the governments should not abandon as long as they want to retain individual responsibility for actions.

(3) Questions of military security are best dealt with under the aegis of the Atlantic Alliance. Apart from a few individual aspects relating to armaments and military technology (Euro-Group, European Programme Group) the West Europeans do not represent an independent political bloc in the Alliance. On the other hand, questions of economic and political security have to be seen as grey zones where coordination between Europe and America should, in fact, be the rule. Nevertheless, it should be decided in each individual case how far coordination should go and what procedure the Europeans should pursue, i.e. EEC, EPC, bilateral or multilateral.

It only makes sense to assign powers in this way if, at the same time, one supplements the arrangement with regulations governing cooperation. Up to now custom, rather than prepared rules, have governed the coordination of EEC external relations and political cooperation of the Nine. In future it would be important for each side to see itself within a given division of responsibilities. Both systems would have to allow greater access to the other, without merging completely, in order to allow an adequate two-way flow of communication as well as being able to take over harmonized analyses and coordinated operational tasks.

There are, in fact, already a number of precedents for these questions as well as pragmatic solutions to the complicated problems of organization and coordination, and so not too many major innovations will be required. The EEC Commission is in the best position to mediate between both systems of opinion-formation and action by dint of its dual participation in EEC *and* EPC bodies. As EEC and EPC activities move closer together and overlap the Commission would, in fact, take on a vital function. The Commission cannot, however, expand this subsidiary function at will. It remains ultimately bound to its sphere of activity within the Community institutions[17]. There will clearly be only limited success in achieving a relaxed and constructive relationship betwen EEC and EPC on the basis of a division of responsibility at the European level as long as the rivalries of the two decision-making structures are not curtailed in the capital cities, and also as long as the political departments and the sections dealing with the EEC affairs in the foreign ministries do not cooperate more closely. The reciprocal participation in the separate processes of information-gathering, opinion-formation and decision-making would have to be dealt with in a more extensive manner. Experience shows, however, that it will be difficult to implement any rapid restructuring of the Nine foreign ministries along similar lines (e.g. using the UK model where EEC and EPC are integrated in one department of the Foreign Office). Nevertheless, in the long term it will not be possible to avoid doing this[18].

The coordinated division of responsibility at an administrative level in the capitals, as well as in Brussels, is aimed at achieving a more comprehensive briefing at the political level. Foreign ministers, as well as heads of state and governments, are obviously free to discuss Community affairs and EPC matters as part of their agenda, but up until now they have lacked sufficiently broad preparatory dossiers for their discussions. The main proposal for improving procedure in complex questions of foreign policy would thus be to better combine central decisions with decentralized preparation and implementation. Cooperation between EPC and EEC aimed at the practical implementation of decisions is not as yet greatly developed compared with work on the preparation of those decisions. One indication of progress in this respect is the number of recent cases of joint representation, i.e. representatives of the Commission and the presidency presenting a common front towards non-member-states. An increasing number of foreign policy problems remain linked to the area of military security and cannot be solved outside the larger context of the Western Alliance. The necessary answers to these problems cannot be secured simply with the help of the traditional diplomacy of the presidency. Until now it has not been possible to achieve the necessary degree of reliability in Atlantic relations, despite political cooperation among the Europeans. The USA still has to cover itself through consultations with the individual member-states as well as their multilateral institutions. Even if bilateralism is still the most reliable basis for cooperation on questions of security policy on both the European and American sides, it will not be able to cope with the increasing demand for coordination on a broader front without increasing the process of harmonization between international institutions. Given carefully composed national delegations, it should not be difficult to achieve consultation and the exchange of information in relations between NATO and EPC; the partners in the Alliance should therefore be encouraged to do so on questions with particular relevance for security. The onus is thus on national administrations rather than on EPC or NATO to create the grounds for improved coordination.

11.6   The question of accountability

There is no doubt that up to now EPC has operated predominantly 'behind closed doors'. This had not been fundamentally altered by the occasional public statements and the common positions of the Nine towards outside states. The same applies to the meagre debates on EPC topics in national parliaments as well as for the, albeit slightly more extensive, dealings of the European Parliament with the activities of EPC. In particular the extensive fund of European agreed positions, the *communauté de vue*, has, until now, not been the subject of broader debate by the political public of the Nine[19]. The basic consensus which has been built up discretely over the years is based primarily on discussions within a closed circle of European diplomats. EPC appears, however, to have already reached a point of its development where the continuation of this practice needs to be seriously reconsidered.

It would certainly be wrong to expose all the separate elements of EPC activities, including actual measures taken in European crisis management, to the public gaze. Nevertheless, this does not rule out the possibility of a continual public discussion on the basic options in European affairs. EPC has become a force in international politics (in conjunction with the EEC and in cooperation with US diplomats) which would justify creating a broader base for common European positions. One is talking here both of the desirability of democratizing European foreign policy and of increasing the long-term effectiveness of an instrument of foreign policy belonging to the Nine.

Admittedly, it will be difficult to achieve an adequate degree of public debate on EPC without at the same time damaging the effectiveness of the system of cooperative exchanges. This difficulty will have to be examined at every stage of the development of EPC. At the beginning of the 1970s such a redefinition of the relationship between EPC and the public was taking place all the time. But from 1975 onwards the problem has clearly become more and more difficult to solve. Thus the members of the European Parliament regard themselves today as 'being robbed of the opportunity at every level of investigating, influencing and testing the common foreign policy of the Community and the Nine member states'. If parliamentarians in Luxembourg or Strasbourg had any say in it, foreign ministers would have to be prepared in future not simply to pass on adequate information on the development and operation of EPC but also 'to allow access to decision-making procedures, which would allow European parliamentarians to influence common foreign policy initiatives and to be involved in the shaping of those policies'. In this connection there have been proposals for an 'Office for Political Cooperation': this would be a bureau centred in Brussels replacing the present administrative mechanisms of EPC. At the same time, the European Council would need to be fully institutionalized and would be answerable to the European Parliament after each of its sessions[20].

As stimulating as the suggestions of the European Parliament might be, they are nonetheless not particularly feasible. There are serious grounds for doubting the value of an 'Office for Political Cooperation'. Establishing yet another bureaucratic 'body' in Brussels would probably serve neither the efficiency of a common foreign policy nor the development of the Nine's integration policy. Similarly, bureaucracies of this sort, even if they work well, do not appeal particularly to the political public at large.

Apart from the assessments and wishes of the European Parliament, which are derived from its particular perspective, the question remains whether in fact an unintentional process of increased access to EPC is not already in progress. As was indicated above, the work of EPC is done less and less in isolation. Its particular feature of operating as an exclusive apparatus parallel to the highly developed procedures of the EEC is beginning to fade. With the intensification of its activities, EPC will increasingly have to consider the Brussels authorities and the European Parliament, and it will have to cope with pressure from them; in this way the process of harmonization may indeed lose its easy-going and secretive atmosphere, possibly with beneficial results. Apart from this, the Nine are being increasingly forced to allow an open debate on basic foreign policy positions, not least by world opinion. One way or another, the Nine will probably be forced both internally and externally to be franker and more explicit about their foreign policy activities.

11.7   Conclusions

Until now the development of EPC has taken a direction which leaves open the question of the shape of European foreign policy in the future. In the absence of new apparatus, EPC will remain, alongside endeavours within the EEC, the most significant attempt of the Nine to further European union in the field of foreign affairs. European foreign policy will, in the foreseeable future, be derived from both these structures, EEC and EPC. This, however, gives little indication of the future shape and the effect of Western Europe as an actor in foreign affairs. Precise details are hard to envisage[21]. At best, one can project possible directions this development could take from the state of things at present.

One possible development would be a simple continuation of the current trends discussed in this volume. If this is the case, it can be expected that EPC will take on more and more tasks (as described at the beginning of this chapter) and will continue to extend its procedures. This quantitative expansion could take place without it being necessary to reach a new qualitative level of foreign policy goals relating either to integration or to specific issues. However, if quantitative amibitions are not accompanied by a corresponding ability to solve problems, then the value of EPC for the shaping of European foreign and integration policy will not be able to grow. This process does not extend beyond a consolidation of the *status quo*; it is possible that it could lead to tensions among the member-states within the various organizations. EPC would be one among several multilateral instruments of the Nine, though without an automatically reliable functional framework.

The pragmatic development of EPC would, on the other hand, further strengthen its instrumental character. An institutional fixation of the procedures of cooperation would be unlikely. Its development into an independent body or its incorporation into the institutional structure of the EEC would have to be rejected as dysfunctional, for EPC 'lives' by dint of its very relaxed and non-binding character. The dual structure of European foreign policy would be preserved.

EPC would certainly not be a significant vehicle for integration, though its actual effectiveness regarding integration could not be denied. Even in its short existence up to now, EPC has been able to identify common European points of view and has brought them to bear in foreign affairs. Further pressure will be exerted on the Nine from outside in order to make them demonstrate their European identity. However, this pressure will, as in previous instances, have an ambivalent effect on common European positions. As long as the apparatus is neither connected with the relevant forces within the Community nor obtains the requisite means to act, nothing is likely to alter the tendency of EPC politics to be reactive in nature. The combining of EEC external relations and EPC would at best prevent the

Nine having to adapt themselves too much to the options of the superpowers in international relations[22].

Instead of a continuation of EPC in its present shape, a second direction for its development can be considered. This could amount to an ultimate reduction in the dynamics of integration policy. In the relationship of tension between Community and national interests, a majority of governments might argue for a standstill in the development of integration. In practice this would mean that politico–psychological jockeying among the Nine, striving for the projection of a national identity and the pursuit of special interests in political and economic affairs, would be of greater importance than commitment to the European ideal (compare the reaction of the Nine in the context of the oil crisis 1973–1974). If this development occurred, EPC would become more of a method for concealing individual national initiatives rather than for the *collective* harmonizations of national interests. European coordination and consultation would be regarded to a large extent as a nuisance. Attempts to reverse this trend, like appealing to the solidarity of the Nine or even threatening excessively egotistic countries with the termination of loyalties in other areas, would no longer have any disciplinary effect. A regression of this sort cannot be ruled out, especially if the Community expands both in terms of membership and of tasks without at the same time 'deepening' relations or without attempting to counteract the growing political and social differences among the partner-states. In this case the already limited effectiveness of EPC would either stagnate or decrease. The tradition of cooperation between the Nine would be impaired, the *acquis politique* in foreign affairs would begin to crumble, the 'diplomatic community' of the Nine would be undermined. It would not be possible to conceal this state from the outside world for long. The Nine would perhaps cease to be a political force to be reckoned with in international relations.

A lower efficiency and a reduced status on the part of EPC would not be without consequences for the Community as a whole. EEC foreign economic relations would lose the support of their diplomatic flank and their foreign policy foundations. The dynamic of integrative development generated by common foreign policy initiatives would be missing. A mentality of indifference towards integration policy would spread to other areas of the Community. Although, within the flexible character of EPC, terminal rifts might be avoided, an apparatus of cooperation which had been emptied of its content and emasculated as an instrument of action would ultimately become unworthy of preservation.

In a third possible scenario for the development of EPC one might envisage entering a phase of dynamic development which, alongside the expansion of topics and procedures, would also contain qualitative improvements of the structure. The member-states might be increasingly prepared to perceive EPC as a central institution of collective foreign policy which is no longer subject to any artificial or extraneous limitations. In particular, the political commitment to a common approach in foreign policy might be strengthened. Deviations would not be allowed. EPC would be able to deal more adequately with problems, namely by encompassing all the various aspects of a given question of foreign policy. Here it would be necessary to initiate a distribution of responsibilities above all with the EEC but also with bodies concerned with security and defence policy. This would not just apply to the processing of information and the analysis of international developments but would also be applied to the processes of decision-making and action. This kind of development is only conceivable if there were a broad public political base in Europe which would promote the common service of foreign policy interests. Also this would depend in turn on the further development of the political infrastructure.

With this variant European foreign policy would come close to the model described by Leo Tindemans in his Report on European Union. This means that a unitary decision-making centre for foreign policy would emerge which still had a dual but coordinated substructure. Alongside the political commitment towards a common foreign policy in agreed fixed areas, there would also be the legal obligation to consult other member-states even on other decisions of national foreign policy. European foreign policy would not simply involve the bundling together of foreign policy instruments which 'happen' to be there[23], but would rest on the basis of its own political identity with its own bodies and a basic conception of integration policy, such as is expressed in the Tindemans Report. The foreign policy sector would play a central role in the integrative development of European Union. European foreign relations would indeed remain a function of the internal development of the Community, but would in turn contribute to that internal development. The changes would come about progressively, leading in time to a situation where the previous limits of consensus among the Nine were reduced comprehensively and the Community would experience a marked thrust towards further integration.

The outlining above of three possible developmental models for EPC is not, of course, meant to suggest that the Europeans have a free choice in this matter. The actual direction of developments will be rather determined by factors upon which the Nine will only have a certain amount of influence.

The direction which the development of EPC has already taken was influenced in part by factors which derived essentially from three sources: the development of the EPC apparatus itself, the political state of affairs within the Nine and finally general developments in the international system itself. These factors have produced a relatively favourable climate for the development and deployment of this new instrument of foreign policy[24].

This trend is not inevitably going to continue. There are some indications, as was mentioned at the beginning of this chapter, which point to an excessive organizational and procedural growth in the development of the

EPC apparatus. It is not beyond the bounds of possibility that EPC, through a further expansion of its tasks without any adequate intensification of its problem-solving capacity, could simply strengthen its reputation as merely an instrument of information and analysis. However, if this activity does not produce any substantial operational advances, the credibility and usefulness of EPC could suffer as well. Western Europe would have yet another set of institutions with decreasing functions. The more ponderously foreign policy decisions are reached in this body, the more a development of this kind will be accelerated. However, in this respect the Nine are faced with a severe test, the outcome of which is quite uncertain. The expansion of the Community to take in twelve members could well place the effectiveness of EPC in doubt, simply by dint of the increased number of participants in the consultation process. The large member-states would be less prepared than before to lay all their foreign policy cards on the table in the extended circle of EPC. The system of cooperation could become an area of argument between 'large' and 'small' states, with the result that for some member-states the harmonization of their foreign policy could become a matter for resentment. A partial withdrawal of individual member-states from the consultation process and a reduction in the rank of the representatives in the various EPC bodies is just as conceivable as the increased endeavours of the large member-states to dominate opinion-formation under the cloak of efficiency. Even though there has been a *de facto* 'directoire' of the major states from the beginning of EPC as well as of the EEC, the weight of this group is likely to be felt even more strongly than before. The interest of the small partner-countries in EPC could thus decrease in the same measure as the dominance of some of the Twelve increases. An even more serious strain on the unanimity of the EPC group could arise from the increasing political heterogeneity of the member-countries. While up to now EPC could be regarded precisely as a promising framework for the mediation of differences within Europe, the disparities in economic, political and military attitudes and goals could become so great that they could no longer be bridged, even by employing greater flexibility. Growing differences in the dependence on raw materials, in the attitude towards protectionist trade policies, in the strike-power of the national armed forces, in the perception of the threat to security, in domestic stability and tolerance are all examples of a generally discernible trend towards increasing heterogeneity, which promises to be even more marked with expansion to twelve countries. One cannot abstract the realization of EPC tasks from this background. The prospects for European Union are becoming visibly worse[25]. The existing multilateral organizations may no longer be in a position to control the disparate dynamics within Europe.

Finally, we must consider the effect on the development of EPC of influences from outside Western Europe. Without having to describe these determinants in detail, it is possible to make the following assessment. In the case of a number of external influences and challenges which are to be found in everyday diplomacy, the Nine are quite able to carry out tasks satisfactorily with the aid of EPC. In contrast to this, the Nine clearly find themselves unable in the foreseeable future to eliminate the threat by one world power or the fact of dependence on the other in any fundamental way, whilst at the same time giving consideration to the demands of the Third World. Rather there has been increased disquiet in all three directions, especially since the prospect of a more independent Europe is questioned within Europe itself. To this extent EPC might be less a means for the Europeans to transform the structure of international relations fundamentally and more a method for adaptation to given structural circumstances. In this way the Nine may still retain the possiblity of being able to participate in the determination of future global developments[26].

Notes

1 For a further discussion of factors affecting West European foreign policy see R. A. Rieber, 'The Future of the European Community in International Politics', *Canadian Journal of Political Science*, Vol. 9, No. 2 (June 1976), pp. 207–226

2 See Wolfgang Wessels, Chapter 1

3 A recent example is the French motion in Belgrade relating to the Final Document of CSCE II which was not supported by the other eight EEC members

4 These case studies were concluded before the Iranian revolution and the Soviet invasion of Afghanistan

5 See Götz von Groll, Chapter 5

6 See Beate Lindemann, Chapter 9

7 See Nicholas van Praag, Chapter 10

8 See David Allen, Chapter 6

9 Ursula Brown utilizes a broader approach to an assessment of the Euro–Arab Dialogue. See 'Der Europaisch–Arabische Dialog – Entwickling and Zwischonbilanz', *Orient*, Vol. 18, No. 1 (1977), pp. 30–56

10 See K. Meyer. 'Der Europaisch–Arabische Dialog am Wendepunkt? Stand und Aussichten', *Europa-Archiv.*, Vol. 33, No. 10 (1978), pp. 290–298

11 See Nicholas van Praag, Chapter 8

12 See Beate Kohler, Chapter 7

13 See Reinhardt Rummel, 'Nene Entwicklungen in der atlantischen Partnerschaft', *Liberal*, Vol. 19, No. 11 (November 1977)

14 C. Pentland, 'Linkage Politics: Canada's Contract and the Development of the European Community's External Relations', *International Journal*, Vol. 32, No. 2 (Spring 1977), pp. 207–232

15 An ability to manage crisis situations in the Mediterranean area after enlargement would be a positive achievement. See Lothar Ruehl, 'Europa Sicherheits probleme im Mittelemeeraum', *Europa Archiv*, Vol. 33, No. 2, January 1978, pp. 33–42

16 See G. Edwards and H. Wallace, *The Council of Ministers of the European Community and the President-in-Office*, Federal Trust Paper, London 1977

17 See Gianni Bonvicini, Chapter 3. Note also that the Political Committee's ignorance of EEC matters will tend to inhibit its cooperation with the Commission. See Nicholas van Praag, Chapter 8

18 See William Wallace, Chapter 4

19 See Wolfgang Wessels, Chapter 1

20 *Draft Resolution on European Political Cooperation*, European Parliament, Political Committee, 14 May 1977 (The Blumenfeld Report). See also the Revised Draft, 12 October 1977

21 Academics have repeatedly stressed the problem of predicting this development with any degree of reliability. See W. Wallace, 'A Common European Foreign Policy: Mirage or Reality?' *New Europe*, Vol. 5, No. 2, Spring 1977, pp. 21–33

22 See R. Dahrendorf, 'International Power: A European Perspective', *Foreign Affairs*, Vol. 57, No. 1, October 1977, pp. 72–88

23 See O. Von der Gablentz, 'Wege zu einer europaischen Aussenpolitik', H. Schneider and W. Wessels (Eds), *Ant dem weg zur Europaischen Union*? Bonn, 1977 (*Europaische Schriften des Instituts fur Europaische Politik*, Vol. 46/47)

24 See David Allen and William Wallace, Chapter 2. See also H. D. Genscher, 'Notwendigtreiten und Moglichteiteneiner europaischen Aussenpolitik', *Europa Archiv*, Vol. 31, No. 13, 1976, pp. 427–432

25 Foreign policy options continue to bear distinct national marks. See L. Ruehl, 'Un point de vue oeust-allemand sur la cooperation politique en Europe occidentale', *Defense Nationale*, Vol. 36, No. 3, March 1978, pp. 65–75: R. Toulemon, 'Europe européene or Europe atlantique?' *Defense Nationale*, No. 1, January 1978: G. Goodwin, 'The External Relations of the European Community – Shadow or Substance?' *British Journal of International Studies*, No. 3, 1977, pp. 39–54

26 See R. Rummel, 'Neu Entwicklungen in de Atlantischen Partnerschaft', *Liberal*, Vol. 19, No. 11, November 1977, pp. 828–840

CHAPTER TWELVE
Postscript 1982
DAVID ALLEN

The purpose of this brief concluding chapter is to review the impact on European Political Cooperation of events and developments since the early years up to 1977 which are the subject of this book. This is of particular interest in view of the fact that many observers consider the dramatic events of the early 1980s to have produced another 'sea change' in the workings of EPC. The events themselves, the Soviet invasion of Afghanistan, the turmoil in Poland and the election of Ronald Reagan to the American presidency, have highlighted what seems to be a general trend in the international system. After a decade in which economic issues dominated international politics, the more traditional substance of diplomacy, namely political–security issues, have returned to the forefront. These are, of course, the very issues that political cooperation was set up to deal with, and their proliferation in recent years has naturally placed a new set of demands and pressures on the machinery discussed in this volume.

Despite the developments mentioned above, political cooperation has essentially continued to develop along familiar lines. The problems discussed in the earlier chapters have been further highlighted but not as yet resolved. Proposals for reforms in procedure still abound and in many of the policy areas little progress has been made. Thus the Euro–Arab Dialogue remains in much the same state that the case study[1] left it in 1977, cooperation at the CSCE follow-up conferences continues but with no significant breakthroughs, coordination at the UN continues along the lines suggested by Lindemann[2] and the problems of relating to the USA remain, if slightly exacerbated by issues such as Afghanistan or the whole question of European nuclear weapons.

Despite a further growth in activity in political cooperation, the basis of a common foreign policy, as opposed to a coordination of national policies, still remains a distant and disputed objective. Rummel's point that political cooperation is selective remains valid; certain areas such as aid and security still remain outside of the cooperative framework, although the question of security has been recently raised in the context of the debates about the replacement of American nuclear weapons stationed in Europe. The 'low degree of political obligation' associated with political cooperation has led to renewed calls for a Treaty and an intensification of the obligation to consult on foreign policy matters. Finally, Rummel's warnings about the dangers of a 'directorate' of the major powers developing, as a result of the difficulties of managing the views of ten states, have been borne out by the growing tensions within the Community arising from the development of bilateral relations between the large states.

Some new developments must also be recorded. First, within the Community the substance of foreign policy cooperation has become of much greater interest to the general public, partly because of the attention given to EPC by the newly elected European Parliament but mainly because the issues themselves have proved to be the subject of controversy. Thus, as European leaders set about the difficult task of presenting a united and distinct European front to an increasingly aggressive and insensitive US administration, they find their own national positions threatened by an increasingly questioning public. Questions of nuclear policy or about the correct response to the activities of the Soviet Union have begun to impinge on the domestic political scene. Inevitably this has had some effect on an EPC process which we have characterized as being, as far as the participating diplomats are concerned, healthily isolated from political controversy and domestic squabbles about the future of the European Communities. Second, it must be noted that in recent years EPC has attracted the attention of other major actors in the international system, many of whom are anxious to form new types of relationship with the Europeans. The best example of this renewed external attention can be found in the case of the Japanese who, at one time, seemed to be seeking an organic link between their own foreign policy activities and those of EPC. At the time of the Iranian 'hostage' crisis not only did EPC itself work quite well in the form of cooperation between the Nine in Tehran, the Japanese increasingly sought to associate themselves with the stances taken by the Community countries. The question of non-member-states associating with the work of EPC has also been raised in the context of deliberations about the UK's continued membership of the EEC. Although the example of Norway is not encouraging for those who would advocate the UK's leaving the EEC but remaining within EPC, arguments along those lines continue to be made in the light of the obvious importance that the major Community states place on their own quadripartite discussions with the USA.

Arguments about the participation of non-member-states in the EPC process return us to a discussion of the overall relationship between EEC and EPC activities. The difficulty of keeping the two apart have been highlighted further by recent developments. The question of a political response to the behaviour of the revolutionary Iranian government involved the use of economic sanctions that were the proper concern of the EEC. The debate about the nature of the European relationship with Eastern Europe in general and with Poland and Yugoslavia in particular revolves around economic matters that again are the responsibility of the Community itself. Any development of a political dialogue, be it with the USA, the Arabs or the Japanese, must involve those areas of policy that member-states have chosen to operate at the Community level. EPC still lacks the traditional 'tools' of foreign policy. To the extent that these exist outside of a purely national and, hence rather ineffective, framework, they exist within the stucture of the EEC. The fate of the EEC itself is thus inextricably bound up with the future development of EPC, and this fact, which was apparent when the present volume was completed, has been further confirmed in recent years.

We have seen in this brief introductory overview that there have been no fundamental alterations in recent years to the fundamentals of EPC, more that certain tendencies previously mentioned have become further highlighted. We will now examine these developments in more detail, covering two broad areas; policy substance and policy procedure. A recent writer[3] has challenged the assessment of two of this book's authors[4] that EPC is best seen as 'procedure as a substitute for policy'. Douglas Hurd's argument is based on the view that recently the areas of agreement and coordinated activity have considerably expanded. However, he himself cites a number of what are essentially procedural developments, such as the expansion of the COREU network, the laying down of agreed rules of procedure, the gathering together of a number of major EPC statements and the practice, initiated by the British, of linking preceding and succeeding presidencies. Nevertheless there has been growth in the area of substantive policy that is worthy of record.

In the Middle East, where European diplomacy has perhaps attracted the most attention, the shape of a common policy is beginning to emerge. The Venice Declaration backed up by the discussions initiated by the successive Luxembourg and Dutch presidencies do indeed represent 'the re-entry of the European countries into Middle East diplomacy'[5]. Whilst no-one pretends that the Europeans can achieve solutions single-handed, their detachment from the immediate interests of the two superpowers may well give them an articulating and arbitrating role that can assist the search for peace in that area. Much the same can be said about the visit of Lord Carrington to Moscow, early in 1981, representing as it did the ability of the Ten eventually to reach a common position on the problems arising from the Soviet invasion of Afghanistan and the US reaction to this.

We have already mentioned the coordination of the Nine's embassies in Iran at the time of the revolution. Here EPC worked well in the face of a very difficult and sensitive challenge. At the UN it is now claimed, with some justification, that the Community countries represent the most cohesive of the various regional groupings that dominate that institution. Some progress has been made in developing a relationship with the ASEAN countries, although to date little progress has been made in Latin America. This may well change with the admission of Spain and Portugal to the EEC and thus also EPC, although enlargement also promises to add to the list of internal problems that EPC has so far fought shy of. Thus just as internationally significant disputes such as that between the UK and Ireland are tabu subjects for EPC, so issues like Gibralter and Cyprus may suffer from becoming internalized. Relations with the USA continue to pose fundamental problems for EPC and here the difficulties are increasingly of a substantive rather than a procedural nature. Whilst the habit of the UK, France and West Germany discussing foreign policy matters with the USA within the context of the Berlin Agreements proves as irritating to the small countries within EPC as the global economic summits do within the framework of the EEC, the real problem lies in the nature of the issues presently under discussion. As in 1973, the Europeans find themselves faced with demands to reconsider fundamentally the basic assumptions of the Atlantic Alliance. Over Afghanistan and Poland, and to a lesser extent Iran, the European countries find themselves divided as to how far they are willing to go along with a hard-line American position. These internal differences of perception naturally inhibit the effectiveness of collective European diplomacy. Similarly American reactions to other areas of European activity, such as the Middle East, tend to be internally divisive. In 1973, as we pointed out[6], the argument was essentially procedural and was solved to a certain extent by the Gymnich formula for transatlantic consultation. Nowadays the consultation process, whilst still a little one-sided, is not the real problem: it is the substance of the policies that are being discussed. Although some European states are undoubtedly more confident of their unilateral positions than they were in 1973, the resolution of Atlantic differences remains fundamental to the successful operation of EPC in most areas.

It is within the context of Atlantic relations that the question of EPC and the discussion of security matters has been recently revived. The basic principle that security issues lay outside the remit of EPC has been challenged by the nature of the issues themselves. The question of the basing of Cruise missiles and the development of the neutron bomb goes to the very heart of European–American relations. The need for a common European position in the face of a determined American stance is apparent: the security issues are entwined with all other aspects of East–West and West–West relations. To this end, EPC has quietly considered security matters without any noticeable embarrassment of the Irish. If ECP was allowed to operate as it has done in the past one suspects that these issues could be discreetly handled and that security considerations could enter the field of EPC activity without the establishment of a major point of principle that could embarrass certain members. However, as we have seen, this is not likely to be the case. The level of public interest in these matters will probably ensure that the question of EPC and security discussions *will* become a matter of principle. Given this degree of public interest it would seem unlikely that individual countries will be able as easily as they have done in the past to disguise national policy positions within common European positions. In the security area the dangers of internal division for the rest of EPC activity are apparent. Whilst some countries may attempt to resolve their internal political situations by pursuing a more neutralist stance, others, frustrated by the lack of a common position, will turn increasingly towards the USA for diplomatic support and reassurance. In displaying a certain insensitivity to the individual European dilemmas the Americans may well unwittingly be successfully achieving the break-up of the limited foreign policy cooperation that the Europeans have thus far developed.

Finally, with regard to substantive policy matters it is important to record that since this original volume was completed the situation within the Community has not improved. We made the point that external effectiveness would depend in the future on the continued development of internal economic policies. This has not occurred; indeed those policies which do exist and which attract the attention of other actors in the international system are themselves under internal attack. This must undermine the potential effectiveness of EPC and enhance in the eyes of the outside world the desirability of continuing to pursue bilateral relationships with individual European states.

If we now turn to recent procedural developments the picture, whilst altered in degree, remains much the same as in 1977. The Community itself has, of course, seen a number of procedural developments. The European Parliament is now directly elected and taking a much greater interest in EPC activities. The European Council has developed a regular pattern of thrice-yearly meetings at which the Community heads of government discuss both EPC and EEC matters. Greece has now joined the Community and negotiations proceed for the eventual entry of Spain and Portugal.

The enlargement of the Community has tended to highlight the problem that affects both the EEC and the EPC decision-making processes. Because EPC is run on the assumption of unanimous agreement many areas of discussion do not get very far. This problem is compounded by the demands that are placed on those officials and ministers who participate in EPC. Even though the actual number of EPC meetings has continued to expand greatly, there is a limit to what can be fruitfully discussed by the representatives of ten member-states, travelling from national capitals and meeting for, at the most, one or two days. The task of organizing these numerous meetings, which falls on the already overburdened presidency, has led to renewed calls for the establishment of some kind of permanent secretariat for EPC. Despite attempts to coordinate the activities of succeeding presidencies and despite arguments of both a theological and practical nature against such a move, there is a growing concern that unless EPC is given some form of permanent institutional identity the whole enterprise will founder. In a speech in Hamburg in November 1980 Lord Carrington, the UK Foreign Secretary, proposed, amongst other things, that EPC could be strengthened by a small but experienced foreign policy staff. This staff, which would continue to be paid by the individual foreign ministries, would be designed to assist the presidency rather than supplant it.

The problem of inflexibility, bought about by the existence of ten member-states, also led Lord Carrington in the same speech to propose that some sort of 'crisis mechanism' might be devised in order to enable EPC to react more speedily to rapid developments in the international system. The need for this sort of rapid reaction was highlighted at the time of the Afghanistan invasion, unfortunately timed as it was for the Community at Christmas, when the presidency was in the process of being handed over. Carrington proposed a 'three-man trigger' whereby any three member-states could declare a crisis to be in existence, thus solving the problem of getting ten states to rapidly reach the same assessment of a developing situation. As Douglas Hurd[7] has pointed out, in such situations it is important to gather together ministers from national capitals who will be framing decisions, rather than ambassadors who will be simply receiving instructions. Thus the meetings of ambassadors either in the country of the presidency or in non-member-states, which at the moment can be convened fairly rapidly, do not in themselves constitute an effective crisis mechanism. Even if these reforms were successfully implemented, EPC would still be characterized by its inability to conduct day-to-day diplomacy. EPC will remain as a mechanism which, in a sense, has its agenda set for it by events in the outside world. It is essentially suited to reacting to events: anything more would require a much closer harmonization of EPC and EEC activities. In the long run this would presumably require a much larger secretariat than that proposed by Carrington; it would, in fact, require the establishment of both a common foreign policy and a common European diplomatic service. To the extent that both these objectives are as far off as they were when this volume was originally completed, Rummel's speculations about the future of EPC remain relevant, despite the passage of time since they were first formulated.

Questions about the possible procedural development of EPC still come up against the fundamental suspicion that EPC was and is designed very effectively to 'do nothing in an apparently positive way' at a time when the member-states of the Community are not in a position, because of their own national circumstances, to do anything else. If this is the case, then there may be dangers in making the EPC process more visible than it is at present. Expectations, both within and outside the Community, may be raised in a way that they have not in the past, which will produce inevitable disappointment in the long term. It has, for instance, been pointed out with regard to the proposed further institutionalization of EPC that NATO, with a large permanent secretariat, still has problems in reconciling the disparate views of its member-states. The difference between NATO and the EEC on the one hand, and EPC on the other, is that, at the moment, disagreements within the discreet EPC framework remain relatively secret and thus less damaging.

Inevitably the smaller states of the Community fear any unstructured EPC developments, but it may well be that they will have to recognize that the price to be paid for a fruitful participation in an increasingly cumbersome EPC framework is some informal form of inner directorate comprising the major states. One could argue that a useful division of labour might be instituted into EPC whereby working groups consisting of a limited number of countries might take the lead on specific issues, whilst at the same time recognition is made of the fact that inevitably the larger powers are going to have an interest in most issues and that they are likely to discuss them amongst themselves as well as in the larger full EPC group. Whilst this sort of development may go against the wishes of those who would like to see the practices of the EEC extended to EPC, they may well prove to be a more practible solution to the problems that the EPC process undoubtedly continues to face at the start of the 1980s.

The conclusion of this brief postscript is that it is still difficult to see exactly where EPC is heading. It has, as Rummel suggested it would, continued to expand along a path that is probably not heading towards the establishment of a European foreign policy. It is still essentially a reactive mechanism which is currently under pressure because there is suddenly a great deal more to react to. Its discreteness, which was once seen as its great merit, is challenged by the breakdown in the foreign policy consensus both within and between member-states. It remains the case that the future development of EPC remains fundamentally bound up with the development of the EEC itself, If further progress is to be made in establishing a European voice in world affairs the member-states need, in the 1980s, not just to consider ways of improving the EPC mechanism but also their whole approach to the development of European integration.

Notes

1 See David Allen, Chapter 6
2 See Beate Lindemann, Chapter 9
3 Douglas Hurd, 'Political Cooperation', *International Affairs*, Vol. 57, Summer 1981, No. 3
4 William Wallace and David Allen, 'Political Cooperation; Procedure as Substitute for Policy', H. Wallace *et al.* (Eds) *Policy-making in the European Communities*, John Wiley, 1977
5 Hurd, 'Political Cooperation'
6 See Beate Kohler, Chapter 7
7 Hurd, 'Political Cooperation'

Index

In subheadings throughout this Index the following abbreviations have been used: CSCE = Conference on Security and Cooperation in Europe; EEC = European Economic Community; EPC = European Political Cooperation.